DEVASTATION!
THE WORLD'S WORST
NATURAL DISASTERS

DEVASTATION!
THE WORLD'S WORST NATURAL DISASTERS

LESLEY NEWSON

DK PUBLISHING, INC.

A DK PUBLISHING BOOK

www.dk.com

PROJECT EDITOR
PETER ADAMS

PROJECT ART EDITOR
PHILIP J. ORMEROD

EDITOR
TERESA PRITLOVE

US EDITOR
JILL HAMILTON

DTP DESIGNER
JASON LITTLE

MANAGING EDITOR
MARTYN PAGE

MANAGING ART EDITOR
BRYN WALLS

CARTOGRAPHERS
DAVID ROBERTS, JANE VOSS, PHILIP ROWLES

PRODUCTION
MICHELLE THOMAS

PICTURE RESEARCH
ANGELA ANDERSON

First American Edition, 1998

4 6 8 10 9 7 5 3

Published in the United States by DK Publishing, Inc.
95 Madison Avenue, New York, New York 10016

Visit us on the World Wide Web at http://www.dk.com

Published in Great Britain by Dorling Kindersley Limited.

Library of Congress Cataloging-in-Publication Data

Newson, Lesley.
    Devastation! the world's worst natural disasters / by Lesley
Newson. -- 1st Amer. ed.
        p.   cm.
    Includes index.
    ISBN 0-7894-3518-7
    1. Natural disasters. I. Title.
GB5014.N48 1998
363.34'9--DC21   98-2567
                                                  CIP

Reproduced by ColourPath, London, England
Printed and bound by Dai Nippon Printing Co., (HK) Ltd.

CONTENTS

INTRODUCTION

MOTHER NATURE IS AN ABUSIVE PARENT. She strikes unpredictably and the blows can come from anywhere. The ground may ripple like the sea, fiery rock and gas may explode from mountains, or the air and oceans may tear the land apart. Sudden changes in the level of the oceans, the composition of the atmosphere, the temperature of the Earth, and the patterns of the seasons can and have killed off all but the hardiest species, or the luckiest.

Human society and the natural world have both been shaped by the blows of natural disasters. Historians tend to explain the shaping of the past in terms of the influence of great leaders and the strategies of their generals. But the whims of nature have been at least as influential; the violence of nature has played a decisive role in many battles. England's tiny fleet could not have defeated the mighty Spanish Armada in 1588 without the aid of the storms howling in from the Atlantic. Natural disasters have made and broken many great leaders. King Yu was made China's first dynastic ruler 4,200 years ago because he dealt with huge floods along the Yellow River by getting teams to dredge out the river channel so the floodwaters could flow away. Unexpected catastrophes also have a profound effect on the human mind, and this has been an important force for social

THE GROUND SPLITS OPEN
Fissures on the tiny Icelandic island of Heimaey split open without warning and covered a nearby town in molten lava and black ash.

change. The Black Death, the plague outbreak that indiscriminately slaughtered one-third of Europe's population between 1346 and 1352, is often credited with sparking the Reformation. Disasters destroy old ways of life and make way for new ones.

NATURE'S IMPACT

By providing vivid accounts of the wide range of natural disasters known to have affected humanity or changed the history of the Earth, this book attempts to give an impression of the magnitude of their effect. Of necessity, the list is far from complete. The governments of some countries still do not allow full accounts of natural disasters to be published, and throughout history the disasters that have befallen rich and powerful nations have been more fully recorded than those that struck poorer areas. Accounts of the many devastating catastrophes that disturbed our ancestors exist only as legends, but traces of the damage that occurred at

THE IMPACT OF WIND AND WATER
Numerous marinas and thousands of homes in Florida were ripped apart by tempestuous waves and ferocious winds when Hurricane Andrew swept across the southeastern United States in 1992.

TREMORS FROM BELOW
Almost 800 multistory buildings in the center of Mexico City collapsed completely when tremors from an earthquake centered 250 miles (400 km) away rocked their foundations. About 9,000 people were killed and 30,000 more were injured.

this time still remain as a record. Scientists have learned how to interpret this record and are slowly piecing together details of these disastrous prehistoric events. Studies of rocks carrying the fossil remains of ancient life forms is yielding evidence of climatic and geological events that made life on Earth almost impossible. Our knowledge of the past is far from complete, however. More is known about the extinction of the dinosaurs 65 million years ago than the demise of the intelligent apes that were our ancestors. Learning about humanity's darkest hours provides an insight into human nature. The reaction of communities affected

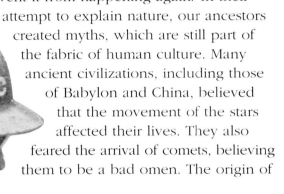

THE THREAT OF FIRE
Forest fires are a perennial problem in the South of France, where long hot spells dry out the trees and allow a single spark to blaze into an inferno.

by natural disasters remains the same all around the world and throughout history. During a disaster there is shock, anger, disbelief, fear, resignation, relief, and immense gratitude for the help and support that is given. After, the same questions are asked: Why did it happen? Who is to blame? Can we prevent it from happening again? In their attempt to explain nature, our ancestors created myths, which are still part of the fabric of human culture. Many ancient civilizations, including those of Babylon and China, believed that the movement of the stars affected their lives. They also feared the arrival of comets, believing them to be a bad omen. The origin of

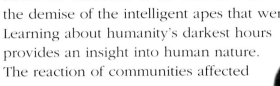

SAVED FROM A FLASH FLOOD
Storms in California often cause flash floods because the ground is too dry to absorb heavy rain. This girl was fortunate that help was at hand when one of these these floods suddenly engulfed her.

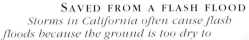

this belief may have been linked to a series of large aerial explosions that shook the Earth some 4,200 years ago. Astronomers have now calculated that a large comet broke up in the Solar System around this time, leaving debris in the path of the orbiting Earth. Fragments of the comet entering our atmosphere are thought to have exploded, causing the fires and other calamities referred to in the legends of many cultures.

The word "disaster" is a legacy of our ancestors' fear. "Aster" is derived from the Greek word for star, so "disaster" means "bad star." The immense power of nature dominated most ancient cultures, whose belief was that nature was not a random force, but was under the direct and total control of their gods. Thunderbolts were the weapons of the Greek god Zeus and the Norse god Thor. The god of the Israelites destroyed his enemies and those who disobeyed him with floods, earthquakes, and other natural weapons. The Hindu god Shiva reflected both the benign and the violent aspects of nature, being both a destroyer and a restorer.

STILL WAITING FOR RAIN
Poor seasonal rains throughout most of the 1980s caused widespread famine across much of Africa. As this 1993 picture of Masai farmers in Tanzania shows, the threat of drought has still not passed.

THE MODERN PERSPECTIVE

During the twentieth century, the advances in science and technology have provided us with a greater understanding of how natural forces sustain and destroy the Earth's environments. We now know why certain parts of our planet are more prone to certain disasters. We have also gained a limited ability to predict when some disasters will strike, and a limited amount of power to alleviate their effects. People in the more affluent parts of the world are showing a willingness to share this knowledge and power with people in the poorer areas. We continue to make mistakes, however, one of the most serious of which is to believe that our understanding of nature and our power to change it are greater than they are.

Scientific investigation has now made us aware that, in the distant past, the Earth has been damaged by natural forces far more destructive than any yet faced by humans. Although we have caused and are still causing major changes to the natural environment, there is no real danger that we will destroy nature itself. Nature will, in time, destroy us.

Lesley Newson

LESLEY NEWSON

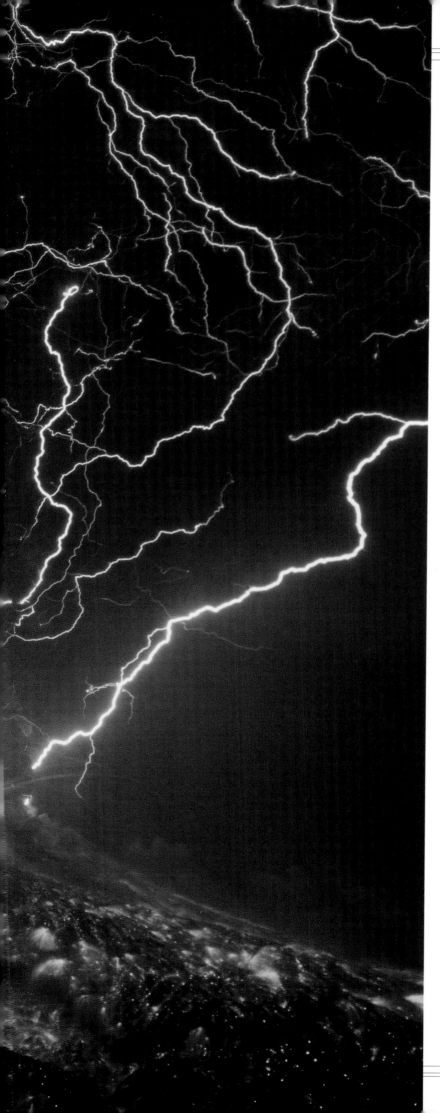

PART ONE

NATURAL DISASTERS

*"When men lack a sense of awe,
there will be disaster."*

LAO-TZU (SIXTH CENTURY BC), *TAO-TE CHING*

THE EARTH IS A ROCKY SPHERE nearly 8,000 miles in diameter. It is surrounded by a shroud of gases more than 60 miles deep. Sandwiched in between is a fragile layer, only a few miles thick, where humans are able to survive. It is perhaps not surprising that in this tiny zone of life there are occasional upheavals that make survival impossible.

This section of the book examines the range of natural disasters, grouped according to their primary cause. Most of the disasters are regarded in two ways: by looking at what has happened to the Earth and also at what has happened to the people involved. Every disaster gives an opportunity to learn about the forces at work within and around the Earth. It is an opportunity to learn about ourselves and what we can do to prevent or lessen the most severe consequences of Nature's destructiveness.

MOUNT SAKURAJIMA, JAPAN
During the eruption of Mount Sakurajima in 1995, a violent lightning storm was generated by the friction of swirling ash particles.

RESTLESS EARTH

EARTHQUAKES AND VOLCANIC eruptions can cause destruction and death in many different ways. When a severe earthquake shakes a city, it not only destroys buildings, but also wrecks the entire infrastructure. Earthquakes can also trigger fires, landslides, avalanches, and huge waves called tsunamis that inundate coastal areas. Some volcanoes release rivers of lava that bury and burn nearby land, but those that erupt explosively are far more deadly. They blast out clouds of molten rock and gases, which shoot high into the atmosphere, disrupting the climate of the entire planet; or they race across the ground, incinerating everything in their path. The ash deposited by these clouds can mix with water to create lethal mudflows.

② MOUNT ST. HELENS
When Mount St. Helens exploded on May 18, 1980, the blast blew away its north face and millions of trees.

⑧ HEIMAEY
When the ground split open on the Icelandic island of Heimaey in 1973, lava and gas shot up into the air.

① SAN FRANCISCO
A powerful earthquake on April 18, 1906 rocked San Francisco and triggered devastating fires.

LISBON ⑨
An earthquake off the coast of Portugal in 1755 toppled many buildings in Lisbon, and triggered vast tsunamis.

③ MEXICO CITY
Hundreds of buildings in the Mexican capital collapsed when an earthquake struck the city in September 1985.

⑦ MOUNT PELÉE
An eruption on Martinique in 1902 blew a cloud of hot gas and ash into St. Pièrre, killing about 30,000 people.

VOLCANO GODDESS
This figure represents Pelé, the Hawaiian goddess of fire who, according to legend, lives in Mount Kilauea.

CHIMBOTE ④
A large earthquake near Chimbote caused widespread damage across Peru and set in motion a deadly landslide on Mount Huascarán.

⑥ NEVADO DEL RUIZ
On November 13, 1985 the eruption of a volcano in Colombia created a river of mud that destroyed Armero, killing about 21,000 people.

⑤ VALDIVIA
A series of offshore earthquakes caused extensive damage in Chile and triggered tsunamis that flooded coasts around the Pacific Ocean.

CALIFORNIAN EARTHQUAKE
The epicenter of the earthquake that shook down these homes in San Francisco in 1989 was 60 miles (95 kilometers) southwest of the city, but its shockwaves still carried enough energy to cause widespread damage.

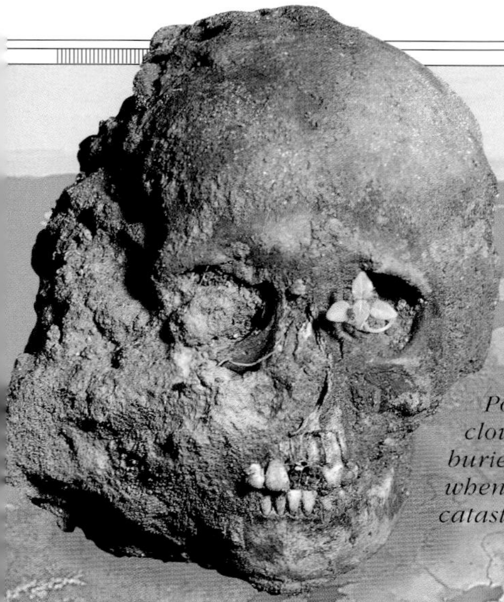

10 VESUVIUS
*Herculaneum and
Pompeii were engulfed in
clouds of burning gas and
buried under volcanic ash
when Mount Vesuvius erupted
catastrophically in AD 79.*

15 KOBE
*A powerful earthquake in
Osaka Bay, Japan, in
January 1995 claimed 6,000
lives and caused extensive
damage in Kobe and other
cities in the region.*

13 TANGSHAN
*A strong earthquake directly
under the Chinese industrial
city of Tangshan in July 1976
killed almost 250,000 people.*

11 SPITAK
*Early on December 7, 1988,
a 15-second tremor wrecked
much of Spitak and 100,000
Armenians lost their lives.*

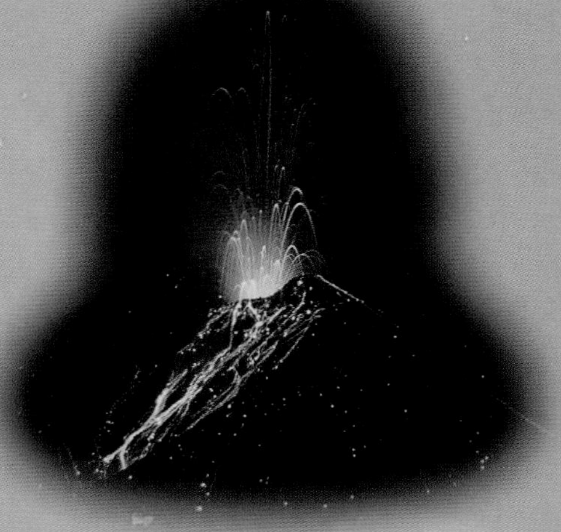

12 KRAKATAU
*About 36,000 people in Indonesia
were killed by vast waves, when
the volcanic island of Krakatau
blew apart in May 1883.*

MEASURING SHOCKWAVES
This seismograph, built in 1885, was
designed to record shockwaves from
earthquakes. Modern seismographs
can detect shockwaves from
anywhere in the world.

14 MOUNT PINATUBO
*The eruption of Mount Pinatubo in May 1991
clogged the atmosphere with volcanic gas and
covered much of the Philippines in ash. The death
toll, though, was below 1,000 due to evacuations.*

VOLCANOES AND EARTHQUAKES

EARTHQUAKES AND VOLCANOES ARE VIOLENT REMINDERS that only a thin layer of solidified rock separates us from the hot, restless interior of the Earth. This fragile skin is broken up into a jigsaw puzzle of plates, which constantly jostle each other as they slowly slide around the Earth's surface. Violent geological upheavals commonly occur near the edges of the plates.

PLATE TECTONICS

The interior of the Earth is unimaginably hot, reaching temperatures of 6,700°F (3,700°C). The decay of radioactive elements inside the Earth would cause a constant increase in temperature if it were not for the circulation of the rock in the mantle carrying heat up to the surface, keeping the core temperature stable.

On top of this cauldron is the Earth's crust, made up of cool slabs of solid rock known as tectonic plates. Currently there are seven large plates and at least eight smaller ones. Underneath, hotter rock near the core slowly wells up. The solid surface rock blocks its rise, but at a rifting boundary the hot rock can push through the weak point between two plates.

Released from the enormous pressure, the rock becomes molten as it rushes upward, escaping from rifts in the form of lava and hot

THE EARTH'S INTERIOR
Beneath a thin, cool crust lies a 1,800-mile (2,900-km) thick layer of hot, viscous rock in the mantle. The Earth's center consists mostly of iron. Vast pressures keep the Moon-sized inner core solid despite the enormous heat.

Continental crust is thicker and less dense than oceanic crust

Crust
Upper mantle
Lower mantle
Liquid outer core
Hot, solid inner core
Oceanic crust is thinner and denser than continental crust

gases. At the surface the lava cools and solidifies into new crust. Most rifts are located on the ocean floor where extruded lava has formed into vast parallel ridges.

As new rock builds up at rifts, the crust on either side of the boundary is pushed away so that, at their other boundaries, plates are being forced against one another. What happens as the plates are pushed together depends on the nature of the rock at the edges of the plates.

Subduction boundaries form where the density of the rock on either side of the boundary is unequal. The denser plate slides beneath its neighbor and is forced into the Earth's hot interior. The rock melts as it slowly sinks. Most of it is absorbed into the mantle, but some rises again to create subduction volcanoes. The Pacific rim is known as the "Ring of Fire" because it is bordered by subduction volcanoes.

A colliding boundary occurs where two plates of the same density push together and rock at the edge of the plates is forced to bend and break. Mountain ranges are formed by the pile-up of rock as two continents collide head-on. The Himalayas are being formed as India and Eurasia collide. At some colliding boundaries two plates grind past each other, creating transform faults such as the San Andreas Fault in California.

THE EARTH'S TECTONIC PLATES
The Earth's surface is made up of a dynamic jigsaw puzzle of tectonic plates. The ceaseless movement of these plates is responsible for most of the world's volcanoes and earthquakes.

LAVA CAULDRON
The Erta'ale Volcano in Ethiopia is one of several craters in Africa's Great Rift Valley. The valley is a massive split in the Earth's crust where molten rock from the mantle rises to the surface.

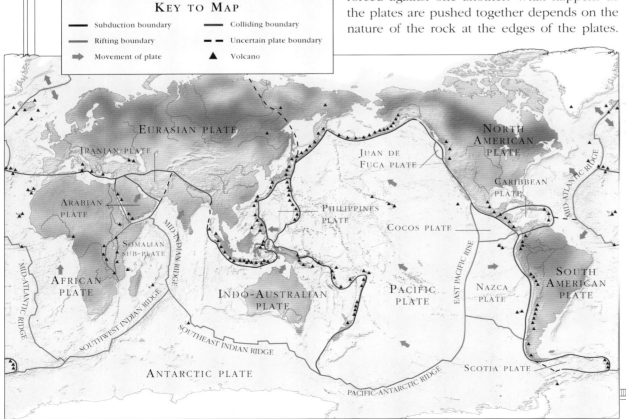

KEY TO MAP

—— Subduction boundary	—— Colliding boundary
—— Rifting boundary	– – Uncertain plate boundary
→ Movement of plate	▲ Volcano

EURASIAN PLATE

IRANIAN PLATE

ARABIAN PLATE

SOMALIAN SUB-PLATE

AFRICAN PLATE

MID-ATLANTIC RIDGE

MID INDIAN RIDGE

SOUTHWEST INDIAN RIDGE

SOUTHEAST INDIAN RIDGE

INDO-AUSTRALIAN PLATE

JUAN DE FUCA PLATE

PHILIPPINES PLATE

COCOS PLATE

PACIFIC PLATE

EAST PACIFIC RISE

NAZCA PLATE

NORTH AMERICAN PLATE

CARIBBEAN PLATE

MID-ATLANTIC RIDGE

SOUTH AMERICAN PLATE

ANTARCTIC PLATE

SCOTIA PLATE

PACIFIC-ANTARCTIC RIDGE

THE SAN ANDREAS FAULT
Clearly visible from above, the San Andreas Fault in California is formed by the collision of the North American and Pacific Plates where they slide past one another.

VOLCANOES

A volcano is an opening in the Earth's crust that allows material known as magma to escape from the mantle to the surface. These openings occur in three ways, each producing a different kind of volcanic eruption.

Hot spot volcanoes form where a local upsurge of magma penetrates the crust. Each of the Hawaiian Islands is a huge underwater mountain, built up over millions of years as the Pacific plate moves over the hot spot.

Rift volcanoes occur at the boundaries of tectonic plates where magma regularly oozes to the surface. Since most rifts are on the seafloor, these eruptions largely go unnoticed. The exceptions are the volcanoes of the Great Rift Valley in Africa and those of Iceland, which is an island formed from lava that has emerged from the mid-Atlantic rift.

The most destructive volcanoes are those that erupt explosively like Mount St. Helens in northwestern United States (see *pp.18–19*) and Mount Pinatubo in the Philippines (see *pp.28–31*). These are subduction volcanoes

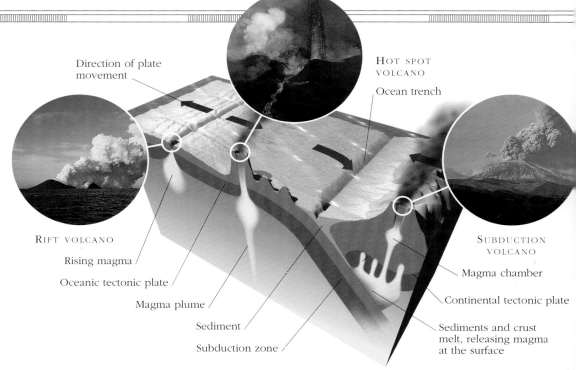

Direction of plate movement

HOT SPOT VOLCANO

Ocean trench

RIFT VOLCANO

Rising magma

Oceanic tectonic plate

Magma plume

Sediment

Subduction zone

SUBDUCTION VOLCANO

Magma chamber

Continental tectonic plate

Sediments and crust melt, releasing magma at the surface

TYPES OF VOLCANO
Rift volcanoes form along the boundary of two plates as they tear apart. Hot spot volcanoes are created by hot magma plumes rising to the surface from deep within the mantle. Subduction volcanoes result from the collision of two plates.

HOT SPOT ERUPTIONS ON HAWAII
Fountains of glowing lava spurt out of Mount Kilauea, Hawaii's largest volcano (below). The boiling rock ejected by Hawaii's hot spot volcanoes forms vast lava flows (left).

and occur where the seafloor is sliding beneath a neighboring plate. As the seafloor slips down into the hot mantle, water, sediment, and the remains of living things are taken down as well. In these hot, high-pressure conditions they undergo chemical changes to become magma, a sticky mixture of molten rock and dissolved gas. This magma rises and becomes trapped in the crust until it breaks through and explodes to the surface.

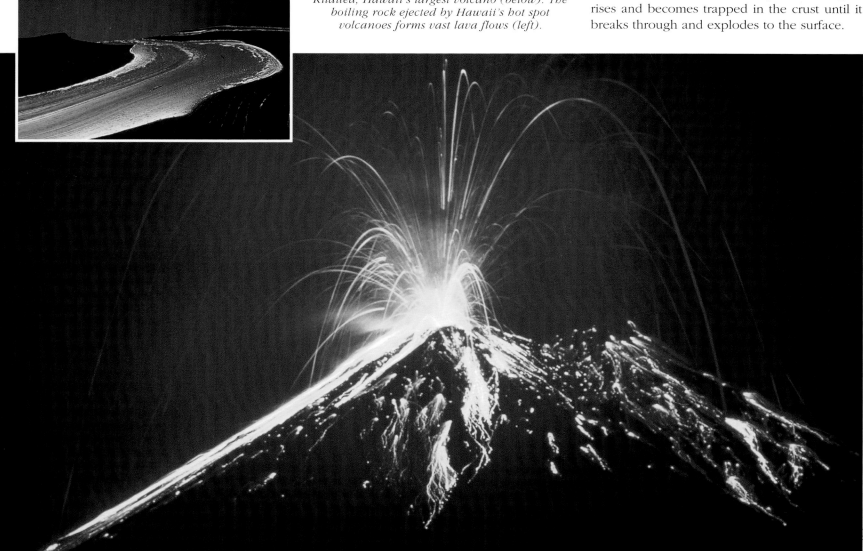

HEIMAEY

VOLCANIC ERUPTION, ICELAND, 1973

GAZETTEER P.134 – SITE NO.108

ON JANUARY 23, 1973 the ground split open on the Icelandic island of Heimaey, near the town of Vestmannaeyjar, ejecting lava 500 feet (150 meters) into the air. Bombarded by swirling black cinders, the island's 5,000 residents made their way down to the harbor and were quickly evacuated. Some returned in an attempt to save their homes and the island's harbor from being engulfed by ash and lava. When the eruption finally ceased five months later, a 1-mile (2-kilometer) lava flow had swallowed a large section of Vestmannaeyjar's harbor, 1,200 homes had been destroyed, but just one life was lost.

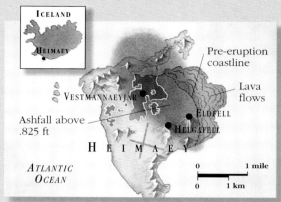

VOLCANIC ISLAND SPLITS OPEN
Heimaey is a 4-mile (6-km) long, 2-mile (3-km) wide island just south of Iceland. The rift that opened in a churchyard on the edge of the town of Vestmannaeyjar formed a new 600-ft (200-m) high volcanic cone.

The island of Heimaey sits astride a 12,500-mile (20,000-kilometer) volcanic rift that runs under the Atlantic Ocean. The island emerged from beneath the waves about 5,000 years ago when lava from the rift exploded to the surface. Despite the danger of the rift opening up again and flooding the island with lava, the people of Heimaey valued their life in Vestmannaeyjar, an excellent natural harbor that they had developed into Iceland's busiest fishing port.

Most of the citizens of Vestmannaeyjar were asleep when a huge fissure opened up on the outskirts of their town. Two night-shift workers returning home in the middle of the night saw what appeared to be flames leaping from the ground and growing into a solid wall of fire. After they raised the alarm, an evacuation of the island was ordered. As the islanders made their way to the boats, planes, and helicopters that would take them to the mainland, the roaring red-hot gash went on growing, nearly splitting the island of Heimaey in two.

Within a few days the huge split, choked by cooling lava, narrowed down to three openings, which continued to throw out hot cinders and spew streams of boiling lava. A team of volunteers returned to try to save Vestmannaeyjar from destruction. They worked around the clock, scraping black mounds of grit and volcanic rock off their houses to prevent them from collapsing and spraying the lava with 6 million tons of seawater in an effort to solidify the flows before they blocked the entrance to their harbor.

When the ground finally closed again on June 26, 1973, a third of the town had been totally destroyed. Most of the residents returned to the island and, because the harbor had been saved, many of them were able to resume their livelihoods.

ADVANCING LAVA
Houses burst into flames as they were engulfed by streams of glowing lava. More than one-third of the houses in Vestmannaeyjar were destroyed during the five-month-long eruption on Heimaey.

WALLS OF FLAME
On the night of the eruption, a wall of flaming lava roared into the air on the outskirts of Vestmannaeyjar, and tore open a gaping fissure that was nearly 1 mile (2 km) long.

MOUNT ST. HELENS

VOLCANIC ERUPTION, US, 1980

GAZETTEER P.129 – SITE NO.89

THE UNITED STATES WAS ALERTED TO the threat posed by volcanoes in May 1980, when Mount St. Helens erupted, killing 57 people. A huge explosion blew away the north side of the mountain and shot out a deadly volcanic cloud that flattened everything within 8 miles (12 kilometers) of the blast. As the shattered mountain collapsed, it smothered the countryside under tons of rock and caused rivers to flood. Erupted ash buried vast tracts of northwest America in gray mud.

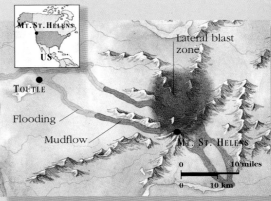

CHAOS IN THE CASCADES
During an 8-hour eruptive phase, Mount St. Helens, which forms part of the Cascade Range in northwest America, turned more than (130,000 acres) 52,000 hectares of beautiful mountain scenery into a devastated wasteland.

Mount St. Helens had several minor eruptions between 1831 and 1857, but then went totally quiet for over a century. By 1980, the beautiful snowcapped mountain was a favorite vacation spot for thousands of climbers and campers. Then, in March of that year, the peace of this wilderness was disturbed when tremors began to shake the foundations of the mountain.

Soon after, Mount St. Helens started to vent ash and rock, and its north face began to bulge as if there were something inside the mountain trying to force its way out. A major eruption seemed imminent, and scientists and journalists gathered eagerly to monitor the proceedings. State officials prevented tourists from coming near the volcano, but there seemed to be no change in the serenely beautiful mountain as the days passed. It seemed as if it might be settling down to rest again.

When 30-year-old geologist David Johnson radioed his colleagues in the nearby town of Vancouver the first thing on May 18, he had nothing special to report. Then at 8:32 am he came on the radio again and announced excitedly: "Vancouver! Vancouver! This is it." Those were his last words. A moderate strength earthquake had rumbled the ground below the volcano. Seconds later, the north face of the mountain began to collapse, providing an escape route for the hot magma inside.

MOUNT ST. HELENS EXPLODES

With a deafening bang that could be heard up north in Canada and down south in California, an explosion blasted out the side of Mount St. Helens, causing instant devastation to areas up to 19 miles (30 kilometers) north of the crater. On a hill 6 miles (10 kilometers) to the north, the mobile hut that sheltered David Johnson and his monitoring equipment was blown off the ridge. Johnson's body was never found. To the south, a team of foresters working less than five miles (8 kilometers) from the crater were unhurt by the crippling northern blast.

A team of geologists circling Mount St. Helens in a small plane at the time described seeing the north flank of the volcano "ripple and churn up" before collapsing in a massive avalanche of rock and ice. The landslide surged down the flanks at speeds of up to 180 mph (290 kph), submerging Spirit Lake and the Toutle River. The debris set in motion mudflows and floods, which extended the range of the devastation.

Mount St. Helens has been quiet since 1980, but a new hazard threatens the Cascade Range – nearby Mount Rainier has begun to rumble ominously.

PARADISE LOST
When Mount St. Helens erupted, its perfectly formed glaciated summit was blown apart, leaving a gaping wound on its northern flank (above). Countless evergreen trees and much of the teeming wildlife that lived here was destroyed by the eruption, which turned the area into a gray wasteland (right).

BILLOWING ASH CLOUDS
After a massive lateral eruption blew out the north flank, volcanic clouds shot skyward and dumped ash on northwest North America.

WASHED DOWNSTREAM
Savage floods tore down valleys, sweeping up vehicles and houses, after the collapse of Mount St. Helens' northern flank.

LAVA BOMB

The explosion of gases inside a volcano may hurl out lumps of molten rock, known as lava bombs, which can be as large as a house or as small as a tennis ball. Some of these bombs form distinctive twisted tails as they fly through the air.

VOLCANIC ERUPTIONS

There is evidence that, at intervals of tens of millions of years, huge magma plumes have penetrated the Earth's crust and spewed out vast amounts of lava and gas (see *pp.98–101*). There have, however, been no catastrophic hot spot eruptions in historic times.

Hot spot activity, like most eruptions of rift volcanoes, has not been responsible for many deaths. The lava produced usually flows out gently, allowing people time to escape. The suffocating mix of dense gases that is often released during these eruptions can be more of a threat than the lava. Poisonous gases released during a major eruption on Iceland in 1783 decimated crops and killed most of the livestock across the island. As a result, 10,000 Icelanders died of starvation.

The worst volcanic disasters are caused by the eruption of subduction volcanoes. These volcanoes often remain dormant for hundreds of years, and then explode into life when the pressure of the magma below them cracks the

NEVADO DEL RUIZ

VOLCANIC ERUPTION, COLOMBIA, 1985

GAZETTEER P.132 – SITE NO.25

AN ERUPTION OF THE REMOTE Nevado del Ruiz volcano on November 13, 1985 caused the second deadliest volcanic tragedy of the twentieth century. The heat of ash and gases released during the eruption melted a large section of the mountain's ice cap. The water surged down the mountain carrying tons of ash, and within minutes it became a cascade of sticky mud known as a lahar. One of these lahars burst out of a canyon upstream of Armero, sending a 130-foot (40-meter) high wave of mud churning toward the town. About 21,000 people were killed in Armero, along with over 1,000 others in neighboring villages.

BURIED IN RIVERS OF MUD
Ejecta from the Nevado del Ruiz eruption set in motion a series of fast-moving mudflows that traveled more than 38 miles (60 km) from the volcano and destroyed many settlements in their path, including the town of Armero.

Nevado del Ruiz is one of many volcanoes in the Andes range of mountains. The ash from past eruptions has enriched the soils in central Colombia, creating excellent farmland. Armero, a town of 23,000 residents, was located about 30 miles (50 kilometers) from the volcano and was built up around warehouses that stored rice, cotton, and coffee grown in the area. The town's low-lying position on the banks of La Lagunilla river made it vulnerable to lahars. When Ruiz erupted in 1845, 1,000 people died when mud flooded down the mountain.

NEVADO DEL RUIZ REAWAKENS
The first sign that the mountain was entering another eruptive phase came in January 1985, when it began venting volcanic gas and steam. On September 11, the situation deteriorated when a small eruption melted part of a glacier on Nevado del Ruiz's ice-capped peak and triggered a series of rockfalls. The meltwater formed a large lake that was held precariously in place by fallen chunks of ice and rock. After preparing a hazard map of the surrounding area, the Colombian Institute of Geological Mining Research reported that there was a high risk of mudflows hitting Armero, should the volcano erupt again.

On November 13, scientists were advising government officials of the risks that Armero faced when Nevado del Ruiz began to erupt. Despite the warning, no action was taken and

THE CHAIN REACTION
The eruption of the 17,800-ft (5,400-m) high Nevado del Ruiz was merely a sneeze, but the heat of the blast was sufficient to melt part of its ice cap.

BURIED IN A SEA OF MUD
Armero was obliterated in a matter of minutes when waves of fast-flowing mud surged through the town, two hours after Nevado del Ruiz erupted.

Earth's crust and pushes up to the surface. As the magma rises, the gas comes out of solution and expands rapidly, blasting molten rock into the air. The magma is often ejected with such force that chunks of rock are hurled over great distances, or the molten rock may be shattered into tiny droplets that are shot high into the atmosphere. These droplets solidify into volcanic ash that blackens the sky and drifts down to bury the land under a thick layer of ejecta as fine as dust, but as heavy as rock.

After the 1815 eruption of Tambora on the Indonesian island of Sumbawa, homes and crops on adjacent islands were crushed under a 3-foot (1-meter) thick layer of fallen ash. The ash also sank into the sea, destroying marine life. It is estimated that about 80,000 people perished in the resulting famine.

PYROCLASTIC FLOWS

Some eruptions eject hot gases and droplets of molten rock in a cloud so dense that, instead of blasting upward, it tumbles out of the crater. These pyroclastic flows hug the contours of the land like a liquid, rolling across the ground at more than 100 mph (160 kph), incinerating everything in their path.

Pyroclastic flows often move long distances from the crater, enveloping wide areas in an unbreathable cloud of scorching gas and ash.

LUCKY ESCAPE
A man carried to safety after the ordeal was one of only 2,000 people to escape the lethal mudflows that destroyed the town of Armero.

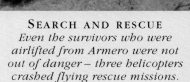

local radio broadcasts urged the residents to remain calm and not to leave their homes.

That night, Nevado del Ruiz was cloaked in a thick cloud and the scientists who were monitoring the volcano did not notice the pyroclastic flow that began blowing out shortly after 9 pm. As the hot ash hit ice near the summit, it became a muddy torrent of water that rushed down the mountain. By the time the scientists had realized what was happening, one mudflow had nearly reached Armero.

A last-minute warning was broadcast on the civil defense channel but was largely ignored. Most people were listening to the local station, which was still broadcasting music, when mud engulfed Armero soon after 11 pm. Many people

SEARCH AND RESCUE
Even the survivors who were airlifted from Armero were not out of danger – three helicopters crashed flying rescue missions.

had already gone to bed and were buried where they lay. Of the few residents who realized what was going on, only the fast runners survived by sprinting up to the safety of high ground.

Armero was not rebuilt after the tragedy, and the town's mud-encased remains are still visible on the La Lugunilla floodplain.

VALLEY OF DEATH
Debris and bodies were swept up by the lethal mudflow and strewn across the valley floor. A few fortunate survivors were carried to safety on the crest of the waves of cementlike mud.

These glowing clouds reach temperatures of up to 1,650°F (900°C), and can burn, boil, or melt everything they envelop in an instant.

The deadliest volcanic disaster of the twentieth century occurred in 1902, when Mont Pelée erupted a pyroclastic surge.

MOUNT UNZEN BOILS OVER
An enormous pyroclastic flow surged down the flanks of Japan's Mount Unzen when it erupted in June 1991. Nearby residents had been evacuated, but in 1792 similar flows claimed 15,000 lives.

FLOODS AND LAHARS

Since the peaks of many terrestrial volcanoes tower above the snowline, flooding is a danger when they erupt. The heat generated can rapidly melt snow and ice on their slopes. The resulting meltwater often picks up volcanic ash as it flows down the mountain, producing deadly mudflows known as lahars. These torrents of sticky mud pick up great speeds and can flatten everything in their path.

When Nevado del Ruiz erupted in 1985, the lahars it created flowed long distances, killing more than 22,000 people (see *pp.20–21*).

Meltwater is not essential for lahars since eruptions are often accompanied by torrential rain. Fast-rising columns of gas and ash shot into the sky often trigger thunderstorms. In the Philippines, heavy rain combined with dense ashfalls to create widespread mudflows both during and after the eruption of Mount Pinatubo in 1991 (see *pp.28–31*).

MONT PELÉE
VOLCANIC ERUPTION, MARTINIQUE, 1902
GAZETTEER P.131 – SITE NO.42

ZONE OF DESTRUCTION
The eruption of Mont Pelée on May 8, 1902 laid waste to 22 sq miles (58 sq km) and destroyed St. Pierre. Subsequent eruptions on May 20 and August 30, 1902 further devastated the region.

IN 1902, ST. PIERRE WAS the largest town on the French colony of Martinique, with some 30,000 inhabitants. The residents of this thriving Caribbean port were used to the rumblings of the 4,583-foot (1,379-meter) high Mont Pelée, located less than five miles (8 kilometers) to the north. Pelée had been emitting gas since 1889, but in April 1902 the mountain began erupting in earnest. By May, people grew fearful as clouds of steam and ash poured from the volcano, darkening the sky and covering the streets like a blanket of snow.

TIMEWARP
Recovered from the ruins of St. Pierre, this pocket watch was melted to a standstill by the heat of a deadly pyroclastic surge that engulfed the town.

LETHAL ERUPTION
On May 5, scores of residents abandoned St. Pierre after water from Mont Pelée's crater-lake was spat out by an eruption. Mud swept away a nearby distillery and 23 of the workers. Far from encouraging the exodus, the editor of the local newspaper, *Les Colonies*, urged the residents to return even though the town now reeked of sulfur, a lava plug in the volcano glowed red, and the eruptions were getting worse.

Two days later, troops were sent to St. Pierre to prevent further evacuations and to calm the residents, who were alarmed by the news that an eruption of the nearby island of St. Vincent had killed 1,700 people. Despite the reassurances of "experts" that Mont Pelée was safe, fears grew when ash-laden clouds of gas began pouring down the Rivière Blanche, just north of the town. In an attempt to prevent a full-scale panic, Governor Mouttet moved to St. Pierre with his wife on the evening of May 7, 1902.

Shortly before 8 am the next day, gaseous magma exploded under the lava plug and burst through the side of the volcano. Under cover of a large black eruption cloud, a lethal concoction of superheated gas and volcanic ash surged down Mont Pelée's southern flank and tore through St. Pierre with terrifying speed. The incandescent cloud was hot enough to melt glass and struck so suddenly that people had no time to take cover, let alone to escape the deadly cloud.

Within seconds, the burning cloud had killed all but two of St. Pierre's residents. Auguste Ciparis, a prisoner incarcerated in the town's underground dungeon, and Leon Comprère-Leander, a shoemaker living on the outskirts of the town, survived the ordeal. The shoemaker later recounted how he was knocked unconscious by a terrible wind that burned his

GHOSTLY REMAINS
The people of St. Pierre fell where they stood when the pyroclastic surge struck (right). The sinister form of Pelée still looms over the town, whose 1902 ruins are a memorial to this tragedy (below).

body and deprived him of air. When he came around, Leon discovered that his whole family was dead and "the entire city was aflame."

In the harbor, 18 vessels were sunk by the conflagration. One ship, the *Roddam*, escaped. A crewman told of people "running hither and thither amidst the flames until a terrible cloud of smoke came, when they fell like flies."

TSUNAMIS

These highly destructive waves are most often triggered by undersea earthquakes (see *p.40*). Tsunamis also occur when the sea is suddenly displaced by a landslide. Studies have shown that the Australian coastline was swamped by huge waves in prehistoric times after a major underwater landslide took place under Hawaii Island, a hot spot volcano in the Pacific.

During the eruption of Krakatau in 1883, tons of volcanic rock and ash were hurled into the sea, creating waves that devastated nearby coastlines and traveled across the oceans.

CLIMATE CHANGE

The most explosive volcanic eruptions cool the entire planet by blasting volcanic ash and gases high up into the stratosphere. Unlike volcanic debris suspended in the lower atmosphere, which attaches to water droplets and soon falls back to earth in drops of rain, the ash and gases that are blasted above the level of clouds can stay aloft for months. This volcanic cocktail is carried around the globe by high-altitude winds and forms a worldwide sunscreen that reduces the amount of the sun's radiation penetrating the atmosphere. The volcanic gas sulfur dioxide has the most long-term effect on global climate because it changes into droplets of sulfuric acid in the upper atmosphere. These droplets allow more of the sun's heat to radiate out into space.

The huge eruption of Tambora in 1815 blasted 19 cubic miles (80 cubic kilometers) of volcanic material into the atmosphere. The volume of ash and gases ejected in this eruption was about eight times more than the Mount Pinatubo eruption in 1991. The 1815 eruption severely disrupted the weather around the world. People in the eastern United States called 1816 "the year without a summer." The prolonged cold and damp

VOLCANIC MONSTER
In the summer following the massive Tambora eruption of 1815, Mary Shelley (left) was on vacation in Switzerland with friends. The constant bad weather that the eruption had caused forced them to stay indoors. The group amused themselves by writing horror stories. Hers was called "Frankenstein."

conditions that year prevented crops from ripening, which resulted in widespread food shortages and famines around the world.

Layers of volcanic ash found in glaciers and sea sediments provide a record of the many volcanoes that have blasted magma into the atmosphere over the ages. The most recent catastrophic volcanic eruption occurred about 75,000 years ago on the Indonesian island of Sumatra. It blasted 200 times more volcanic debris into the atmosphere than Pinatubo and created a 25-mile (40-kilometer) wide crater on the island that filled with water and is now known as Lake Toba. Some scientists believe that the global cooling that followed the eruption of Toba triggered one of the coldest phases of the last Ice Age (see *p.96*).

INDONESIAN VOLCANOES
Tambora's huge water-filled crater dominates the Indonesian island of Sumbawa (left). Below are some other peaks in a chain of 130 volcanoes that runs the length of the Indonesian islands.

KRAKATAU

VOLCANIC ERUPTION, INDONESIA, 1883

GAZETTEER P.139 — SITE NO.11

ON AUGUST 27, 1883 ONE OF THE VOLCANOES on the tiny Indonesian island of Krakatau erupted with such force that the explosion almost totally destroyed the island, leaving a 960-foot (290-meter) deep crater in the ocean floor. The blasts and heavy ash falls triggered tsunamis, which struck the coastlines of Java and Sumatra with waves up to 130 feet (40 meters) high. The waves swept far inland, destroying hundreds of villages and killing about 36,000 people.

WAVES OF DEATH
As Krakatau blew apart on August 27, 1883, it triggered gigantic tsunamis that devastated the coastlines of Java and Sumatra, washing away the towns of Teluk Betong, Kalimbang, and Merak, as well as many other villages.

THE CONTINUING THREAT
Since 1927 frequent small eruptions have built the Anak Krakatau (Child of Krakatau) volcano within a sunken crater that was formed when Krakatau island blew apart in 1883.

SWEPT ASHORE
The steamer Berouw *was swept up in a tsunami that submerged the Sumatran town of Teluk Betong and was deposited deep in the jungle.*

In 1883, the small jungle-clad island of Krakatau was uninhabited, but fishermen often visited it to pick fruit and collect wood. The island was made up of a row of three volcanoes that straddled a 4-mile (7-kilometer) wide crater formed during an earlier massive eruption, which was dated to around AD 416 by scientists.

There had been no eruptions on Krakatau since 1680 until, on May 20, 1883 a series of loud explosions signaled that the island was stirring again. Over the next three months the eruptions on the island grew fiercer as one of Krakatau's volcanoes began to belch out steam, ash, and chunks of pumice. No one on the nearby islands of Sumatra and Java was concerned by the eruptions on Krakatau until 1 pm on August 26, when explosions and earthquakes began to shake their houses.

At 5:30 am the following day a series of five awesome explosions began, which together almost totally obliterated Krakatau. Lethal ash-laden clouds tore across the narrow Sunda Straits, burning many villagers on the coast of Sumatra. The vast majority of the 36,000 deaths, however, were caused by massive tsunamis that ravaged the coastlines of Java and Sumatra. Enormous waves swept the debris of boats and villages far inland, before they washed back, clogging the sea with drowned bodies.

VESUVIUS

VOLCANIC ERUPTION, ITALY, AD 79

GAZETTEER P.135 – SITE NO.11

IN AD 79, THREE ROMAN TOWNS, Stabiae, Herculaneum, and Pompeii, were destroyed when Mount Vesuvius erupted. The towns, situated around the Bay of Naples, were buried under tons of volcanic ash and lay frozen in time for many centuries. Excavation of the ruins has given archaeologists an extraordinary insight into everyday life in Roman times. It has also allowed scientists to determine the sequence of the eruption, which is estimated to have killed 16,000 people.

CARBONIZED FIGS
FOUND AT POMPEII

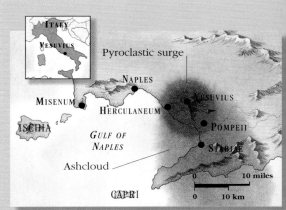

VESUVIUS'S MOST FAMOUS ERUPTION
Towns as far away as Stabiae were buried in ash and pumice during the eruption of Vesuvius in AD 79. Most victims died when Herculaneum and Pompeii were engulfed by clouds of burning gas surging from the volcano.

Pompeii was a successful market town and a port that traded in the produce of the many farms in the area. The farmland owed its high fertility to the presence of mineral-rich ash from previous eruptions of Mount Vesuvius, which had lain dormant for hundreds of years. A severe earthquake shook Pompeii in AD 63, and the repairs were still not finished 16 years later, when disaster struck again.

FACING AN UNCERTAIN FUTURE
Vesuvius, towering over the ruins of Pompeii, has erupted 50 times since AD 79. The most lethal killed 18,000 in 1691. Despite the risk of more eruptions, the area is still densely populated.

EYEWITNESS ACCOUNTS

We owe much of our knowledge of the AD 79 eruption of Mount Vesuvius to the Roman writer, Caius Pliny. He was 18 years old at the time and was living approximately 19 miles (30 kilometers) away in the town of Misenum. On August 24, he saw "a great cloud" rising from Vesuvius in the shape of a pine tree. Pliny's uncle, who was in charge of the Roman fleet in

CAPTURED IN STONE
This dog became encased in ash. When its body decomposed, it left behind a hollow that was used as a mold to recreate its death throes.

the area, promptly set sail to rescue friends who lived in Pompeii. As he crossed the Bay of Naples, ash rained down onto the ship, growing hotter and denser as he approached the shore. The crew described falling "stones blackened, burned, and broken by the fire" and "vast sheets of flame and tongues of fire" that burst from Mount Vesuvius.

The conditions became so bad that the ship could not reach Pompeii, but Pliny's uncle and his crew managed to land at Stabiae. Having landed, they found that high winds and turbulent seas made escape impossible.

BURNED AND BURIED
Many of Herculaneum's residents were burned alive by surges of searing hot ash and gas. The surges were followed by dense flows of pumice and ash, which entombed the victims.

THE FINAL DESTRUCTION

In Stabiae, the residents had abandoned their homes. Many of the people hurrying through the streets had cushions tied to their heads to protect themselves from the hail of ash and pumice that was rapidly burying their town. Pliny's uncle, who was in his mid-fifties, did not survive the bombardment, but some of his friends managed to escape and bring home his body and a first-hand account of their ordeal.

There are no surviving first-hand accounts of how Pompeii and Herculaneum were destroyed, but archaeological research shows that both were rapidly engulfed by "tongues of fire" similar to the one Pliny's party had seen burst from the mountain. Scientists believe that most of the victims at Herculaneum died when a surging cloud of burning gas struck the town at around 11:30 pm on August 24. Skeletons that were found in the ruins were huddled together under 66 feet (20 meters) of ash, in positions that suggest the people had died suddenly and together. Most of Pompeii's victims are believed to have died at around 6:30 am the next day, when the town was engulfed by a later surge of burning gas. After the eruption, the towns were forgotten until the ruins were discovered in 1709.

PREDICTING ERUPTIONS

More than 500 land-based volcanoes are known to have erupted in the last 3,000 years, and are consequently classified as active. Theoretically, they could erupt at any time, and about half a billion people live in areas that are at risk from active volcanoes.

The most devastating eruptions are usually preceded by days, weeks, or even months of lesser eruptions. The warning signs can be misleading, however. In 1976, a cautious French Government evacuated the Caribbean island of Guadeloupe after earth tremors suggested that La Soufrière, a volcano that had killed 1,600 people in 1908, might erupt again. When no eruption followed, the authorities were heavily criticised. Nowadays, Scientists monitor eruptions in the early phases, all over the world, and they also study areas around past eruptions. If the scientists' findings indicate that a volcano is likely to erupt explosively or suddenly eject a pyroclastic flow, evacuation is recommended. Evacuating early, to be on the safe side, is often not an option because of the difficulty in providing food and shelter for large numbers of evacuees. In addition, local people are disrupted financially, and they may be tempted to return to their homes before the main phase of the eruption begins.

LIVING WITH VOLCANOES

Several active volcanoes in Japan are monitored continuously so that people can be evacuated promptly if a severe eruption looks likely. This monitoring successfully predicted a major eruption of Mount Unzen in 1991. Thousands of local people were evacuated from the area and, as a result, the only people who died were scientists and television crews who had elected to stay within the evacuation zone. Huge dams have been built near some volcanoes, to divert lava and mudflows away from cities, so that the buildings will also have a chance of surviving an eruption. The last major eruption of Sakurajima in southern Japan was in 1914, but the volcano still has about

CLOUD OVER THE CARIBBEAN
Volcanic clouds, blasted out of the Soufrière Hills volcano on Montserrat, have covered most of this Caribbean island in ash. The volcano has killed more than 30 people since it erupted in 1995.

150 minor eruptions every year. People in the nearby city of Kagoshima, and in settlements close to the volcano, are drilled regularly on the evacuation procedures they must follow, should the eruptions become more violent.

Frequent eruptions on the tiny Caribbean island of Montserrat have forced two-thirds of the population to evacuate since the Soufrière Hills volcano came back to life in 1995.

JAPANESE CHILDREN AT RISK
Children who live at the foot of the Japanese volcano Sakuraǰima wear hardhats on their way to school to protect them from ash and cinders erupted by this highly active volcano.

MOUNT PINATUBO

VOLCANIC ERUPTION, PHILIPPINES, 1991

GAZETTEER P.137 – SITE NO.92

THE MASSIVE ERUPTION OF MOUNT PINATUBO in June 1991 was the most violent volcanic event of the twentieth century. The mountain blasted out more than 2 cubic miles (10 cubic kilometers) of ash and gases into the atmosphere, and lowered temperatures around the world. Falling ash destroyed 42,000 homes on the island of Luzon and smothered 200,000 acres (80,000 hectares) of land. Despite careful monitoring and the timely evacuation of more than 200,000 local residents from the surrounding area before the main eruption, nearly 900 people died as a consequence of Mount Pinatubo's devastating explosions.

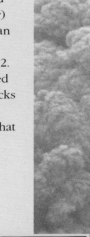

THE IMPACT OF MOUNT PINATUBO
During a series of eruptions in June 1991, pyroclastic flows incinerated land up to 11 miles (17 km) from Mount Pinatubo's summit, and heavy ashfalls were swept into mudflows that destroyed homes up to 38 miles (60 km) away.

Mount Pinatubo is one of 22 volcanoes located in the Philippines. The 5,440-foot (1,700-meter) high mountain had been dormant for more than four centuries before it reawoke in 1991. The first sign that it was waking up came on April 2. Local people noticed rumbling sounds followed by clouds of steam and ash escaping from cracks in the volcano. A nun went to the Philippines Institute of Volcanology in Manila and stated that the mountain, which she could see from her village, had just blown up.

Within three days, scientists had set up an observation post and installed instruments to monitor the waves of small earthquakes that

THE EXPLODING MOUNTAIN
Palls of volcanic gas and ash hung over Mount Pinatubo in June 1991 following a succession of major explosions, which blew apart the top 660 ft (200 m) of the mountain.

CLOUDS OF DESTRUCTION
Pinatubo ejected huge clouds of volcanic gases. Weighed down by droplets of molten rock, rivers of superheated ash fell back to earth and flowed across the ground at more than 50 mph (70 kph).

RIVERS OF MUD

Fallen ash lay more than 330 ft (100 m) deep on the upper slopes of Mount Pinatubo. When rain fell, the ash became a gray slurry that continued to churn down valleys, destroying roads, bridges, and villages long after the eruptions ended.

threatened a major eruption in the near future. Volcanologists from around the world arrived in Luzon with instruments to detect bulging on Pinatubo's flanks and measure changes in the level of gas emissions. They also prepared a hazard map of the area by studying existing volcanic deposits, which revealed that Mount Pinatubo had erupted very violently in the past. Fearing that it was about to do so again, they evacuated people living right next to the volcano.

THE FINAL COUNTDOWN

Late in May, there was a tenfold increase in the amount of sulfur dioxide in the volcanic gases, suggesting that magma inside the volcano was rising fast. In June, the situation worsened, prompting further evacuations. On the morning of June 12, there was a series of explosions within the volcano. Bombs of molten rock were hurled out, along with ash and gases, creating a 13-mile (20-kilometer) high mushroom-cloud. Highly destructive clouds of burning ash tore down Pinatubo's flanks and along river valleys, searing everything in their path. Further eruptions over the next two days spewed out even more ash, turning the sky black and covering fields and houses in a thick gray blanket.

At dawn on June 15, the most devastating phase of the eruption began and continued for two days. Two huge explosions blasted out of the side of Mount Pinatubo and burning ash clouds scorched land lying up to 11 miles

(17 kilometers) from the volcano's summit. A total of 19 eruptions poured out a column of volcanic debris that hung 25 miles (40 kilometers) over what was left of Mount Pinatubo.

The destruction on Luzon caused by Mount Pinatubo was compounded by Typhoon Yuna, whose arrival coincided with the main phase of the eruption. Torrential rains soaked the falling ash as it settled on rooftops, turning it into a concretelike substance. The weight of the wet ash collapsed thousands of buildings and was responsible for many of the 300 deaths that occurred around the time of the eruption.

Volcanic debris laid waste to much of the northern Philippines, forcing 200,000 people to be relocated. More than 500 people died of disease and exposure in the tent cities, where refugees were given temporary shelter, and hundreds more were killed by mudslides. In addition to the tragic loss of life, damage to farms, shops, and factories in the region left 650,000 people without an income. Much of the local infrastructure also had to be rebuilt and recovery costs exceeded $10 billion.

RAKING THE ASHES

Thousands of people who were evacuated from the area returned to find their houses had collapsed under the weight of sodden ash.

A GLOBAL SUNSCREEN
Satellites tracked the volcanic ash and gases thrown into the atmosphere by Mount Pinatubo. A month after the eruption, the volcanic clouds had circled the Earth, blocking out sunlight and reducing temperatures worldwide.

DARKNESS AT NOON
After Mount Pinatubo exploded on June 15, 1991, the skies remained black all day for weeks on end as the 25-mile (40-km) high ash column slowly settled over Luzon. People carried umbrellas to ward off showers of gritty ash.

LOST HARVESTS
Millions of dollars' worth of crops were destroyed and over a million people were severely affected when Mount Pinatubo erupted. In time, however, the ash deposited on Luzon will enrich its soil.

EARTHQUAKES

Well over 10,000 earthquakes are recorded around the world each year. Some are related to the movement of magma under volcanoes. Others are caused by the weight of water in reservoirs. The strongest and most devastating earthquakes, however, are triggered by the relentless motion of the Earth's plates.

When plates meet, movement occurs along faults at or near the boundary. If the rock is fragile, the two plates grind past each other easily. If the rock is strong, however, instead of crumbling under the pressure, it becomes more and more distorted until it eventually breaks and allows the plates to move with a jerk. At the moment of rupture the pieces of rock snap back to their original shape like a spring, releasing stored energy as a series of shockwaves known as seismic waves.

Two kinds of seismic waves radiate out from the point of rupture, known as the focus. Primary or "P" waves travel like sound waves and produce vibrations in the air. They are responsible for the loud roar or rushing wind noise that people often report hearing shortly before the shaking of an earthquake begins. Compared to the slower-moving secondary or "S" waves, which make the ground shudder with a backward and forward motion, "P" waves cause little damage. When they reach the surface, both kinds of waves set off other vibrations that cause the ground to undulate and to shake from side to side.

The more energy released during a quake, the more potentially destructive it is. Scientists use recordings of seismic waves to determine and compare the magnitude of earthquakes. The best known scale for describing the magnitude of earthquakes is the Richter scale, named after the American seismologist Charles Richter, who devised it in 1936.

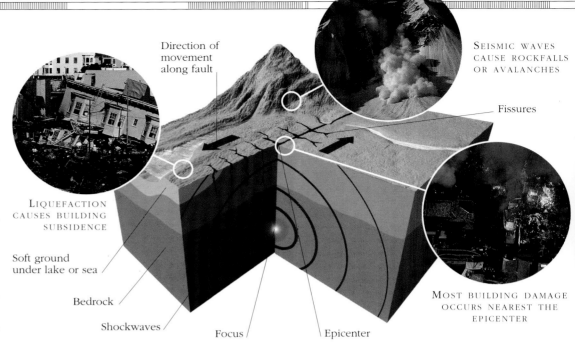

Direction of movement along fault

SEISMIC WAVES CAUSE ROCKFALLS OR AVALANCHES

Fissures

LIQUEFACTION CAUSES BUILDING SUBSIDENCE

Soft ground under lake or sea

Bedrock

Shockwaves

Focus

Epicenter

MOST BUILDING DAMAGE OCCURS NEAREST THE EPICENTER

EARTHQUAKE DAMAGE

Areas nearest the epicenter often suffer the most ground movement in an earthquake. Towns built here are the worst damaged. Loose soils near lakes and seabeds liquefy, causing subsidence in towns built here. Seismic waves cause avalanches or rockfalls in mountainous areas.

CRACKED EARTH

Huge fissures tore apart the earth in Anchorage, Alaska, when a 9.2-magnitude earthquake struck in 1964. Fortunately, casualties were light due to the remoteness of the earthquake's epicenter.

MEXICO CITY

EARTHQUAKE, MEXICO, 1985

GAZETTEER P.130 – SITE NO.76

A HUGE 8.1-MAGNITUDE EARTHQUAKE just off the west coast of Mexico on September 19, 1985 produced shockwaves powerful enough to be felt from Texas to Guatemala. As a result of differences in ground conditions, the death toll in coastal towns near the focus of the earthquake was much lighter than that of 250 miles (400 km) away in Mexico City, where about 9,000 people died. A further 30,000 people were injured and 1,000,000 were left homeless.

In 1985, scientists were carefully monitoring the movement of the tectonic plates off the Mexican coast because the Cocos Plate, which should have been sliding gently under Mexico, had jammed. The buildup of tension near the plate boundary indicated that a powerful earthquake was imminent. No one suspected that such an earthquake would have major consequences for Mexico City, which had expanded rapidly to house almost 19 million people. The city's builders, without realizing the dangers of long-range seismicity, had sunk the foundations of multistory buildings into the wet clay and sand of a former lake bed lying under the heart of Mexico City.

toppled to the ground or broke their bases and collapsed in lethal heaps of rubble and twisted steel. While most of the million or so buildings outside the city center were untouched by the earthquake, nearly 800 of the newer structures within the city center collapsed and 6,500 other buildings in the area were damaged. The buildings worst affected were between

AN UNUSUAL EARTHQUAKE
Although a number of ships were destroyed by tsunamis and hundreds of people died in the coastal region near the epicenter, the main damage was confined to the center of Mexico City and the nearby Morelos District.

seven and 16 stories high. Later studies revealed that these structures started to sway because their resonance matched that of the shockwaves. The level of movement was particularly violent above the lake bed, because there the soils acted like a drum, intensifying the vibrations.

PREPARING FOR FUTURE QUAKES

The earthquake that hit Mexico City in 1985 taught engineers many lessons about the long-range effects of seismic waves and led to stricter building codes being imposed in the city. How effective these changes will be is bound to be tested. A fresh buildup of stress along the Cocos Plate promises more earthquakes in the future.

SELECTIVE DAMAGE
The quake mostly affected high-rise offices, apartment buildings, and municipal buildings, but left many smaller structures alone.

DANCING STREETS

The earthquake occurred at 7:18 am, when many of Mexico City's citizens were crowding into the downtown streets on their way to work. As the seismic waves passed underneath the city, they resonated through the ground. Just as a tap with a knife causes a crystal glass to ring with vibrations, the nature of the ground caused it to increase the amplitude of the seismic waves.

The waves rocked Mexico City for three full minutes, causing many tall buildings in the city center to start swaying wildly. Some of these buildings bent over and crashed into their neighbors. Others swayed so far that they

HOSPITAL EMERGENCY
The multistory Benito Juárez Hospital collapsed like a house of cards, crushing the patients and staff inside. Miraculously there were survivors, including two babies found alive after 10 days.

SPITAK

EARTHQUAKE, ARMENIA, 1988

GAZETTEER P.135 – SITE NO.113

IN DECEMBER 1988, A 6.9-MAGNITUDE TREMOR and the landslides it triggered caused major damage across 154 square miles (400 square kilometers) of Armenia and northeastern Turkey. The Armenian town of Spitak, which stood closest to the earthquake's focus, was virtually destroyed and most of its 25,000-strong population was killed. In Leninakan, Armenia's second-largest city, 80 percent of the buildings were destroyed. The earthquake affected 700,000 people living in the area, and the death toll was estimated at more than 100,000.

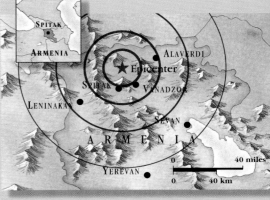

SMALL BUT DEADLY
The destructive potential of the Armenian earthquake was increased dramatically because its focus was very shallow, just 10 miles (15 km) below the surface, and because violent movement occurred along a fault that ran under Spitak.

In 1988, Armenia was one of the 15 republics in the Union of Soviet Socialist Republics. For this reason, the majority of factories and apartment buildings in Armenia were built to designs that were standard throughout the Soviet Union. Despite the fact that engineers had modified these designs to strengthen buildings in earthquake-prone Armenia, the changes were not sufficient for the buildings to withstand the severe earthquake that struck the country at 11:41 am on December 7, 1988. Some buildings, although damaged by an earthquake, will remain standing long enough to allow most of their occupants to escape. However, the precast concrete-framed structures common in Armenia collapsed almost instantly during this earthquake, crushing and suffocating people in a chaos of rubble and dust.

The 30 seconds of violent shaking also cracked roads and collapsed bridges. Rock and

earth in the surrounding mountains were dislodged and cascaded into valleys, bringing even greater destruction to stricken areas.

A NEW BEGINNING

For many years the Soviet Union had strictly controlled the reporting of bad news, but by 1988 the Soviet leader, Mikhail Gorbachev, was encouraging openness. As a result, the disaster received widespread media coverage, and people around the world were able to see the suffering the earthquake had brought about.

One positive effect of the tragedy was that old rivalries between former Cold War enemies were laid aside in order to assist the Armenians. Heat-seeking devices were sent in to help locate people still trapped under the rubble, and food, blankets, and clothes were given to the thousands of survivors who had been made homeless and were stranded out of doors in the freezing winter conditions.

Since gaining its independence in 1990, Armenia has suffered a political upheaval that has made rebuilding its cities difficult.

BURYING THE DEAD
Thousands of coffins were shipped to Leninakan after the earthquake so that the city's many victims could receive a proper burial.

BURIED ALIVE
Rescuers scoured the ruins of Spitak with dogs and heat-seeking equipment for weeks in the hope of locating trapped survivors. Despite subzero temperatures, some people were rescued long after the earthquake.

BUILDING DAMAGE

Most of the people who die during earthquakes are killed by collapsing buildings and falling masonry. In many earthquake-prone regions, traditional building materials, such as wood, straw, and clay, were used because they were relatively light. Consequently, people were less likely to be crushed beneath the wreckage if their homes collapsed. Because these traditional buildings have now been replaced by modern brick and concrete structures, the risk of dying in an earthquake has vastly increased.

Buildings made of brick and concrete are extremely vulnerable during an earthquake. The shaking that occurs forces buildings to bend and, although these materials have the strength to bear heavy loads, they are brittle and break easily when bent. Many of the people who died in the Spitak earthquake were crushed beneath concrete or smothered by dust when the buildings they lived in collapsed. Reinforcing concrete with steel can save lives because it makes buildings more flexible. This helps to prevent a building from collapsing completely, even when it is badly damaged, and gives the people inside a better chance of escaping.

The severity of shaking to which a building is exposed during an earthquake depends on the nature of the ground it is built on. Buildings founded on bedrock sustain the least damage. Those with foundations in loose sedimentary soils or reclaimed land are the most vulnerable because these materials contain numerous air gaps, which intensify the surface movement of seismic waves. Also, groundwater is forced upward and fills

CRUSHED AND TWISTED
This book was recovered from a building that collapsed when the Macedonian city of Skopje was struck by an earthquake in 1963.

these gaps, and the saturated ground liquefies, turning into a soft slurry that can no longer support the weight of the buildings above it.

It has also been found that constructing a building on saturated clay increases the severity of shaking during an earthquake. In this case, it is the stiffness of the ground that is the problem. A burst of seismic waves can make the ground resonate so that the shaking lasts for several minutes rather than a few seconds. The seismic waves that passed through

Mexico City in 1985 resonated under the downtown area for three minutes and caused many buildings to collapse (see *p.33*).

One commonly used scale for quantifying the level of earthquake damage in a given area is the Modified Mercalli Intensity Scale. This scale assigns a value of I to areas where an earthquake can be detected by instruments but causes no damage. It ranges up to intensity XII, which describes areas where most of the buildings are totally destroyed.

CRUSHED CARS
Apartments in the Northridge area of Los Angeles collapsed when an earthquake struck the city in 1994. Although it caused $15 billion worth of damage, only 60 lives were lost.

BUILT ON SHIFTING SAND
During the Loma Prieta earthquake, which struck San Francisco in 1989, buildings in the Marina District suffered worse damage than those nearer to the epicenter because they were built on sandy ground that liquefied when the quake struck.

SAN FRANCISCO

EARTHQUAKE, US, 1906

GAZETTEER P.129 – SITE NO.38

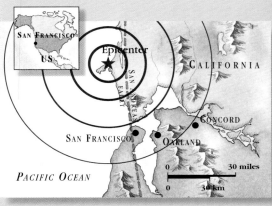

THE SAN ANDREAS FAULT RUPTURES
The earthquake, focused to the north of San Francisco, had an estimated magnitude of 8.3 and sent two massive jolts along the San Andreas Fault, which runs through the city.

THE DEADLIEST EARTHQUAKE ever to strike the United States plunged San Francisco into chaos at 5:13 am on April 18, 1906. The quake itself damaged many buildings, but the fires that followed caused far greater destruction. They burned for three days, consuming two thirds of the young city and completely obliterating the central business district. The combination of building collapse and fires forced tens of thousands of people to flee the city and is estimated to have killed over 500 people. Economic losses were vast, and several insurance companies, overwhelmed by the many claims, were bankrupted.

THE MARINE DISTRICT SWAYS
Houses built on land reclaimed from San Francisco Bay swayed drunkenly during the earthquake as the ground that held their foundations was jolted and liquefied.

During the gold rush in the latter half of the nineteenth century, San Francisco grew from a small village to a booming frontier town. By 1906 it had matured into a major city with a population of more than 300,000. Uncontrolled growth of the city had created a thriving, bustling patchwork of ostentatious public buildings, opulent mansions, hastily built warehouses, and squalid shantytowns inhabited by an exotic mix of immigrants from around the world. Aware that fire could spread rapidly between the city's tightly packed wood-framed buildings, Fire Chief Sullivan had warned that more money had to be spent on firefighting equipment in order to prevent a disaster.

A CITY UNPREPARED

On April 18, there was still little firefighting equipment available. Sullivan, who had drawn up detailed contingency plans for tackling a city-wide blaze, lost his life in the earthquake, which struck in two waves at 5:13 am. The first and strongest tremor

EMERGENCY MEASURES

Troops were drafted to help the emergency services and a state of martial law was declared by Brigadier General Funston without the approval of the President.

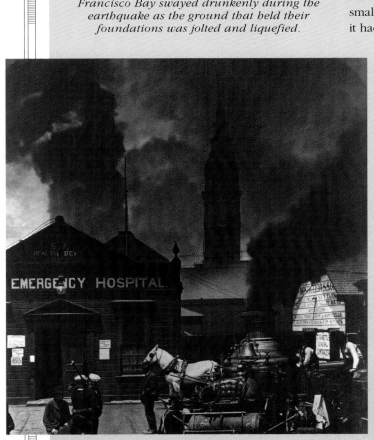

lasted 40 seconds. When the tremor ceased, there was 10 seconds of uneasy calm, followed by a further 25 seconds of violent shaking.

Police Sergeant Cook, who was patrolling the city streets that morning, reported that the road was behaving like ocean waves rushing toward him. John Barrett, editor of the *San Francisco Examiner*, reported how the jolts made buildings "dance and jiggle like jelly" as they bent, swayed, and bulged. Carthorses on their morning delivery rounds began to whinny nervously and then panicked as the buildings broke up and chunks of masonry plummeted to the streets below.

SAN FRANCISCO REACTS

As survivors emerged from shattered buildings, fires began to break out all around them. Many collected any possessions they could carry and set off on foot to find a place where they would be safe. Others remained to help free the dead and injured from the rubble. Some people took advantage of the chaos to loot the wrecked and abandoned buildings and get drunk.

Although there was little wind that day, the fire department could not contain the fires. Due to shattered water mains, they were left without water. As the fires spread relentlessly, 15,000 troops were called in to help with evacuation, rescue, and firefighting efforts. The troops were given orders to shoot all looters on sight. Army engineers and firefighters resorted to blowing up buildings in order to create firebreaks, but their efforts often did more harm than good. Twelve hours after the quake, the Chinatown district was set on fire when an explosion

WATCHING THE CITY BURN
San Franciscans emerged from their damaged houses and watched helplessly as fires slowly completed the destruction of their city that the earthquake had started.

flung blazing mattresses into a tangle of rickety wooden buildings. Chinatown burned rapidly, and it is impossible to tell how many people died in its maze of subterranean streets, which were off-limits to all but the Chinese residents.

San Francisco was rebuilt within four years and continues to thrive. It now has one of the strictest building codes in the world, which helped save thousands of lives when another major quake struck the city in 1989.

COMMERCIAL CENTER IN RUINS
The charred remains of grand hotels, banks, and department stores line Market Street, where businessmen risked death to rescue their valuables.

FIRE

In some earthquakes building collapse is not the main cause of the death, only the trigger. After the Great Kanto Earthquake struck Japan in 1923, fires began to sweep through the city minutes after the shockwaves toppled houses. Many of the fires were started when charcoal grills, which had just been lit to cook lunch, overturned. Fueled by high winds, the fires swept through vast swathes of Tokyo and the neighboring port of Yokohama, incinerating half a million homes. Most of the 143,000 who died during the earthquake were killed by fire.

The earthquake that struck Kobe, Japan, in 1995 (see *pp.46–49*) demonstrated clearly that modern cities are just as vulnerable to fire. Gas pipes running under the streets are likely to be ruptured by seismic waves and, no matter how quickly the supply is shut off, there is a moment when clouds of escaping gas can be ignited, setting off fires. A similar disruption to water mains frequently occurs, making it nearly impossible to bring these explosive conflagrations under control.

LANDSLIDES, AVALANCHES, AND FLOODS

Earthquakes often cause changes to natural features that can have disastrous consequences for people living nearby. By dislodging loose rock, soil, and snow, seismic vibrations in mountainous areas are liable to trigger serious rockfalls, landslides, and avalanches. Almost half of the people killed in an earthquake that struck Peru in 1970 died when a massive avalanche buried two towns and almost all of their 25,000 inhabitants (see *Chimbote*, right).

The earthquake with the highest recorded death toll, around 830,000, occurred in the Shaanxi province of China in 1556. Many of the victims were living in caves and were buried under tons of rock when the caves collapsed during a period of intense shaking.

Floods are caused when an earthquake or landslide disrupts the course of a river. A major earthquake near Assam, India, in 1950 caused extensive landslides in the Himalayas, temporarily damming the Subabsiri River. The force of the tremors also smashed a dam on the Brahamaputra River. The resulting floods swamped an area of over 42,000 square miles (110,000 square kilometers).

DANGERS BELOW
The Northridge earthquake, which hit California in 1994, caused extensive damage to the streets of Los Angeles and to the pipes running beneath them. Escaping gas started many fires.

CHIMBOTE
EARTHQUAKE, PERU, 1970
— GAZETTEER P.132 – SITE NO.22 —

THE TRADITIONAL BUILDING material used by the people living on the slopes of the Andes in Peru is *quincha*, a mix of clay and sticks. While it is easily shaken apart, *quincha* is ideal in a land where earthquakes are an inevitable part of life because it is so light. If a *quincha* house collapses, the occupants will usually escape with only minor injuries. By 1970, however, many of the houses in Peru were built of brick or concrete. These houses proved far more lethal in the huge earthquake that struck on May 31.

The massive 7.7-magnitude quake had a focus 16 miles (25 kilometers) west of the fishing and industrial port of Chimbote, where half the buildings were destroyed. Nearly 3,000 of Chimbote's 200,000 residents were killed during the earthquake, and many more were injured. The earthquake and the landslides it triggered also destroyed communication lines across Peru, so it took several days for the extent of the damage to emerge.

THE FULL HORROR EMERGES
When rescuers reached stricken towns and villages up and down Peru's coastline, they found more and more dead, injured, and homeless. But the worst-affected area was 41 miles (65 kilometers) inland at the foot of Mount Huascarán, where a massive chunk of rock had shaken loose near the peak. The rock had fallen onto the snowy slopes far below, causing a lethal avalanche. About 1,765 million cubic feet (50 million cubic meters) of rock and ice then hurtled down a valley, carrying away the town of Ranrahirca and its 5,000 residents. Past Ranrahirca,

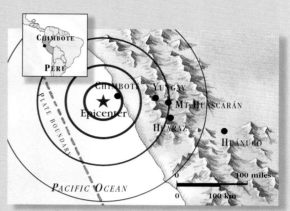

UNDERSEA QUAKE DEVASTATES PERU
Over 600 miles (1,000 km) of coastline was affected by the earthquake. Inland the quake dislodged rock on Mount Huascarán, which set off the twentieth century's most lethal avalanche.

one edge of the huge flowing landslide split off to the right and plowed through the mountain resort of Yungay, killing all but 92 of the town's 20,000 residents in a matter of minutes.

In all, about 66,000 Peruvians died in the earthquake, and the death toll continued to rise because of the difficulties in getting medical help and relief to survivors, many of whom were stranded outside in freezing conditions. It took Peru many years to recover from the sheer scale of the destruction.

SANCTUARY IN THE CEMETERY
The earthquake triggered an avalanche that flattened the town of Yungay, killing almost all its 20,000 residents. Only 92 people survived, by fleeing to Cemetery Hill – the highest ground in the town.

VALDIVIA
EARTHQUAKE, CHILE, 1960
— GAZETTEER P.132 – SITE NO.18 —

BITTER EXPERIENCE HAS taught Chileans to fear the violent earthquakes that frequently shake their country. Memories of the 50,000 lives lost in central Chile during a devastating quake in 1939 were still painful when tremors began to rock the region again in May 1960.

Shortly after 6 am on Saturday, May 21, a 7.7-magnitude earthquake struck near Valdivia, causing heavy casualties and forcing tens of thousands of Chileans to flee into the streets. This was just the start of an eight-day-long earthquake ordeal that seriously disrupted more than 56,000 square miles (145,000 square kilometers) of Chile as tremor after tremor shook the country. The severest quake hit around 3 pm on Sunday, May 22, and registered 8.7 on the Richter Scale. The ground shook for three full minutes, toppling thousands of buildings and unleashing countless landslides and avalanches in the Andes. Within days, a number of Chilean volcanoes began spewing out lava.

PACIFIC-WIDE TSUNAMIS
After the tremors died down sea levels rose dramatically along the Chilean coast, breaching harbor walls and flooding towns. Most coastal dwellers abandoned their homes and moved inland as soon as they saw the telltale signs of a tsunami. Their fears were justified. About 15 minutes after the quake, sea levels dropped abruptly, washing boats and ships out to sea.

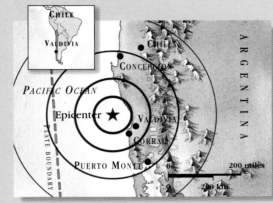

THE GREAT CHILEAN EARTHQUAKE
A 625-mile (1,000-km) long slab of oceanic crust plunged under South America after rock in the seafloor snapped, triggering earthquakes that ravaged central Chile and tsunamis that swamped coastlines around the Pacific rim.

Half an hour later a 33-foot (10-meter) high wave crashed ashore, punching down the walls of houses. As the ocean retreated, it drained the bays and harbors, sucking the shattered remains out to sea. At Corral, men who came down from a nearby hill to try to salvage their boats were drowned when another massive wave swept through the town. There was nothing left to salvage by the time the third wave struck.

The Chilean coast, being closest, was the first to be hit, but tsunamis spread out in all directions from the epicenter. The wave that reached Hawaii 15 hours later still carried enough energy to produce a 36-foot (11-meter) high wall of water that flooded Hilo, killing 61 people. The waves swept on to batter the Philippines, New Guinea, New Zealand, and Japan. Since the Japanese were not warned of the tsunami threat, the country was totally unprepared when waves up to 20 feet (6 meters) high struck, killing at least 119 people.

The death toll of 5,000 in Chile would have been much higher had people not heeded the warning of foreshocks. The economic losses, however, were crippling and widespread famine was averted only by a major Red Cross relief effort.

VALDIVIA IN RUINS
Survivors wander through the wrecked remains of Valdivia, which was devastated by a series of violent earthquakes. Around 400,000 buildings in central Chile were destroyed by the quakes.

TSUNAMIS

Earthquakes beneath the seafloor are very common. Although many of these earthquakes cause little direct damage, they may trigger sea waves that can flood coasts around the ocean. These have been called tidal waves, possibly because their approach sometimes seems like a rising tide. They are now usually called by their Japanese name, tsunami. The earthquake that occurred off the coast of Chile in 1960 (see *Valdivia*, left) triggered tsunamis that flooded coasts all around the Pacific Ocean.

Tsunamis occur when an earthquake is accompanied by the rupturing and sudden collapse of a section of seafloor. Water rushes into the space where the seafloor used to be, which sets the surrounding water in motion. The disturbance creates ripples, which radiate out from the collapsed seafloor. In deep water, the ripples form wide shallow waves that travel at speeds of up to 600 mph (1,000 kph). When the waves reach shallower water, their forward motion is slowed by the seafloor and the waves are forced to rise up. A tsunami that is barely visible in midocean can swell up to become a 33-foot (10-meter) high wave when it breaks on the shore.

In 1946, an earthquake in the North Pacific near the Aleutian Islands triggered a 115-foot (35-meter) high tsunami that destroyed a local lighthouse and killed five people. Nearly five hours later, a 40-foot (12-meter) high wave smashed into the Pololu Valley on the island of Hawaii. Most of the island's capital city, Hilo, was submerged by a smaller tsunami. More than $26 million worth of damage was inflicted on Hilo and 165 people lost their lives.

CRUSHED BY A WAVE
Fishing boats, vehicles, and coastal properties were wrecked when a 33-ft (10-m) high tsunami hit the island of Okushiri in 1993. The wave, which was born in the Sea of Japan, killed 240.

WALL OF TERROR
Residents of Hilo, Hawaii, run in terror from a tsunami that flooded the city in 1946, killing 165 people. Following the tragedy, a tsunami alert center was founded on the island.

TANGSHAN

EARTHQUAKE, CHINA, 1976

GAZETTEER P.137 – SITE NO.86

THE TERRIBLE EARTHQUAKE that hit northeast China on July 28, 1976 was the most disastrous in modern times. It was focused directly under the industrial city of Tangshan, which was almost completely destroyed by a massive tremor that measured 8.3 on the Richter Scale. The massive jolt struck suddenly and was responsible for the deaths of one tenth of Tangshan's population. It also caused severe damage well beyond the city. In total, more than 240,000 people died and 164,000 were severely injured as a result of the destructive effects of the main earthquake and the hundreds of aftershocks that followed.

CHINESE TRAGEDY
The main tremor created a zone of complete devastation that spread 18 square miles (47 square km) from the epicenter at Tangshan. The Chinese capital of Beijing and the port of Tianjin were also damaged by the quake.

In 1976, Tangshan was a thriving mining and manufacturing center. It had grown rapidly since Mao Tse-tung became Chairman of the People's Republic of China in 1949 and its population had just exceeded one million.

On July 28 the night shift was hard at work in Tangshan's coal mines when, at 3:42 am, a fault situated just 7 miles (11 kilometers) under the city gave way. The shockwaves left the miners trapped underground, wondering what had happened to their families at the surface.

The scene above matched their worst fears. As the first burst of shockwaves reached the surface, some people said they heard a sound like a whistling wind. Others claim it was an

ear-splitting bang. The initial vibrations were small but very rapid. Then, seconds later, the ground made a "sifting motion" accompanied by several violent jolts up and down.

Within 10 seconds, most of the buildings in Tangshan and its suburbs had become piles of broken rubble, shrouded by a massive cloud

of dust. About 86 percent of the population was buried in the debris, but miraculously only 16 percent was fatally wounded. As many as 300,000 people were able to free themselves and by dawn these survivors had formed teams that set about rescuing hundreds of thousands of other people trapped in the rubble. While the

TANGSHAN IN RUINS
The powerful earthquake that ruptured directly under Tangshan reduced 90 percent of the city to rubble. Almost the entire population was trapped in the 650,000 buildings that collapsed.

SOLDIERS TO THE RESCUE
Over 100,000 officers and men from the People's Liberation Army were dispatched to Tangshan to assist with the rescue operation and to help build 370,000 shelters before the onset of winter.

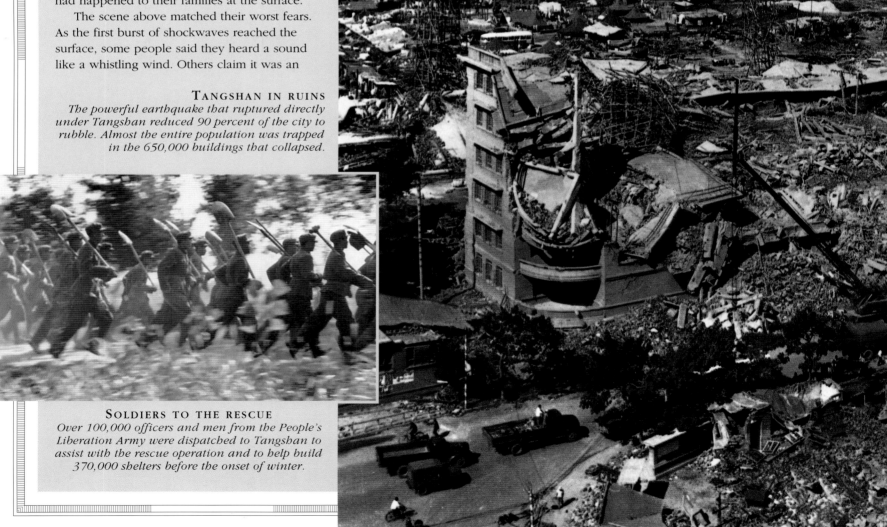

frantic search for loved ones continued, other teams were formed to salvage food and clothes for the rescued survivors. More than 700,000 people needed medical care and medical teams worked 12- to 15-hour days, even though many were injured themselves. Vital equipment lay buried in the ruins of the hospitals, so doctors had to operate amid the wreckage, using crude instruments sterilized in boiling saltwater. The patients were operated on without the aid of medication because acupuncture was the only anesthetic available.

THE RESTORATION OF TANGSHAN

Soon after the earthquake, 180,000 medical workers, builders, and troops were rapidly recruited from neighboring districts and sent to the aid of Tangshan. They brought vital medical supplies and pumps to lift drinking water from wells. Food was parachuted in. After months of relief work, the rebuilding of Tangshan began. It took ten years

BEFORE AND AFTER
Only one corner of this five-story brick hospital in Tangshan's mining district was left standing after the earthquake, which collapsed nearly all of the brick buildings in the city.

and an enormous investment of labor and resources to complete the task. The strategic location of the city and the rich coalfields that lay below it made rebuilding worthwhile, despite the cost of clearing away the ruins and the risk of more devastating earthquakes occurring in the future.

TWISTED TRACKS
Some 42,000 workers were needed to repair Tangshan's shattered railroad tracks. One line was replaced within 6 days so supplies could be sent in and the injured evacuated.

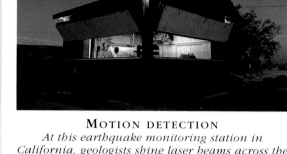

MOTION DETECTION
At this earthquake monitoring station in California, geologists shine laser beams across the San Andreas Fault. This enables them to measure rock movement on either side of the fault.

PREDICTING EARTHQUAKES

Major earthquakes occur when the rock at the edge of tectonic plates resists the inevitable movement of the plates. Geologists know an area is at risk when they monitor the buildup of stress in rock trapped by the arrest of movement across a fault. On this basis, scientists predict that several of the world's largest cities, including Tokyo, San Francisco, and Los Angeles, are likely to be struck by a major earthquake, maybe within a generation. Yet there is little sign of people abandoning these cities. Unfortunately, geologists cannot detect precisely when rock is going to give way, so it is usually impossible to evacuate people before an earthquake begins.

However, numerous changes have been detected in the movement of groundwater and in the way electricity is conducted by the soil prior to earthquakes. It has also been observed that animals behave strangely several hours before an earthquake.

Chinese scientists have attempted to develop these observations into a system for detecting earthquakes. In 1975, their methods appeared to be working since they successfully predicted that an earthquake would hit Haicheng in northeast China. After detecting characteristic changes in the ground, the scientists noticed that snakes were waking up from hibernation and rats were swarming, so they recommended evacuating the city. Within 12 hours a major earthquake struck. Although Haicheng was badly damaged, the death toll was light. The timely evacuation did involve an element of luck, however, since foreshocks warned the authorities that an earthquake might occur soon. Tangshan was not so lucky. No foreshocks preceded the 1976 earthquake.

LIVING WITH EARTHQUAKES

It has been suggested that the 1995 Kobe earthquake provided a foretaste to the sort of disasters that will hit many of the world's large cities at some time in the future. The world's wealth is becoming increasingly concentrated in a small number of huge cities, many of which are in geologically unstable areas. Since the earthquakes cannot be prevented, and the cities will not be moved, the only option is to make sure the buildings and their residents have the best chance of surviving a quake.

To help target areas at risk, engineers draw up seismic hazard maps. In addition to giving broad estimates of the location, timing, and magnitude of future earthquakes, engineers also assess the danger of landslides, ground

DRILLING FOR DISASTER
Children in Californian schools are given lessons on what to do in the event of an earthquake. The hope is that when tremors strike they will be able to protect themselves, rather than panicking.

liquefaction, flood, fire, and other hazards that could make an earthquake more destructive. Authorities in earthquake-prone areas can then avoid building in regions where the damage from the quake is likely to be highest.

To gain a fuller knowledge of potential hazards, engineers visit the sites of major earthquakes to discover which types of structures stood up best and which collapsed. These findings are then passed on to urban planners in earthquake-prone areas so that they can reinforce dangerous buildings and provide architects with information that will

allow them to design buildings and other structures that will remain standing when subjected to different types of seismic shaking. Unfortunately, constructing buildings of the necessary strength is expensive and can only be afforded in the wealthiest areas. A 6.9-magnitude quake that struck San Francisco in 1989, where tight building regulations exist, killed just 65 people. An earthquake of the same magnitude that hit Armenia a few months earlier, where less money was available for building, killed 100,000 people (see *p.34*).

After each earthquake, specialist teams review the performance of the emergency services. Knowledge of the unforeseen problems that arose helps in improving earthquake procedure. It also assists in formulating suitable education programs for earthquake-prone areas that teach local residents what to do when the ground begins to shake.

BAD VIBRATIONS
Recorded in England in 1923, the wildly fluctuating lines on this seismic chart show the 8.3-magnitude and duration of the "Great Kanto" earthquake, which struck Tokyo.

Start of earthquake   Highest magnitude waves

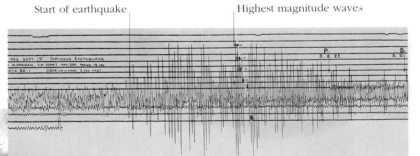

TOKYO PAST AND PRESENT
Much of Tokyo collapsed or was destroyed by fire (left) when the 8.3-magnitude "Great Kanto" earthquake struck in 1923. Modern Tokyo (below) is still vulnerable to the effects of a major quake, despite stringent building codes.

LISBON

EARTHQUAKE, PORTUGAL, 1755

GAZETTEER P.134 – SITE NO.56

A MASSIVE 8.5-MAGNITUDE EARTHQUAKE off the southwest coast of Portugal on November 1, 1755 inflicted widespread destruction on the Iberian Peninsula and across northwest Africa. Scores of magnificent palaces and cathedrals in the Portuguese capital of Lisbon were reduced to rubble by the force of the tremors or by the raging fires that broke out among the ruins and burned for a week. Lisbon's harbor district was further damaged by the impact of ferocious waves that swept in from the sea an hour and a half after the earthquake. Some 60,000 people lost their lives in the earthquake, 15,000 of whom lived in Lisbon.

EUROPE'S STRONGEST EARTHQUAKE
The earthquake's focus lay under the sea near the boundary between the North African Plate and the Eurasian Plate. Its tremors were felt as far north as Scotland and some of the tsunamis it set off crossed the Atlantic to strike the West Indies.

When the sun rose in the east on November 1, 1755, Lisbon was a rich and confident city. Gold was flowing in from the Portuguese colony of Brazil, along with goods from Africa and India. This trade had financed the building of many ornate palaces and churches that were filled with great works of art and literature from around Europe. The Roman Catholic residents of Lisbon believed that their good fortune depended on faith in God; the Jesuits, who were based in the city, taught the people that their salvation depended on the strict observance of Catholic rituals.

LISBON IN FLAMES
Few people tried to fight the fires that broke out after the earthquake and were burning out of control when tsunamis struck the city.

THE WRATH OF GOD

At 9:30 am, the faithful were gathered together in churches and cathedrals all over Lisbon to celebrate All Saints' Day. While priests were intoning mass, the ground began to shake, walls swayed, and huge chunks of masonry began falling on congregations across the city. Over a period of 10 minutes, three violent tremors wrecked large areas of the Portuguese capital.

Fearing more damaging shocks, most of the survivors fled in panic from the unstable ruins, mindless of the many fires that were starting to spread across

VOLTAIRE
In a poem that describes the events of the Lisbon earthquake, Voltaire concluded that man is weak and powerless, doomed to an unhappy fate on Earth.

Lisbon. Those who headed for the harbor in the hope of fleeing by boat were soon dealing with a new terror. At around 11 am, the first tsunami heaved itself at the harbor. One survivor told of the wave rising "like a mountain.... It came on foaming and roaring, and rushed toward the shore with such impetuosity that we all immediately ran for our lives." As the survivors watched Lisbon burn and grieved for their losses, it was natural for them to inquire why God had destroyed their churches and killed the faithful on All Saints' Day. The question was taken up by scholars all over Europe, many of

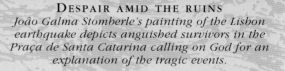

DESPAIR AMID THE RUINS
João Galma Stomberle's painting of the Lisbon earthquake depicts anguished survivors in the Praça de Santa Catarina calling on God for an explanation of the tragic events.

whom rejected mystic and religious reasons in favor of a quest to find a scientific explanation for the cause of this disaster. This enquiry led in time to the development of modern geology.

This revolution in thinking was reflected by the practical actions of Portugal's chief minister, the Marquês de Pombal, who quickly assumed charge of rebuilding Lisbon after the earthquake and forced the Jesuits to leave the city.

KOBE

EARTHQUAKE, JAPAN, 1995

———— GAZETTEER P.138 – SITE NO.37 ————

THE 7.2-MAGNITUDE EARTHQUAKE that struck Kobe on January 17, 1995 was the most powerful earthquake ever to strike a modern city. Twenty seconds of shaking destroyed much of Kobe and caused widespread damage to surrounding areas, including Japan's second-largest city, Osaka. The earthquake and the 142 fires that it triggered damaged about 180,000 buildings and burned 247 acres (100 hectares) of Kobe, killing 6,310 people and injuring 43,000 more. Damage to this important industrial center was a severe drain on Japan's economy. It has been estimated that rebuilding will take 10 years and cost $147 billion.

EARTHQUAKE IN OSAKA BAY
The earthquake was focused 13 miles (20 km) under the northern tip of Awaji-shima Island. A fault running under Kobe ruptured. Kobe bore the brunt of the destruction, but buildings were damaged as far away as Kyoto.

Before the earthquake, Kobe, on the island of Honshu, was best known as the home of the world's most pampered cattle. Visitors paid large sums of money to sample morsels of beef from cattle reared on beer and body massages. The elegant wooden buildings and cramped streets of old Kobe were also a popular attraction.

On January 16, 1995, scientists and engineers gathered in Osaka for a workshop on Urban Earthquake Hazard Reduction, which was due to start the next day. The aim of the workshop was to promote better earthquake awareness in this part of Japan. The region had suffered little seismic activity in recent years and was not as well prepared as other parts of Japan, where frequent earth tremors and simmering volcanoes had provided regular reminders that their country straddles one of the most unstable parts of the Earth's crust. The workshop was never held, but by sunset the following day local officials needed no convincing that their plans for dealing with a major earthquake were woefully inadequate. The proof lay all around them.

SHAKEN AWAKE

Most people were still sound asleep when the shaking began at 5:46 am. Like everyone else in Japan, the people of Kobe had been drilled since childhood to crouch under a strong table or in a doorway until the tremors stopped and then to go outside as quickly as possible. Some people never had a chance to move, but died in bed when their homes collapsed. Some forgot the drills, panicked, and ran outside into a hail of falling masonry. Thousands more were trapped inside their ruined houses and apartment buildings.

BUCKLED STREETS
Parts of Kobe's subway system collapsed during the earthquake, causing the streets above the fractured tunnels to buckle.

TRAPPED IN THE RUBBLE

Although most of Kobe's new buildings had survived 20 seconds of violent shaking, about 56,000 older buildings collapsed. Worst affected were the traditional wooden houses in Kobe's historic center and the apartments that sat on unstable ground overlooking Osaka Bay.

As dawn broke that cold January morning, the muffled cries of trapped survivors could be heard around the city. Some people remained entombed for up to five days because rescue teams possessed few fiber-optic cameras and no search dogs to pinpoint their whereabouts. During the ordeal, thousands of people died of their injuries or were killed by the fires that swept through Kobe after the quake.

UNTAMED FIRES
Kobe's firefighters had great difficulty putting out fires due to a lack of water (above). Many of the city's old wooden buildings (right) were consumed by fire because water supplies ran dry a couple of hours after the earthquake.

KOBE'S HIGHWAY FLIPS OVER
The Hansin Expressway collapsed during the earthquake, crushing 12 drivers in their vehicles. At 5:46 am the road was almost deserted, but two hours later it would have been jammed.

BURNED-OUT REMAINS
The fires that burned for 24 hours after the earthquake forced survivors to flee central Kobe, leaving their possessions, as well as their missing friends and family, behind.

LESSONS TO LEARN
Engineers examine the remains of the Hansin Expressway to work out why a 1,815-ft (550-m) long section collapsed, even though it had been strengthened before the earthquake.

SEARCHING THE REMAINS
Some 30,000 troops were dispatched to the Kobe area to help search the ruins for bodies and to provide assistance to the 300,000 residents who were made homeless by the earthquake.

HISTORIC CENTER DESTROYED
The narrow streets and alleys of traditional wood-framed buildings in the heart of Kobe crumpled during the earthquake and then became a lethal firetrap as flames swept through the area.

RAGING INFERNOS

The fires began almost as soon as the shaking had started. Gas escaping from ruptured pipes was ignited, setting buildings on fire before the supplies could be shut off.

Firefighters struggled to get through streets blocked with debris and the dense traffic that had built up as thousands of people tried to flee to safety. They had great difficulty fighting the fires they managed to reach, since damage to the underground mains had severely disrupted water supplies and their hoses dried up. Where possible, water was pumped from the harbor or streams. Luckily, the wind was calm and the fires did not spread too rapidly.

KOBE'S LEGACY

The Kobe earthquake showed how vulnerable a complex modern city can be to the destructive forces of a major earth tremor. Apart from the hundreds of thousands of people who were left homeless and jobless by the earthquake, around one million households were left with no gas, electricity, or water. Kobe's high-speed railroad service was also disrupted for six months, and the city's port took more than a year to become fully operational again.

Three days after the disaster, the authorities admitted being overwhelmed by the relief task. In summing up Kobe's effects on the Japanese people, Professor Katsuki Takiguchi from the Tokyo Institute of Technology stated: "The most valuable lesson...is that...Japan is not earthquake-proof. We always believed that Japan was ahead of everybody else. It turned out we were not."

TECTONIC UNCERTAINTIES

In December 1994, Mexico City was shaken by tremors, and clouds of condensing steam began to bloom from Popocatepetl, a volcano located on the southern edge of the city. Teams of volcanologists flew in to monitor the volcano and study deposits from earlier eruptions to help predict what the mountain would do next. For centuries, Popocatepetl's only activity has been the occasional ejection of gas and steam, but the studies revealed that the volcano is capable of much more. For tens of thousands of years, there have been major eruptions every thousand to two thousand years. The last of these, in about AD 800, covered the pyramid at Cholula in ash, mud, and pumice. An even larger eruption about 23,000 years ago buried the area that is now Mexico City – and home to almost 30 million people.

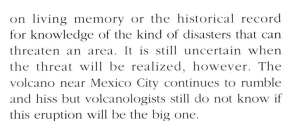

VOLCANIC THREAT
Vestmannaeyjar, on the tiny island of Heimaey, is one of many towns built close to an active volcano. During an eruption here in 1973, most of the town was destroyed.

The pattern of previous volcanic eruptions and earthquakes shows that history repeats itself, but history also teaches that the greatest losses of life occur when the event is unexpected. The huge earthquake that struck Lisbon in 1755 (see *p.45*) overwhelmed the city's residents because there was no record of a disaster of this scale ever having struck Portugal before. Where volcanoes and earthquakes are infrequent, not only are people less prepared, but the severity is often greater because tectonic stresses have built up over centuries. Because scientists have learned to interpret the signs of previous tectonic upheavals, we no longer need to rely

STUDIES IN THE UNITED STATES
Seismologists in California examine the soil for evidence of previous earthquakes. Their findings help them determine the seismic hazards of the region and predict the scale of future quakes.

on living memory or the historical record for knowledge of the kind of disasters that can threaten an area. It is still uncertain when the threat will be realized, however. The volcano near Mexico City continues to rumble and hiss but volcanologists still do not know if this eruption will be the big one.

Similar uncertainty hangs over cities such as Vancouver on Canada's west coast. A little way offshore, three tectonic plates grind against one another, driven by the same forces that have caused earthquakes and volcanic eruptions south of the border and in Alaska to the north. Vancouver has never suffered severe earthquake damage, but scientists warn that the deep offshore earthquakes that have shaken western Canada many times this century are harbingers of far greater things. The region's recorded history only began 200 years ago when European explorers first arrived, but native legends tell of terrible disasters. The ground

LIVING WITH THE AFTERMATH
Volcanic dust erupted by Mount Pinatubo in 1991 collapsed thousands of houses in the Philippines. Heavy rains washed the dust into lethal mudflows, which killed more people than the eruption itself.

HISTORY REPEATS ITSELF
The Bay district of San Francisco was devastated by earthquakes in 1906 and again in 1991. In both disasters, the tremors caused widespread subsidence and fires swept across the area.

reveals that forests of huge trees have been periodically overturned by massive tsunamis triggered by offshore earthquakes, the most recent of which was about 300 years ago.

North America's east coast is one of the most geologically stable parts of the world, but it is still at risk from tsunamis. Scientists warn that the next eruption to take place in the Canary Islands could send towering waves across the Atlantic to strike New York. The Canaries, like the Hawaiian Islands, are a chain of large hot spot volcanoes. The floor of the ocean around these islands is littered with evidence of huge lava slides that triggered vast tsunamis in the past. In 1949, an eruption on La Palmas in the Canaries almost caused one of these landslides as the explosion created huge fissures that nearly split the island in two. Scientists fear another eruption could open the cracks and send half of the island crashing into the sea.

HIDDEN DANGERS
Over the last few decades, strict building codes have ensured that new homes and offices are better able to withstand the violent upheavals of an earthquake. Gas and water mains remain dangerously vulnerable, however.

VIOLENT SKIES

EACH YEAR devastating storms claim many thousands of lives and cause billions of dollars' worth of damage to property and crops. The mighty cyclones that rise from tropical waters are the most powerful, but the large storms that form in colder regions bring the crippling effects of snow as well. Thunderstorms, which are tiny in comparison, are just as damaging because of their sheer number. Every day, tens of thousands of thunderclouds form, battering the earth with torrential rain, hail, and lightning. The most powerful winds occur in tornadoes, vicious whirlwinds that extend down from the largest thunderstorms, flipping cars over and tearing houses apart.

STORM GOD
This carving of Shango, the god of thunder and lightning, is used in dances of the Yoruba people of Nigeria to bring essential rain.

JARRELL ②
In May 1997, a single 2,600-ft (800-m) wide tornado ripped through Jarrell, Texas, claiming the lives of 27 residents.

③ GALVESTON
The turn of the century brought disaster for Galveston, Texas. In 1900 a big hurricane destroyed half of the town and killed 6,000 of its residents.

④ TRI-STATE TORNADO
The tornado rampaged across Missouri, Illinois, and Indiana, and killed 689 people.

⑥ STORM OF THE CENTURY
In March 1993, much of the eastern United States was brought to a standstill by huge snowfalls.

① BIG THOMPSON RIVER
In July 1976, a thunderstorm poured water for several hours on the Rocky Mountain National Park in Colorado. It caused a flash flood on the Big Thompson River that claimed 139 lives.

⑤ HURRICANE ANDREW
In 1992, a tropical cyclone sliced across southern Florida, causing about 25 billion dollars' worth of damage. It then caused severe damage in Louisiana and was the most costly storm of all time.

TORNADO THREAT
Tornadoes are the biggest threat to life and property in many parts of the United States, destroying everything in their path. This tornado was one of several to touch down in Cantrall, Illinois, in a single day. The tornado caused no serious injuries, but 30 Cantrall residents were left homeless.

WEATHER PLANE
The observations of airborne weather stations, coupled with those of satellites and ground stations, give warning of the formation of storms.

CYCLONE 2B ⑦
Low-lying islands were submerged beneath the 20-foot (6-meter) high storm surge of a cyclone that hit Bangladesh in 1991. More than 120,000 people were drowned.

WIND MEASUREMENTS
Invented in 1846, spinning cup anemometers are used to measure windspeeds in most weather stations around the world. As the cups rotate, the number of rotations in a given time is recorded. This antique instrument, known as an anemograph, is clockwork driven and records average windspeeds on graph paper as the cylinder rotates.

⑧ **CYCLONE TRACY**
On Christmas Day, 1974, the northern Australian town of Darwin was torn apart by a tropical cyclone that brought with it winds that blew at speeds of up to 150 mph (240 kph).

SEVERE STORMS

THE MOTION OF THE EARTH'S OCEANS AND ATMOSPHERE is like blood circulating in a living organism. This swirling, chaotic movement distributes water and regulates temperatures around the globe, creating a multitude of environments where living things can thrive. During severe storms, however, the air and sea move with such speed and violence that they threaten these environments and the life they support.

TURBULENT AIR

The Earth is constantly bombarded by solar energy – more than a million joules for each 10 square feet every second. The Sun's rays warm the land and seas, causing water to evaporate. As heat radiates off the Earth's surface, it increases the temperature of air near the ground so that the air expands, loses density, and carries the water vapor upward.

By causing warm, humid air to rise, the Sun's energy drives the circulation of air and water around the whole planet. During storms vast amounts of energy are violently released as rapidly rising air cools in the atmosphere and water vapor condenses into clouds of droplets, which may fall as rain.

The tropics, which lie nearest the equator, receive more direct sunlight than areas nearer the poles. It is therefore the hottest part of the planet and the region where humid air rises most rapidly. Here, rainstorms are frequent, torrential, and usually brief. These cloudbursts sometimes build into larger disturbances as the rising air forms a zone of low pressure that sucks in denser air from surrounding areas.

Air movement diagram labels

- Polar cell
- Temperate cell
- Tropical cell
- Trade winds
- Westerlies
- Polar Easterlies
- TEMPERATE LOW (60° NORTH)
- SUBTROPICAL HIGH (30° NORTH)
- EQUATORIAL LOW (EQUATOR)
- SUBTROPICAL HIGH (30° SOUTH)
- TEMPERATE LOW (60° SOUTH)
- Direction of Earth's rotation
- At the poles, the Sun's rays strike at an angle and the heat is diffused
- At the equator, the Sun's rays strike directly and the heat is concentrated

AIR MOVEMENTS
As the Earth orbits the Sun, the Sun's rays strike its surface unevenly. The temperature differences this creates keep the atmosphere in constant motion. All types of weather, including winds and storms, arise from the interplay of warm rising air and cool sinking air.

Under the right conditions, groups of storms may join together over the oceans and build into a huge storm called a tropical cyclone.

Just as warm air expands and rises, so cool, dry air contracts and sinks. Falling air masses create high-pressure areas in which the skies are clear of clouds and the humidity is low. High-pressure conditions are common in polar regions, where low temperatures chill the air all year round. They also often occur at subtropical highs, where air shot high up into the atmosphere by tropical storms cools and sinks as it moves toward the poles. Strong winds emanate from these high-pressure regions when air is

sucked toward low-pressure areas in the tropics or temperate zones. These winds veer sideways instead of blowing directly north or south because the Earth's motion is far faster at the equator than it is at the poles. This phenomenon, known as the Coriolis effect, also causes rising air masses to spiral.

In temperate zones, the worst storms are created by the chaotic mixing of cold air surging down from the poles with warmer air blowing up from the subtropics. Depending on local conditions, these storms may unleash rainfall, snow, hail, or lightning, and bring howling winds known as gales. A few mid-latitude storms also produce terrifying vortices of spiraling air known as tornadoes.

Due to the large number of factors that affect the precise way in which air mixes, it is usually impossible to predict the weather accurately more than a few days in advance.

MAIN STORM ZONES
Many of the worst storms begin in the tropics, where high temperatures create violent thunderstorms. Some of these storms develop into tropical cyclones. In temperate zones, gales, blizzards, and thunderstorms can be triggered when cold polar winds collide with warm air masses.

DOUBLE TROUBLE
On the shores of Lake Okeechobee, Florida, a 300-foot (91-meter) high radio mast is dwarfed by a massive lightning streak and a waterspout – a tornado that sucks water up into the clouds.

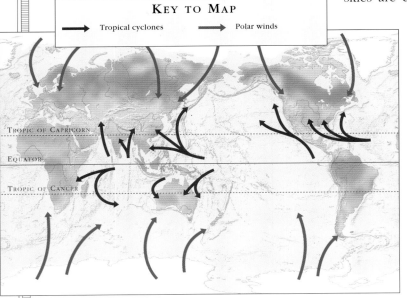

KEY TO MAP
→ Tropical cyclones → Polar winds

TROPIC OF CAPRICORN

EQUATOR

TROPIC OF CANCER

THUNDERSTORMS

Every moment of the day, there are some 2,000 thunderstorms in progress around the world. Although they are relatively small and short-lived compared to cyclonic storms, these ferocious cloudbursts cause, collectively, at least as much damage as larger storm systems.

Thunderclouds form when air near the ground is much warmer than the air above it. Being less dense, the warm air shoots upward and cools, causing the water vapor it carries to condense into towering clouds that can be over 10 miles (16 kilometers) high. While warm air continues to surge up from below,

cooled air at the top of the cloud starts to sink, turning the inside of the cloud into a chaos of updrafts and downdrafts.

Few thunderstorms last more than a couple of hours, but in that time they can release over 26 million gallons (100 million liters) of water. Such downpours can turn a gentle river into a raging torrent, as the residents of Vaison-la-Romaine in southern France discovered in 1992. A 50-foot (15-meter) high wall of water surged down the Ouvèze River and rushed through the town, killing 38 people.

When the water falls as hail, there is often severe crop and property damage; sometimes people are injured or even killed. Hailstones

LIGHTNING SCULPTURE
The path of a lightning bolt is sometimes etched permanently in sand. The air surrounding the bolt reaches 40,000ºF (22,000ºC), which is hot enough to melt the sand and fuse the grains.

BIG THOMPSON RIVER
THUNDERSTORM, US, 1976
GAZETTEER P.129 – SITE NO. 86

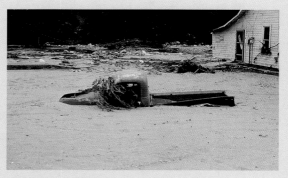

SWEPT DOWNSTREAM
Many of the victims died trying to escape in cars which, like the pickup truck above, were swept downstream. Houses fared no better – the cabin below was just one of 418 destroyed.

ON THE MORNING OF JULY 31, 1976, the banks of the Big Thompson River seemed like an ideal place to camp for 3,000 or so visitors who had come to enjoy the spectacular Rocky Mountain scenery. None of them suspected that a disaster was just hours away when an towering eight-mile (13-kilometer) high thundercloud developed in the area and heavy rain began to fall at 6:30 pm.

Unlike most thunderstorms, which drift along on prevailing winds and only produce short-lived downpours, this thunderstorm stood perfectly still, releasing 12 inches (30 centimeters) of rain over a period of four-and-a-half hours. On hitting the ground, the torrential rainfall coursed down the Rocky Mountains in thousands of cascading rivulets, swelling the

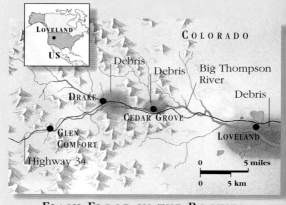

FLASH FLOOD IN THE ROCKIES
On July 31, 1976, a prolonged thunderstorm over the Rocky Mountain National Park in Colorado triggered a disastrous flash flood along a 25-mile (40-km) stretch of the Big Thompson River.

numerous mountain streams that emptied into the Big Thompson River. This caused the river to swell. By 9 pm the swell had reached a narrow canyon along the Big Thompson River. Here the floodwater was temporarily blocked and within minutes water levels rose 17 feet (five meters). Suddenly the great slug of water broke free and began to roar downstream. Floodwater rode the canyon like a bobsled, sloshing high up the wall on the outside of the bends. For many people, the first warning of its approach was a strange, unfamiliar sound, described by some as being like that of a freight train. The wall of water drove a cloud of dust before it, making it very hard for people to find an escape route in the gloom.

The flood lasted only a couple of hours, but in that time it picked up trees, cars, tents, and houses, killing 139 people. The force of the water was so strong that road bridges collapsed and a stretch of Highway 34 was destroyed.

form when water at the warm base of a cloud attaches to ice crystals and freezes around them when swept up to the cloud's frigid top. The worst hail disaster on record struck India in 1888, when hailstones the size of baseballs battered Moradabad, killing 246 people.

Lightning is among the deadliest products of a thunderstorm, however. In the United States alone, about 100 people die each year after being struck by lightning. The movement

FLASH FLOOD IN FRANCE
Muddy waterfalls cascade down the crumbling buildings as the Ouvèze River churns its way through the town of Vaison-la-Romaine, France, following a severe thunderstorm in the area.

FORKED LIGHTNING
In this time-lapse photo, a thunderstorm over Tuscon, Arizona discharges successive lightning flashes. Such displays are common in summer.

of water droplets and ice crystals within a thundercloud creates vast opposing electrical charges, and lightning is discharged when the negative and positive charges connect. The air around the bolt becomes four times as hot as the Sun's surface and expands at supersonic speed with the familiar boom of thunder. Lightning strikes are also responsible for starting many fires and, in the years since the invention of gunpowder, they have triggered a number of devastating explosions.

SUPERCELL ALERT
*Most tornadoes form within large
thunderclouds known as supercells. The
powerful updrafts in these storms are also
responsible for violent hailstorms.*

TORNADOES

A tornado is a writhing funnel of rapidly spinning air that descends to the ground from the base of a large thundercloud. At the heart of a tornado is a low-pressure vortex, which acts like a huge vacuum cleaner, sucking up air and anything the tornado encounters on

VIOLENT TOUCHDOWN
Debris picked up by this tornado, which struck Pampa, Texas on June 8, 1995, was found up to 60 miles (96 km) from the town.

the ground. Ferocious rotational winds blow around this vortex at speeds of up to 300 mph (500 kph) and are capable of lifting houses off their foundations, flipping large trucks high into the air, and tearing the hides off cattle.

Tornadoes, which are sometimes called twisters, occur in many parts of Europe, Asia, and Australia but are most frequent and most violent in the United States, especially in the Midwest. A record-breaking 1,293 twisters struck the United States in 1992. Of these, 57 were powerful enough to produce winds

FUNNEL CLOUD
When a vortex extends down from the base of a thundercloud, it often assumes a blue-gray tinge as moist air condenses in the low-pressure funnel. When it reaches the ground, the tornado darkens instantly as it snatches up dust and anything else it encounters on its path of destruction.

TRI-STATE TORNADO

TORNADO, US, 1925

GAZETTEER P.129 – SITE NO.53

ON MARCH 18, 1925, a single, very fast-moving tornado killed 689 people and injured 1,980 when it tore through the midwestern states of Missouri, Illinois, and Indiana. For most of its duration, it followed the course of a ridge, along which lay a string of mining towns and scattered farms.

The Tri-State Tornado was formed inside a thunderstorm with a cloudbase traveling very close to the ground. This may account for the great stability of the vortex, which touched down near Ellington, Missouri. By the time the tornado had reached nearby Annapolis, which it virtually destroyed, it had already begun carving an unusually broad path of destruction across the

state. The death toll increased when the usually tornado-wise farmers in rural areas were caught unaware. The sky around the tornado was so dark, and the air so full of dust and debris, that they could not see the funnel at the storm's center until it was too late.

The Tri-State was at its deadliest and most destructive during the forty minutes it spent in Illinois. Spiraling winds flattened the village of Gorham, killing or injuring half of its residents. Descending on the town of Murphysboro, the tornado went on to kill a further 234 people. Unabated, it then struck De Soto, where 69 more lives were lost. In West Frankfort, 800 men who were working down a mine were left in darkness when the tornado knocked out their electricity supply. On reaching the surface, the miners found that their homes had been destroyed, 127 of their friends and family had been killed, and 450 others had been injured. Tragedy also struck the nearby village of Parrish, where 22 people died. The damage in Illinois caused directly by the tornado was made worse by fires that broke out in the rubble. Among the many dead were scores of schoolchildren, who were crushed to death inside brick schoolhouses.

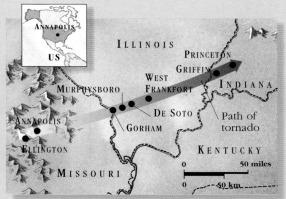

RECORD-BREAKING TORNADO
The Tri-State tornado is the longest-lasting, fastest, and most destructive on record. In three-and-a-half hours, it traveled 220 miles (350 km) at speeds of up to 73 mph (117 kph).

THE FINAL ANALYSIS

When the Tri-State Tornado reached Indiana, the terrible vortex began to destabilize, but it still had sufficient strength to kill another 71 people before returning to the sky beyond Princeton. Its three-and-a-half hour journey is by far the longest on record, and showed how much damage a major tornado can cause.

BROKEN HOMES
Two young survivors comfort one another in Murphysboro, Illinois, after they and about 8,000 others were left homeless. It took days to find and identify the remains of those killed.

UNBELIEVABLE DESTRUCTION
Griffin, Indiana, was unrecognizable in the aftermath of the tornado. Homes and possessions were destroyed, and familiar landmarks such as these trees, torn up by the roots, were lost forever.

TORNADO ALLEY

A massive tornado churns through a wheatfield in Kansas, one of the four American states that lie along "Tornado Alley." The American Midwest is the most tornado-prone region on Earth.

SWIRLING WATER

In 1965, a massive waterspout developed off the Spanish coast, dwarfing the pier at Gerona. Six people were killed when the waterspout collapsed, dumping tons of water onto the pier.

greater than 150 mph (240 kph) and wreak havoc wherever they touched down. Most of these occurred in spring and summer, but 1992 was also unusual for producing a spate of 94 twisters in 48 hours during November.

Scientists still cannot predict exactly when and where a tornado will form, but studies have shown that they are most likely to occur after warm air punches its way up through an overlying body of cool air. The collision of air masses causes the powerful updrafts to form into turbulent thunderclouds known as supercells. If the spiraling intensifies, a vortex may emerge from the base of the cloud and become a tornado if it touches the ground.

The destructiveness of a tornado depends not only on the diameter of its base and its wind speed, but also on its duration and what it encounters on the ground. In 1896, a small and not particularly violent tornado touched down in a densely populated district of St. Louis, Missouri. The devastation it wrought in only a few minutes claimed 306 lives.

JARRELL

TORNADO, US, 1997

— GAZETTEER P.129 – SITE N0.100 —

ABOUT 400 PEOPLE lived in Jarrell, Texas, in the spring of 1997. Some of them worked in the city of Austin, but had chosen to live and bring up their children in this quiet farming community, where everyone knew each other.

Early on the morning of Tuesday, May 27, the heat was oppressive, as warm, moist air blowing up from the Gulf of Mexico collided over Texas with cold, dry air from the north. At around noon severe thunderstorms began developing to the north of Jarrell. Before long, a tornado touched down near Waco, destroying a house and three mobile homes. Shortly after this, another tornado touched down at Morgan's Point, near Temple, wrecking 50 boats at the Marina.

At 3 pm, as the darkening thunderclouds continued to move southward, the emergency service in the Jarrell area was put on full alert. Within an hour, the siren in Jarrell blared out an imminent danger alert minutes after a group of funnels were sighted at 3:43 pm over a farm one mile (two kilometers) to the north of the town. As the funnels moved across a field of wheat, they formed into a single 2,600-foot (800-meter)

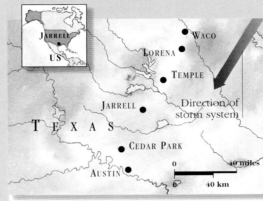

TORNADOES ACROSS TEXAS

The thunderstorms that formed over Texas on May 27, 1997 are reported to have produced 11 tornadoes. Five of these caused significant damage and killed a total of 30 people.

wide tornado. The winds that whipped around this monstrous vortex were strong enough to rip the hides off cattle and to hurl several big 10-ton combine-harvesters across the field. The tornado then swung east toward a subdivision of Jarrell known as Double Creek.

Many of Double Creek's residents were sheltering from the tornado inside their homes, but within 20 minutes 27 of them were dead. After the slow-moving tornado had gone, all that was left of 45 of Double Creek's 50 homes were the concrete foundations. Miraculously, some people survived. Tornadoes killed three other people in Texas that day, when more funnels touched down around Austin.

KILLER TORNADOES IN TEXAS

The tornado (left) that touched down to the north of Jarrell killed 14 children and 13 adults. Another tornado (above) tore the roof off a store in Cedar Park, killing one person and injuring seven others.

TRACKING TORNADOES

In the parts of the United States where the risk of severe tornadoes is greatest, extensive early warning systems have been developed in an attempt to reduce the deadly consequences of these vicious whirlwinds. Since 1977, Doppler radar has allowed meteorologists to detect a developing tornado while it is still inside a thundercloud by identifying the spinning air of a vortex up to 25 minutes before it emerges. This gives extra time for warnings to be issued and for people to find shelter.

Although new technology allows potential tornadoes to be tracked inside thunderclouds, the resources do not exist to track every single thunderstorm. Forecasters need to be selective about the storms they track because less than one percent of storms spawn tornadoes. To

STORM CHASERS IN AMERICA

Mobile tornado research laboratories like this one are driven to areas where large thunderstorms are building up. The trucks carry Doppler radar which detects vortices developing in the clouds.

get a better understanding of why tornadoes form, the National Severe Storm Laboratory in Oklahoma began a project called VORTEX (Verification of the Origin of Rotation in Tornadoes) in 1994. Using an array of mobile Doppler radar units, high-altitude balloons, and "tornado-proof" gauges, this organization has tracked hundreds of tornado-spawning storms from formation to touchdown.

These efforts have been backed by an army of amateur tornado-chasers, who radio in news about touchdowns and then risk their lives to capture these twisters on video. However, some twisters still strike with little or no warning, leaving people little time to take cover when a vortex drops down from the clouds. Once a tornado touches down, no one can predict how it will behave. In 1974, a family were cowering in a closet when a tornado struck their Indiana home. After it had passed they opened the door to find their house gone. The twister had carried away everything but the closet.

TROPICAL CYCLONES

Each year 60 or so huge storms develop over tropical oceans, generating winds of more than 73 mph (118 kph). These storms, called hurricanes in the Americas, typhoons in the Far East, and cyclones in Australia and India, are known collectively as tropical cyclones.

Tropical cyclones develop only where the water temperature is greater than 76°F (24°C) and when the winds are calm. In these hot, humid conditions, numerous thunderstorms develop, as warm air near the surface rushes upward and condenses into towering clouds. When these thunderstorms occur more than five degrees from the equator, the rotation of the Earth sometimes causes them to band together around a low-pressure center. Instead of dying out after a few hours, this storm

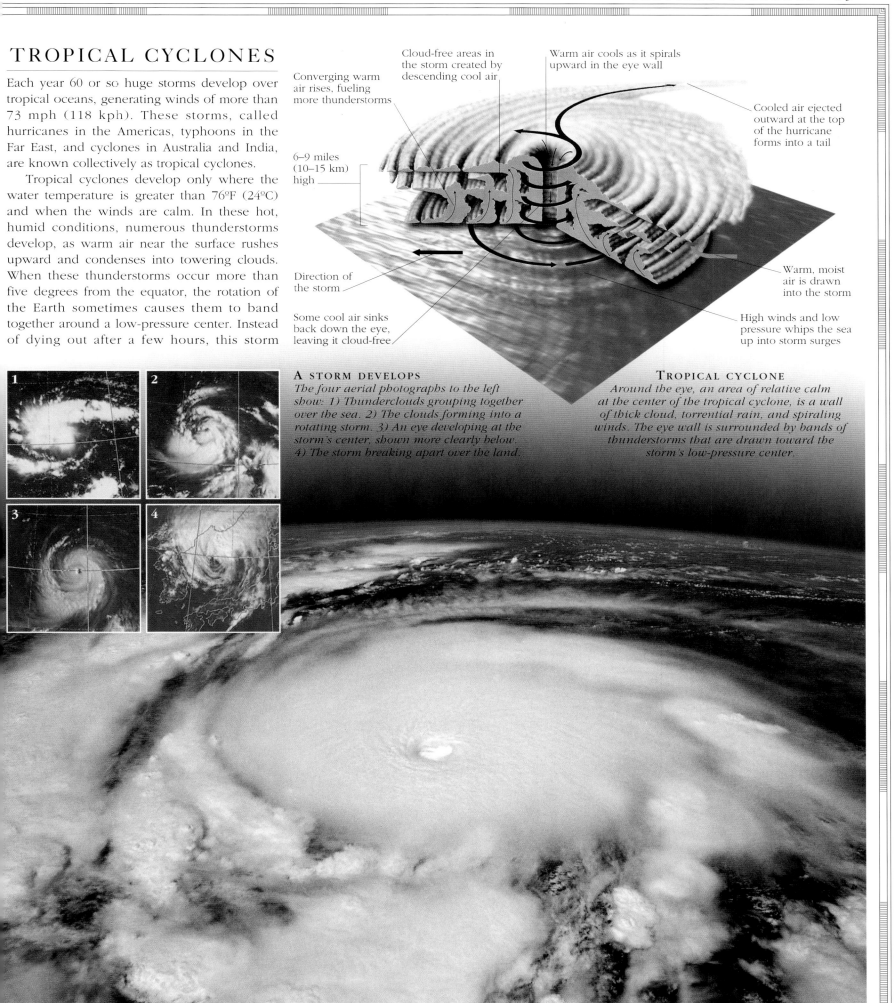

Cloud-free areas in the storm created by descending cool air

Warm air cools as it spirals upward in the eye wall

Converging warm air rises, fueling more thunderstorms

Cooled air ejected outward at the top of the hurricane forms into a tail

6–9 miles (10–15 km) high

Warm, moist air is drawn into the storm

Direction of the storm

Some cool air sinks back down the eye, leaving it cloud-free

High winds and low pressure whips the sea up into storm surges

A STORM DEVELOPS
The four aerial photographs to the left show: 1) Thunderclouds grouping together over the sea. 2) The clouds forming into a rotating storm. 3) An eye developing at the storm's center, shown more clearly below. 4) The storm breaking apart over the land.

TROPICAL CYCLONE
Around the eye, an area of relative calm at the center of the tropical cyclone, is a wall of thick cloud, torrential rain, and spiraling winds. The eye wall is surrounded by bands of thunderstorms that are drawn toward the storm's low-pressure center.

HURRICANE ANDREW

TROPICAL CYCLONE, US, 1992

GAZETTEER P.129 – SITE NO.95

IN THE EARLY HOURS OF MONDAY, AUGUST 24, 1992, one of the fiercest-ever tropical cyclones hit the United States mainland and sliced across 60 miles (100 kilometers) of southern Florida. In the storm's path were the homes and offices of 355,000 people in the densely populated suburbs of southern Miami. The high winds and floods brought by Hurricane Andrew created a zone of devastation larger than the city of Chicago and caused about 25 billion dollars' worth of damage. The storm raged on over the Gulf of Mexico, causing a further 2 billion dollars' worth of damage in Louisiana. Despite the damage it inflicted, Hurricane Andrew killed fewer than 50 people.

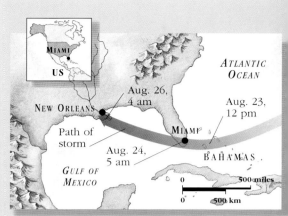

A VERY COSTLY DISASTER
High pressure to the north of Hurricane Andrew steered the storm westward across the Bahamas and southern Florida. In the Gulf of Mexico, it veered northwest and struck Louisiana.

COASTAL ASSAULT
Southern Florida was pounded by 145-mph (230-kph) winds when Hurricane Andrew hit its Gold Coast. The force of the winds ripped boats from their moorings (left) and caused the sea to surge 17 ft (5 m) above its normal level. Many coastal resorts were damaged by the resulting sea floods.

Southern Florida was badly damaged by five severe hurricanes between 1945 and 1950, but for over four decades the Florida mainland had escaped the ravages of a major hurricane strike. During this lull, developers had transformed the remote farms, wetlands, and small towns south of Miami into a sprawling suburb.

The first reports of Hurricane Andrew gave the people of Florida little cause for concern. Although winds reached hurricane speed just after sunrise on Saturday, August 22, they were not rotating around a well-defined eye, and the storm was heading on a track that would take it comfortably north of Florida.

On Saturday evening, the situation changed dramatically. A well-defined eye grew at the center of a huge mass of clouds, and Andrew's winds started to gain strength. Around this time, the storm veered to the west and began heading in the direction of southern Florida.

By Sunday evening, aircraft tracking Hurricane Andrew reported wind speeds of up to 150 mph (240 kph). Television and radio stations broadcast hurricane warnings and more than a million people fled north. Those who decided not to leave were advised to ride out the storm in one of the public hurricane shelters or to stay in a concrete house.

CLOUDS OF DESTRUCTION
This satellite image shows the spiraling clouds of Hurricane Andrew engulfing most of Florida as the storm passed over its southern tip on August 24, 1992.

TRAIL OF DESTRUCTION

At midnight Andrew struck the northern Eleuthera Island in the Bahamas, causing much damage and four deaths. The storm calmed a little over the shallow waters around the Bahamas, but the winds began to pick up strength again as the hurricane crossed the deep, warm water east of Florida.

At 5:05 am on Monday August 24, Andrew crossed Biscayne Bay, whipping up a 17-foot (5-meter) high storm surge that flooded

A HURRIED ESCAPE

Florida motorists faced fierce winds and lashing rain as Hurricane Andrew headed their way. More than a million people evacuated their homes before the brunt of the storm struck the Miami suburb of Homestead.

SWEPT AGAINST THE SHORE

Power boats in South Gables harbor were swept into a tangled heap by violent winds and pounding waves when Hurricane Andrew struck Florida. In a matter of minutes, the storm had wrecked approximately 15,000 vessels.

WIND DAMAGE

Hurricane Andrew tore a 25-mile (40-km) wide corridor of destruction across Dade County in southern Florida. The storm's winds, strong enough to knock down buildings, picked up a rented truck in Cutler Ridge and dumped it on top of a warehouse.

the Florida coastline south of Miami, destroying hundreds of homes and leaving many businesses gutted. The storm proceeded to move across the southern tip of Florida at 20 mph (32 kph).

Andrew was about 500 miles (800 kilometers) in diameter but its fiercest winds, which formed a wall around the eye, carved out a band of destruction 25 miles (40 kilometers) wide. In this zone winds gusted at up to 200 mph (320 kph).

As Hurricane Andrew advanced across Florida, it dragged boats from the water and piled them up on the shore, flipped cars and light aircraft over, and mowed down plantations of trees. Some houses imploded as glass in their windows was sucked inward and their roofs flew off. Trailers were mercilessly smashed to pieces – the pieces becoming deadly shrapnel as the wind hurled the twisted wreckage around.

COUNTING THE COST

Andrew spent just four hours in Florida. In that time it had destroyed 80,000 homes and badly damaged 55,000 more. The people who fled their homes came back to find southern Miami changed beyond belief. In the oppressive heat that followed, there was no electricity and no water supply. Not surprisingly, many people resorted to scavenging food and drinks from the wrecked homes and stores. In some areas people began to steal valuables as well.

The healing of the region began with the arrival of 16,000 troops and a flood of helpers who brought relief. Despite their assistance, it has been estimated that 25,000 survivors of Hurricane Andrew left Florida for good.

SURVEYING THE DAMAGE
This trailer park was flattened by the swirling winds of Hurricane Andrew (below). A mother and her daughter survey the ruined remains of their home, after its roof was ripped off by the storm's violent winds (left).

HURRICANE GILBERT
Hurricane Gilbert rampaged across Jamaica for eight hours in September 1988. Kingston airfield and many other parts of the island were badly damaged by lashing winds and rains.

NO PARKING
NO WAITING

system expands as more and more air is sucked into its low-pressure heart. Rather than simply rising, the hot, moist air spirals up into a tightening vortex of rotational winds. If the pressure continues to drop, the wind-speeds increase dramatically and a distinctive eye begins to develop at the center of the rotating storm.

The conditions that create a tropical cyclone only exist in the tropics but, once formed, the cyclone can travel thousands of miles across oceans to strike coasts in temperate regions.

WIND AND RAIN DAMAGE

Once an eye develops, the most powerful winds and most turbulent updrafts concentrate around it in a great tower of whirling cloud known as the eye wall. Here, the air rises so rapidly that rain falls in solid sheets and winds can gust at more than 200 mph (320 kph). Some tropical cyclones even spawn tornadoes, adding to the suffering that these storms bring.

It is the enormous size of tropical cyclones, as well as their power, that makes them so devastating. Some grow to more than 500 miles (800 kilometers) in diameter, and travel similar distances each day, causing widespread damage. One cyclone that crossed the Indian Ocean in 1952 dumped six feet (two meters) of rain on the Reunion Islands in 24 hours.

The largest storms develop over the Pacific Ocean, the widest expanse of tropical ocean in the world. Typhoon Vera, which hit Japan's

TORRENTIAL RAINS IN MEXICO
Residents of Acapulco struggle to contain the violent flash floods that swept through their town after Hurricane Pauline struck this Mexican seaside resort on October 9, 1997.

central island of Honshu in 1959, unleashed torrential rains and ferocious 130-mph (210-kph) winds on an area 450 miles (700 kilometers) across. Because the damage was so widespread, it was more than a week before the authorities could gauge its extent. Whole towns had been submerged by swollen rivers or seawater that had been swept inland. The storm left more than a million people homeless. Diseases such as dysentery soon spread as people resorted, in desperation, to drinking polluted water. The final death toll was 5,041.

Most tropical cyclones lose power quickly when they cross land, but this was not the case with Hurricane Hazel. After hurtling ashore in South Carolina on October 15, 1954, it swept right across the United States, hitting Toronto in Canada, where it killed 56 people.

CYCLONE TRACY

TROPICAL CYCLONE, AUSTRALIA, 1974

GAZETTEER P.139 – SITE NO.24

IN THE EARLY HOURS OF CHRISTMAS DAY, 1974, Cyclone Tracy blasted the northern Australian town of Darwin with 150-mph (240-kph) winds. Nearly 90 percent of the town's buildings were damaged or destroyed by the storm, and more than half of its 40,000 residents were left homeless. Despite the scale of devastation, casualties were remarkably light. Only 50 bodies were found amid the wreckage of the town itself, and 25 more bodies were recovered aboard the many wrecked vessels in Darwin's harbor.

A CHRISTMAS SURPRISE
Many tropical cyclones develop in the Arafura Sea and track southwest across the Timor Sea. Unusual weather conditions on Christmas Eve 1974 caused Cyclone Tracy to veer southeast, however, straight into Darwin.

SCATTERED DEBRIS
Cyclone Tracy destroyed everything that made it possible for the 40,000 residents of Darwin to survive in the intense heat of north Australia. Within a week of the disaster, over 20,000 people had been airlifted to other parts of the country.

Darwin's excellent harbor allowed agriculture and mining to develop in Australia's Northern Territory, and the town had grown rapidly in the 1960s and early 1970s. Tropical cyclones have frequently developed in the nearby Arafura Sea, but Darwin was not designed to withstand severe weather, since it was felt that the town was well protected behind Melville Island.

Meteorologists realized that this assumption was wrong when early on Christmas Eve 1974 Tracy made an unusual 90-degree turn past Melville Island and headed straight for Darwin. Despite clear advanced warnings, the residents settled down to enjoy Christmas, believing that even if the storm hit, at least families would be together and safe in their homes.

The leading edge of the storm swept into Darwin at around midnight, and worshippers at St. Mary's were forced to abandon mass when torrential rains flooded the cathedral. By 1 am, hurricane-speed winds made driving impossible. An hour and a half later many homes, offices, and warehouses began tearing apart as winds of more than 125 mph (200 kph) ripped through the town. Tracy's furious barrage continued to worsen until about 4 am, when the still eye at the center of the tropical cyclone passed directly over Darwin, bringing with it a sudden calm. The respite was short lived. Scores of people were caught in the open when winds on the other side of the eye wall resumed Tracy's assault.

Within five years of the disaster, Darwin had regained its 1974 population. The new town, however, was built to withstand even a cyclone of Tracy's ferocious power.

SURVEYING THE WRECKAGE
After the disaster Jim Cairns, Australia's Deputy Prime Minister, stated that "Darwin looks like a battlefield, or Hiroshima." An airforce doctor said "the city looks like a giant rubbish dump."

STORM SURGES

Most of the people who die during tropical cyclones are killed by the sea. When these storms hit land, they usually bring the sea with them. Huge waves and exceptional tides, known as storm surges, often overwhelm coastal defenses, destroying harbors and the boats in them. Then the sea sweeps far inland, flooding homes and covering large areas of farmland with salt water. When coastal districts are not evacuated, the death toll is often catastrophic.

A survivor of the great 1938 hurricane, which decimated coasts in the northeastern United States, described a 40-foot (12-meter) high storm surge approaching Long Island. "I thought it was a thick and

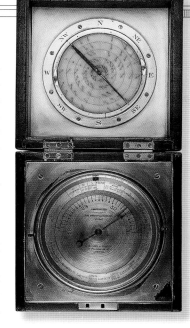

SEASONAL WAVES
An Atlantic hurricane batters the island of Antigua in the West Indies with ferocious winds and surging tides. These storms threaten the area in the summer and in the autumn.

EARLY-WARNING DEVICE
Before modern meteorology, seamen in tropical waters used barocyclometers to gauge the air pressure and wind direction of approaching storms.

high bank of fog rolling in fast from the ocean...when it came closer, we realized it was not fog. It was water." The 1938 storm went on to decimate in the region of 14,000 homes and numerous businesses. At a seafront hotel on Rhode Island, surging seawater poured into the ground floor lounge and drowned some of the guests. The movement of air in and around a tropical cyclone produces these high seas in two ways: first, powerful winds whip up huge waves that radiate out in all directions from the center of the storm. The largest waves develop in front of the storm, where the sea is disturbed by the storm's forward

TERROR IN THE CARIBBEAN
Coastlines in the Dominican Republic were swamped by huge surges when Hurricane David struck the island in 1979, killing over 1,300 people.

movement. In the Pacific Ocean, waves up to 80 feet (25 meters) high are reported to have been generated by tropical cyclones. Secondly, sea levels rise because of the low barometric pressure that develops within a tropical cyclone, causing the surface of the sea beneath the storm to bulge upward by up to 20 feet (6 meters) above its normal level.

The deadliest storm-surge disasters have occurred on marshland reclaimed from the sea and on unprotected sand spits like Galveston (see *p. 70*), which was almost totally submerged when a surge washed across it in 1900. Worst affected of all is the Bangladesh region, where more than a million people have died this century due to the destruction caused by a succession of deadly tropical cyclones.

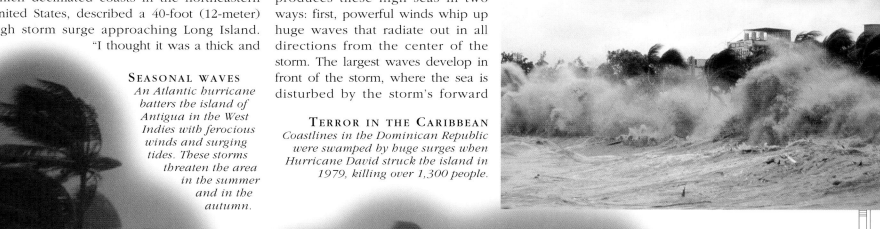

GALVESTON HURRICANE

TROPICAL CYCLONE, US, 1900

GAZETTEER P.129 – SITE NO. 33

AT THE BEGINNING of the twentieth century, Galveston was the premier city in Texas and, based on per capita income, its citizens were the fourth richest in the United States. This success was largely due to the location of the city at the mouth of Galveston Bay, a superb natural deepwater harbor. The busy Texan port was highly exposed to storm damage, however, because it was built on a low-lying sand spit that rose less than 6 feet (2 meters) above sea level.

Dawn on September 8, 1900 brought squally showers and waves that pounded the beach at Galveston. By midmorning, wind speeds were up to 40 mph (60 kph) and were increasing fast. As the storm approached, the barometric pressure dropped lower and lower, and the sea level rose higher and higher. The streets started to flood, and people ran to the bridge that connected Galveston Island to the mainland. However, the bridge was soon covered by rising water, and escape became impossible. By midafternoon, half of Galveston Island was under water.

In the eye wall of the storm, winds blowing at more than 110 mph (170 kph) whipped up huge sea waves, which crushed wooden buildings and washed them away. Numerous stone and concrete buildings also disintegrated because their foundations were ripped out of the

NORTH AMERICA'S DEADLIEST STORM
The violent hurricane that struck Texas on September 8, 1900 destroyed over half of Galveston. The storm killed 6,000 residents, one-seventh of the city's population.

sandy soil. Survivors told of being washed out of their homes and tossed about by the waves until they found something to cling to.

When the storm finally passed over, half of Galveston was gone. Although the city never achieved its former prominence, it was rebuilt with a protective sea wall. The wall proved its worth when the severe hurricanes that struck the city in 1915 and 1961 caused only minor damage.

FORECASTING CYCLONES

When a severe tropical cyclone hauls millions of tons of water onto low-lying coastal land, the only way to ensure personal survival is to be somewhere else. For the many millions of people living on cyclone-threatened coasts, the best protection is to receive warnings of an approaching storm early enough for them to reach a place of safety.

Ships, aircraft, and satellites equipped with devices to monitor weather conditions allow forecasters to observe the development of tropical cyclones far out to sea and to track their course. While general alerts can usually be issued well in advance, it is difficult to know exactly where tropical cyclones will

HUNTING FOR HURRICANES
When multiple thunderstorms develop at sea, forecasters fly out to monitor the movement of the storms in specially equipped airplanes known as "hurricane hunters."

strike, since the path they take is often erratic and cannot be predicted precisely. Even in the 1990s, forecasts given 24 hours before a cyclone strikes are only accurate to within about 100 miles (160 kilometers). This leaves authorities with the difficult choice of either evacuating an area early that may receive little damage, or waiting until the eleventh-hour before issuing specific warnings. Forecasts are only useful if the infrastructure exists to inform the people at risk about the danger and to transport them to a place of safety before the storm arrives. It is also vital that everyone takes the threat seriously. When Hurricane Camille hit the United States in 1969, one of the first things to be destroyed was a beachfront apartment where 25 people were celebrating the storm's arrival. Only one of the party survived.

PICKING THROUGH THE WRECKAGE
The hurricane that struck Galveston in 1900 destroyed 2,600 houses and left about 10,000 people homeless. Many of the houses were toppled by high winds (right). In the worst-hit area (above) the damage was compounded by storm surges, which reduced the houses to splinters.

CYCLONE 2B

TROPICAL CYCLONE, BANGLADESH, 1991

GAZETTEER P.136 – SITE NO.93

BANGLADESH IS ONE OF THE POOREST and most densely populated countries in the world, and much of it is made up of a vast delta created by the Ganges and other powerful rivers which flow down from the Himalayas. This low-lying delta is prone to major river floods, but the greatest loss of life occurs during tropical cyclones. One such storm, known as Cyclone 2B, struck the Bangladesh coast on April 29, 1991, bringing with it 146-mph (235-kph) winds and a lethal 20-foot (6-meter) high storm surge. About 140,000 people died when ferocious waves submerged exposed coasts and islands at the mouth of the delta.

TRAGEDY IN BANGLADESH
Cyclone 2B laid waste to 500 miles (800 km) of coastline and clogged up Bangladesh's main harbor at Chittagong with the hulls of wrecked ships. Many of the storm's victims lived on islands off the coast of Bangladesh in the Bay of Bengal.

Of the nine deadliest storms this century, seven have hit Bangladesh. Despite the risks, families continue to crowd onto the exposed islands and the mudbanks along its coast because the land here is very fertile and yields sufficient crops to meet their pressing need for food.

In the last week of April 1991, satellites began tracking Cyclone 2B as it roared up the Bay of Bengal. Warnings were broadcast on the radio and people were urged to go to one of the new

BRINGING IN THE DEAD
A victim of Cyclone 2B is carried to burial by surviving family members, four days after the storm. The grim task of recovering the bodies of victims washed out to sea lasted for weeks.

storm shelters that were constructed after a major cyclone devastated this part of Bangladesh in 1970, with the loss of more than 500,000 lives.

About 100,000 people huddled in the shelters survived Cyclone 2B, which hammered coastal districts for nine hours. Many other people in the area, however, were stranded in mud and straw huts, which offered little protection from the ferocious winds and waves that decimated the region. Many of the offshore islands were swamped completely. Across Bangladesh, more than one-and-a-half million homes were destroyed and one million cattle drowned.

THE RUINS OF SANDWIP ISLAND
Caught in the path of Cyclone 2B, the island of Sandwip is swamped by the storm. One survivor reported that 30,000 people on the island were swept out to sea by huge waves and that two-thirds of them drowned.

AFTER THE STORM
Because many roads in the region had been washed away, getting relief to the survivors was extremely hard. In the worst-hit areas, the threat of starvation was extremely severe because the waves had ruined crops and the salt-soaked land became temporarily infertile.

Lessons were learned in this disaster, and, when another big cyclone hit the delta in 1997, early evacuations and the provision of more shelters saved many thousands of lives.

THE GREAT STORM OF '87
Many rare trees in London's Kew Gardens and millions of other trees across southern England were uprooted by a ferocious gale in October 1987. Nineteen people died during the storm.

CANADA FREEZES OVER
In Montreal, trees were split apart by the cold and collapsed under the weight of ice when a series of ice storms chilled northeastern Canada for days on end in January 1998.

GALES AND BLIZZARDS

The storms that brew in temperate regions do not reach the violent intensity of the most powerful tropical cyclones, but they tend to last much longer over land. A large temperate storm has a diameter of more than 1,000 miles (1,600 kilometers) and will batter a wide area with pounding rains and high winds – often called gales. They may also be accompanied by a deadly feature never seen in tropical storms – the fierce snowy cold of a blizzard.

These storms are sometimes called cyclones because, like tropical cyclones, they grow into large rotating masses of rising air. However, they are more often referred to as lows or depressions, because of the low barometric pressure that develops in the area where air is rising. Unlike their tropical counterparts, lows are large frontal storms, which occur where cold polar air meets warm tropical air. The warm air is forced upward, rising rapidly in a tight spiral to form a large rotating storm cloud.

FROZEN IN THE FIELDS
During the ice storms that tore across Canada in 1988, temperatures plunged below -40°F (-40°C) and Arctic-cold winds chilled the air further, killing tens of thousands of cattle.

BLIZZARD IN NEW YORK

During a blizzard that struck the eastern United States in 1996, New York was buried under at least 20 in (51 cm) of snow, and 23 people lost their lives.

In the Northern Hemisphere, about 20 lows develop every day. A few of them, such as the "Great Storm" in 1987, produce fierce gales that unleash gusts of more than 100 mph (160 kph). The worst storms usually occur in winter when the temperature contrast between the polar and tropical air masses is greatest. When these air masses collide, deep depressions form, which are pushed along by prevailing winds high in the atmosphere. In 1968, a depression brought 125-mph (200-kph) winds to Scotland, killing 16 people. The hurricane-force blizzards then swept down across Europe, dumping heavy snowfalls as far south as Iran.

North America has suffered many severe blizzards in recent years, including "the Storm of the Century" *(see right)*, which killed at least 243 people in 1993. Large parts of the eastern United States were again brought to a standstill by a blizzard in January 1996, which buried Philadelphia under more than 30 inches (76 centimeters) of snow. Two years later, more than a million households in the province of Quebec were left without power when a raging ice storm collapsed thousands of electricity poles in the area.

North America also endures powerful mid-latitude storms that blow in from the Atlantic. The most powerful of these on record was the "Halloween" storm, which pounded coasts in New Jersey and New England with massive waves for 114 hours in November 1992.

STORM OF THE CENTURY

BLIZZARD, US, 1993

GAZETTEER P.129 – SITE NO.96

THE EXCEPTIONAL THING about the Storm of the Century was its scale. Never before or since has a storm forced the closure of every major airport in the eastern United States. Huge snowfalls paralyzed the region, until the snow had been cleared and services restored. The blizzard was responsible for at least 243 deaths and $3 billion-worth of damage.

Undoubtedly, the damage and death toll would have been greater had it not been for the weather forecasters, who provided early warning of the storm's arrival. Days before the storm struck, satellite images revealed that a huge cold air mass was moving down from polar regions. When the polar air reached the Gulf of Mexico, it collided violently with warm, moist air in the region. The ensuing storm tore across Cuba, bringing with it hurricane-force winds, torrential rain, and mountainous waves that completely destroyed 1,500 houses and badly damaged 37,000 other properties.

The storm swung sharply to the north and grew colder. Florida was battered by ferocious winds and, for the "Sunshine State," unusually heavy snowfalls. All across the southeastern United States, heavy snowfalls caused roofs and power lines to collapse as the blizzard moved northward. Winds of up to 125 mph (200 kph) whipped up the Atlantic Ocean. In the state of North Carolina, 200 beachfront houses were wrecked by storm surges, and 60 inches (152 centimeters) of snow was dumped onto the Appalachian Mountains.

In the northern United States and Canada, where blizzards strike every winter, people were more prepared for the snowy

SNOW SMOTHERS EASTERN SEABOARD
From March 12 to 14, 1993, a huge low-pressure system overwhelmed all of eastern North America, from Cuba to Canada. It brought with it high winds, freezing conditions, and heavy snowfalls.

conditions. However, the hurricane-force winds continued to damage properties and create huge waves. On Long Island, New York, 18 homes were washed into the sea. Further north, off the coast of Nova Scotia, 33 sailors drowned when their boat was swamped and sunk by massive 66-foot (20-meter) high swells.

Most experts agreed that such a large storm only hits America once every 100 years, and it was therefore named the Storm of the Century. Its arrival, however, coincided with a succession of unusually severe winter storms that have troubled the United States since 1989.

SNOWFALLS IN NEW YORK
Over 10 in (25 cm) of snow was dumped on New York between March 12 and 14, 1997. Although this amount is not exceptional, the conditions were made far worse by freezing winds that piled the snow into deep drifts.

GATHERING STORM CLOUDS

On July 26, 1927, a bolt of lightning from a thunderstorm raging over the state of New Jersey struck in the worst possible place – a navy ammunition depot – detonating a store of TNT. The explosion set off a chain reaction. One after another, warehouses around the arsenal blew up, hurling heavy artillery shells into the surrounding hills. Thirty people were killed and hundreds more were injured.

Precisely when and where a storm strikes is a matter of chance, and the degree of suffering it causes depends in part on how willing and able the people who are affected have been to prepare and protect themselves. Inadequate protection of an explosives store against lightning seems like gross negligence, but it would be wrong to blame negligence for all the deaths and injuries that occur when storms happen to strike in the wrong place.

PROTECTIVE MEASURES

In every society, and in each geographical region, decisions have to be made about what kind of weather protection to have and how much to spend on it. For the millions of families that farm on the islands of the delta in Bangladesh, the risk of being drowned by the storm surge of a tropical cyclone is extremely high. However, for many years it was felt that the cost of abandoning the most exposed land, or building hundreds of storm shelters to protect the people living there, was too great. The cost of this decision in human lives has been been enormous. Two tropical cyclones, which swept across the region in 1970 and 1991, each killed more than 100,000 people.

The decisions are difficult, even in wealthier countries. For the last two decades, cutbacks have forced governing bodies to invest less in weather protection measures. The failure of the British Meteorological Office to forecast "The Great Storm" of 1987, which blew down 15 million trees and caused about two billion dollars' worth of

FORKED LIGHTNING IN ARIZONA
The invention of the lightning rod in 1766 has greatly reduced the damage this hazard causes to buildings. However, lightning still kills more than 100 people in the United States each year and every so often causes widespread disasters.

THREAT IN THE PACIFIC
The lethal winds that whipped around the eye of Hurricane Emilia in 1994 threatened the Hawaiian Islands in the central Pacific, which are even more exposed to storm damage than the eastern seaboard of the United States.

CITY TORNADO
Tornadoes are rare in big cities but in 1997 one threatened the inhabitants of Miami, who were lucky to escape without loss of life.

damage in southern England, has been blamed on budget cuts. Many of the ships that once monitored weather in the Atlantic had been decommissioned and forecasters, relying mostly on satellite data, were unable to gauge the severity of the developing storm.

PREPARING FOR STORMS

For economic reasons, the measures set up to deal with severe weather are designed to cope with expected, rather than exceptional conditions. For example, winters in England have been relatively warm for about 25 years. Because there have been few heavy snowfalls during this period, investment in snow-clearing equipment has been low. As a result, the country is extremely vulnerable to heavy blizzards. Meteorological records clearly show that Britain gets several severe blizzards every century. In February 1947, for example, several days of heavy snows, high winds, and freezing temperatures left snowdrifts up to 20 feet (6 meters) deep. To cope with the disruption this caused, troops were called in to clear roads and railroads, and airforce planes dropped food parcels on remote villages. The return of warm weather brought a rapid thaw and severe floods. To assume that blizzards as severe as the one in 1947 will not strike Britain again would be irrationally optimistic.

Similar optimism occurs on the other side of the Atlantic. The people who built homes and marinas along the Florida coastline in the 1980s should not have been surprised by the level of damage that Hurricane Andrew caused in 1992. Worse hurricanes had struck the state in the 1940s and 1950s, and the lack of a major hurricane since then was only a lull. People living in New England and New York should also take heed, because both areas have been hit by big hurricanes earlier this century.

COASTAL HAZARDS IN NORTH AMERICA
During Hurricane Andrew, huge waves crashed into houses along the Florida coastline. Records reveal that hurricanes have damaged coastlines as far north as Newfoundland in the past.

ANDREW'S IMPACT
For more than 30 years, mainland Florida had escaped the destructive winds and storm surges of a major hurricane, but in 1992 its luck ran out. The southern suburbs of Miami bore the main brunt of the damage.

SEA-CLUSION
MIAMI. FLA

PATTERNS OF CHAOS

VIOLENT STORMS are not the most deadly blow that the weather can deal. Far more deaths have been caused by marked changes in weather patterns. Tens of millions of people have died in famines this century when crops have failed due to a lack of rain. Millions more have died when crops were destroyed by excess rain that caused flooding. Some changes in weather patterns are caused by random fluctuations, others by long-term climatic change, and some are triggered by catastrophic events, such as a meteor impact or massive volcanic eruptions. The Earth has been through many changes in its long history, and there have been periods when environmental upheavals have made it uninhabitable for many life forms. Now we face the possibility that our own activities may cause drastic changes to the climate.

NORTH SEA ⑤
Rising sea levels, high tides, and a raging storm caused the North Sea to flood coastal areas of northern Europe.

PLEISTOCENE ICE EPOCH ②
In the Pleistocene Period the Earth suffered a succession of ice ages, during which large parts of North America and Eurasia were buried under massive sheets of ice.

① THE AMERICAN DUST BOWL
Low rainfall in the Midwest during the 1930s brought ruin to tens of thousands of farmers as crops failed and the topsoil was blown away by the wind.

④ CRETACEOUS EXTINCTION
Up to 75 percent of species living on Earth became extinct 65 million years ago, including the dinosaurs. Many scientists believe that a meteorite caused this catastrophe.

③ MISSISSIPPI RIVER
Unusually heavy rainfall across the United States in 1993 raised water levels in the Mississippi and many of the rivers that fed into it, causing them to burst their banks and flood a vast area.

THREATENED BY GLOBAL WARMING
The polar ice caps and glaciers like the Perito Moreno Glacier in southern Argentina are being slowly melted by an increase in the average global temperature. The meltwater is causing sea levels to rise, which brings about a change in the flow of ocean currents.

⑦ GÖMEÇ
Exceptionally heavy snowfalls in eastern Turkey in January 1992 were responsible for devastating avalanches that engulfed several villages in the area, including Gömeç.

⑨ PERMIAN EXTINCTION
A succession of massive volcanic eruptions in Siberia about 250 million years ago contributed to bringing about the largest mass extinction in the Earth's history.

⑩ YANGTZE RIVER
Prolonged and torrential monsoon rains caused the Yangtze and numerous other rivers in China to burst their banks in 1991. One-fifth of China's population was adversely affected by the resulting floods.

⑥ COTE D'AZUR
After months of poor rain, fires raged out of control in southern France in July 1985, causing great damage along one of the most beautiful stretches of coastline in the world.

MECHANICAL CALENDAR
This eighteenth century orrery mechanically tracks the motion of the planets throughout a calendar year. As farmers are all too well aware, the weather does not follow such an orderly passage through the seasons.

⑧ ETHIOPIA
Millions of people died of starvation and diseases of malnutrition after several years of poor rains parched much of Africa. The famine was most severe in Ethiopia.

ASH WEDNESDAY FIRES ⑪
At the end of the long, dry summer of 1983, a number of bushfires started along Australia's southern coast on February 16, 1983. High winds caused them to burn out of control, and 71 people lost their lives in the flames.

CLIMATE EXTREMES AND MASS EXTINCTIONS

DESPITE ADVANCES IN TECHNOLOGY, humans continue to suffer droughts, floods, and a host of other natural disasters. In studying these and earlier much larger upheavals, scientists are coming to realize that the Earth's climate relies on a delicate interaction of natural factors which, when disrupted, can create conditions that threaten all life on this planet.

CLIMATE AND CHANGE

The concept that each region of the Earth has a stable climate is a consequence of our brief human lives. Records going back many generations reveal that some areas have suffered the effects of sudden, radical climatic changes. These upheavals have transformed farmland into desert, caused coastlines to disappear beneath the sea, and allowed glaciers to engulf valleys. Our ancestors blamed evil gods or bad luck for these fluctuations. Today, people look for scientific explanations, which we hope will allow us to predict and prepare for environmental change.

Human activities, such as deforestation and the burning of fossil fuels, seem to affect the climate, but they are only part of the problem. Dramatic climatic change is a natural feature of our planet. Many of the most damaging climatic shifts of recent times have been been linked to fluctuations in the movement of winds and ocean currents. The best known of these shifts is El Niño, which occurs when warm surface water in the western Pacific shifts eastward, leaving behind

droughts in Australasia and Indonesia, while bringing unusually heavy rain to large areas in North, South, and Central America.

Such climatic fluctuations occur frequently, but more profound changes are brought about by the slow but inexorable movement of the continents across the Earth. When continents block the flow of warm ocean currents to the

THE EL NIÑO PHENOMENON
These satellite images show, in red, rises in the surface temperature of the Pacific Ocean at the end of 1994 and, in blue, a marked fall in the amount of cold water.

poles, as they do at present, ice caps form. Ice caps are currently giving the Earth a colder, more unstable climate than it has experienced in much of its history. Within the last two million years, the Earth has suffered nine phases of extreme cold, when huge ice sheets have covered large parts of the globe before retreating back to the poles. The advance and retreat of the ice sheets coincides with cyclic shifts in the tilt and orbit of the Earth. These shifts affect the amount of the Sun's energy that the Earth absorbs, which alters temperatures and can have a major effect on the climate.

Many other factors affect how much energy the Earth absorbs from the Sun. Comet strikes and major volcanic eruptions both blast dust and gases into the atmosphere, which can severely reduce the levels of sunlight reaching our planet, as can dust from a meteor breaking up in space. Biological changes can also affect the levels of carbon dioxide in the atmosphere and alter temperatures profoundly. Five times in the Earth's history, these and other natural factors have combined to make most of the planet virtually uninhabitable and have caused the sudden extinction of more than 60 percent of the animal and plant species.

TEMPERATURE AND EXTINCTION CHART
This graph plots the major species extinctions that have occurred since complex life forms developed on Earth about 570 million years ago, and shows the alterations in global temperature since then.

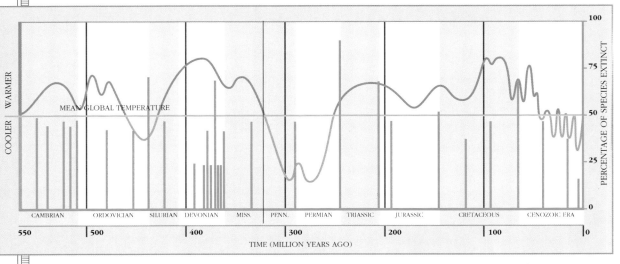

CLIMATIC FLOODING
Georgia was overwhelmed by vast floods during 1994 after heavy rains drenched the southeastern United States, causing a number of local rivers to burst their banks.

FIRES IN THE WEST
During 1988, several months of unusually dry weather in the western United States caused forest fires in Yellowstone Park to burn out of control.

DROUGHTS

Any area that receives significantly less rainfall than normal over a sustained period will suffer a drought. Most of the damage and suffering caused by the relative lack of water occurs in areas such as North Africa and the midwestern United States, where climate fluctuations bring droughts that often last for several years.

The cause of these climate fluctuations is not yet well understood. The climate of Saharan Africa is becoming drier as part of a very long-term cycle that has, over the last 10,000 years or so, turned once-fertile grasslands into the largest hot desert in the world. The spread of the desert has caused rivers and lakes to dry up over much of North Africa. It has also become very difficult for people living in this region to survive the shorter-term cycles of extreme drought that occur periodically. In Southeast Asia, Australia, and perhaps Africa, the decline in annual rainfall is linked to the phenomenon known as El Niño and Southern Oscillation (ENSO).

When farmers plant their seeds, they take a gamble on the weather. In subtropical regions that lie close to a desert, the risk of the rains failing is very high. Farmers are

DUSTSTORM IN AFRICA
During dry spells, strong winds whip the parched topsoil up into swirling clouds of dust. The fertility of the land continues to decline as more and more soil is blown away.

usually able to survive a single bad year by slaughtering their livestock for food, or by selling their cattle and other possessions in order to buy new seed for planting at the beginning of the next growing season. If rainfall is scarce for a second year, however, farmers have no goods left to sell, and food shortages become acute.

Crop failure leaves the fields exposed, and the fertility of the ground diminishes as the parched topsoil is blown away by the wind. The constant hunger and fear of the future in a prolonged drought have a devastating effect on a community. Malnutrition leaves the population, especially children and the elderly, more prone to infection, and babies die as their mothers' milk dries up. If the drought persists, the community is faced with mass starvation, and people are forced to abandon their homes to go in search of food.

DROUGHT'S LEGACY
Thousands of cattle died in Kenya in 1984 (left), in a drought that affected 20 African countries. A long cycle of drought is causing many of Africa's deserts to grow bigger, including, the Namibian Desert (below).

THE AMERICAN DUST BOWL

DROUGHT, US, 1932–40

GAZETTEER P.129 – SITE NO.63

DUSTSTORMS IN THE MIDWEST

It has been estimated that from 1932 to 1935, the wind lifted 850 million tons of soil from the once-fertile prairie farms. Much of the Midwest was transformed by the drought into a region known as the American Dust Bowl.

FROM 1932 TO 1940 the North American Midwest suffered a long drought that left tens of thousands of farmers destitute. Millions of acres of plowed fields became as dry as dust and the parched topsoil was blown away in huge black clouds. Thousands of people died of starvation, or of lung diseases caused by breathing the dust-laden air. The drought also forced more than 350,000 people to abandon the region and move to other parts of the United States.

In the early nineteenth century, when the first wave of settlers crossed the area now known as the American Dust Bowl, it was experiencing one of its periodic droughts. The area was so dry that they named it the Great American Desert and moved swiftly on to greener lands farther west. During the 1860s, however, several rainy years transformed the area, enabling the farmers who subsequently settled there to reap good harvests, until 1887, when drought struck again.

In the early twentieth century, the situation improved again and a new generation of hopeful farmers arrived and prospered until 1932. That year, the fields were plowed and planted as usual, but no rain fell, and nothing grew. With no covering of vegetation, the topsoil dried to a fine dust and was swept away by hot, dry winds. As the drought persisted, more and more soil was lost in repeated periods of strong wind, which

became known as duststorms. One storm in May 1934 blew up a black cloud that stretched from Alberta to Texas, sprinkling soil from what was once fertile farmland onto ships that were sailing 300 miles (500 kilometers) out in the Atlantic.

In March 1935, the wind blew unceasingly for 27 days. Roads and farms were buried by choking dust, and the area became a featureless wasteland. The days became as dark as

night, and roofs caved in under the weight of the dust. Farming also collapsed during the drought and, with so much of the precious topsoil gone, it appeared to many farmers as though their land would never be worth cultivating again.

When the rains returned in 1941, fewer than half of the farmers were left in the region. Finally aware of the fluctuating nature of the climate, they developed practices to protect the land during droughts. Half of the plowed land was returned to grass, and rows of trees were planted as windbreaks.

DRIVEN FROM THE LAND

Duststorms, like the one that swept through Missouri in 1937 (above), forced 350,000 people to leave the Midwest. Packing only what they could carry, many families became destitute as there was little other work at this time.

ETHIOPIA

DROUGHT, AFRICA, 1981–85

GAZETTEER P.133 – SITE NO.41

DROUGHT CAUSED CROP FAILURES AND FAMINE across 20 African countries in 1984 and 1985, but the suffering was most severe in Ethiopia, where there had been low rainfall and poor harvests since 1981. The country was in the middle of a civil war and millions of people were forced to flee from the fighting to search for food. Many of the refugees were close to death before their plight became widely known. Although there are no accurate mortality figures, it is estimated that at the height of the famine more than 20,000 children were dying each month.

A FOUR-YEAR DROUGHT
Over half of Ethiopia was devastated by the drought. When crops failed for the second year running, 50,000 farmers flocked to the cities to sell their possessions for food. After two more years without rain, millions were starving.

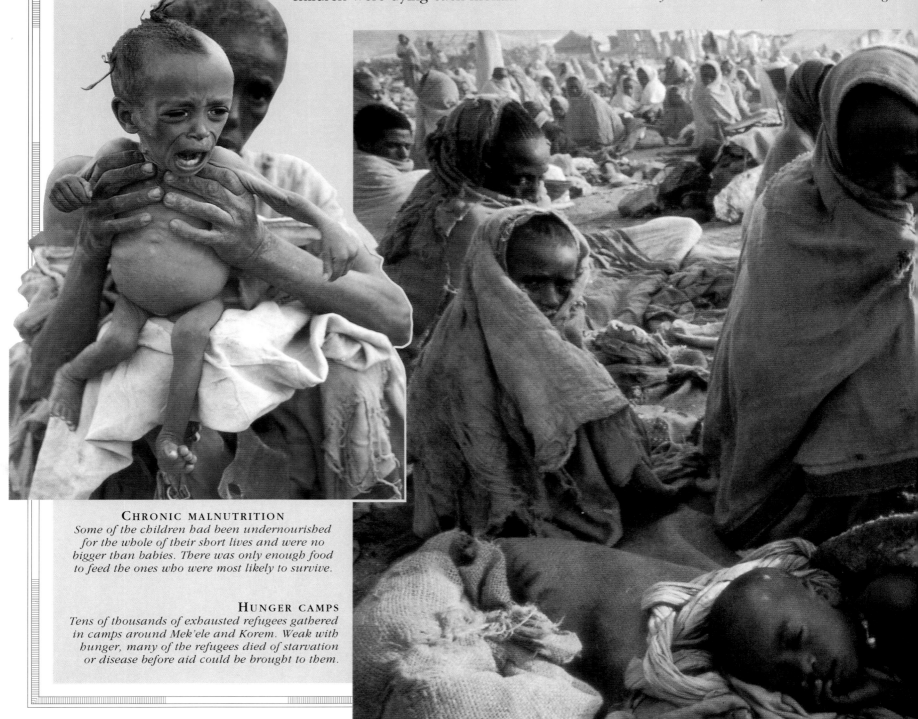

CHRONIC MALNUTRITION
Some of the children had been undernourished for the whole of their short lives and were no bigger than babies. There was only enough food to feed the ones who were most likely to survive.

HUNGER CAMPS
Tens of thousands of exhausted refugees gathered in camps around Mek'ele and Korem. Weak with hunger, many of the refugees died of starvation or disease before aid could be brought to them.

Ethiopia is a mountainous country lying beside the Red Sea in northeast Africa. For most of the year it experiences a desert climate, but around June moist tropical winds veer up from the south and bring a short rainy season. In good years this rainy season lasts from June to September and allows crops to flourish. However, in bad years the rains are virtually nonexistent, or do not come at all, and the crops wither.

The rainfall had been good in the 1950s and adequate in the 1960s, but the weather pattern deteriorated in the 1970s. The amount of rainfall dropped and there were severe droughts in 1972,

BARREN LAND
In the 1980s, drought parched Ethiopia and forced tens of thousands of people to leave their land. Many of them had to walk hundreds of miles in a desperate quest to find food.

1973, and 1974. Even before the famine of the 1980s began, 1,000 Ethiopian children were dying each day of diseases related to malnutrition.

The most serious drought began in 1981 and continued to afflict much of Ethiopia for the next four years. Food shortages were already critical in 1982 and by 1984 the lack of rainfall began to

affect more and more of Africa. It is estimated that during 1984 more than 150 million people faced starvation in 20 African countries.

In Ethiopia, the government was engaged in fighting a civil war and did little to provide famine relief to the millions of starving civilians in the country. In the worst-affected regions, the entire populations of towns and villages abandoned their homes and walked toward the cities in a desperate search for food. Weak with hunger, many of the refugees were not strong enough to finish the journey. Tens of thousands of them, unable to walk any farther, gathered in makeshift camps near Mek'ele and Korem.

RELIEF WORK
In October 1984, a BBC Television news crew first reported on the plight of the refugees. The report revealed that even at the camps there was not enough food to feed everyone. In order to save lives, relief workers were forced to select which refugees they could help, knowing that those to whom they could not give food would die. The images of starving children that appeared around the world caused a wave of public concern. The relief organizations immediately received a flood of donations, but the ongoing civil war made it hard to get the aid to the famine-affected areas inside Ethiopia.

The rains returned to Ethiopia in 1985, but remained patchy until the 1990s, when plentiful rainfall made farming productive once more. Few people doubt, however, that there will be more droughts.

FOOD AID
Once the extent of the crisis became known, donations poured in from around the world. The money raised made it possible to distribute food to all the survivors of the famine.

FIRES

Fires are inevitable in environments that suffer even short periods of drought. The vegetation, which flourished during the wet season, dries out and can easily be ignited by lightning. The fires that start this way are often extinguished by rain, or burn out when they reach water or an area with little combustible material.

Far from being totally destructive, fires often have a beneficial effect. By burning up dead vegetation, fires clear the land for new growth, and the season after a fire is often a time of rapid regeneration. Many plants and animals

BUSHFIRE IN AUSTRALIA
An average of 15,000 bushfires are recorded in Australia each year, making it one of the most fire-prone countries on Earth.

THE 1988 YELLOWSTONE FIRE
More than 720,000 acres (290,000 hectares) of Yellowstone Park, Wyoming, were destroyed in North America's largest forest fire this century.

have evolved to cope with the regular cycle of fire and regrowth. People living in fire-prone areas, however, face the constant danger of being left without food or shelter because their homes and crops, which cannot be moved, are vulnerable to the destructive effects of fire.

While most fires burn slowly enough to allow people and animals to escape, a few spread rapidly and unpredictably. Disastrous fires like these most frequently occur after a

ASH WEDNESDAY FIRE

FIRE, AUSTRALIA, 1983

GAZETTEER P.139 – SITE NO.25

AROUND 15,000 FIRES BURN in the Australian bush each year. In February 1983, however, the fire risk was especially great because the periodic shift in global weather patterns linked to El Niño had brought Australia an extremely hot, dry summer. Temperatures soared to 104°F (40°C)

on a regular basis. As a result, streams, wells, and finally the huge reservoirs that supplied freshwater to people in the state of Victoria, dried up.

It remains a mystery why so many bushfires started at once on February 16, 1983. Some may have been the work of arsonists. Sparks from broken powerlines were blamed for others. After they started, the fires grew quickly. Driven along by a fierce wind, the flames ripped through the tinder-dry bush at 100 mph (160 kph).

The public was kept informed on which way the fires were heading, but a sudden change of wind direction had lethal consequences. People who thought themselves safe, suddenly realized

THE DAY AUSTRALIA CAUGHT FIRE
Several fires started almost simultaneously across southern Australia on February 16, 1983. The fires raged for 48 hours, and left scores of farmers bankrupt, 8,500 people homeless, and 71 dead.

INSTANT INFERNO
The parched Australian bush burned with such intensity that trees exploded and homes were consumed in minutes (below). Fighting the flames (left) was extremely hazardous because the fires were swept around by strong winds.

that they were in grave danger and tried to flee to safety. Some of them were unable to escape because the dense smoke made it impossible to see either the fire, or where they were going.

In the minds of most Australians, the 1983 fires remain the most terrifying. Although there have been several massive bushfires since then, none have claimed nearly as many lives.

AERIAL ASSAULT
Aircraft were used to help douse the fires in Yellowstone Park that raged out of control throughout the summer of 1988 and continued to burn until September.

severe drought and burn most fiercely when the winds are strong. On October 8, 1871, fierce winds drove fires across 400 square miles (1,036 square kilometers) of Wisconsin. Nine towns were destroyed and more than 1,500 people were killed in and around Peshtigo. The fires spread so rapidly that by the time the Peshtigo residents realized the danger it was too late to escape.

SMOKE CLOUD OVER SUMATRA
Forest fires burned out of control in Indonesia in 1997–1998, enveloping much of Southeast Asia in dense smoke for months on end.

CALIFORNIA BURNS
In 1994, fires swept out of control on the outskirts of Los Angeles, California, creating firestorms that caused millions of dollars' worth of damage.

THE HUMAN FACTOR

In the 1970s, biologists found that expensive programs to fight forest fires and bushfires do not protect most habitats but, instead, interfere with the cycle of fire and regrowth that shape them. As a result of these findings, fires started by lightning were allowed to burn unhindered in many national parks, provided that they did not threaten human lives or property. The policy worked very well at the Yellowstone National Park in the Northwest until the dry summer of 1988. When

CHARRED REMAINS IN SYDNEY
In December 1997, a bush fire ravaged the Australian state of New South Wales and swept into the suburbs of Sydney. Two firefighters lost their lives fighting the blaze.

rainfall did not come to extinguish the flames naturally, park wardens decided to send in firefighters. By this time, however, the fires were impossible to control and did not finally die out until the autumn snows started to fall. By that time, 1.6 million acres (648,000 hectares) of prime forest had been destroyed.

Wildfires are not a natural part of the life cycle in tropical rainforests, and the disastrous consequences of using fire to clear areas of rainforest were seen in 1997. When the expected monsoon rains did not come to extinguish deliberately lit fires in Indonesia and Malaysia, the fires burned for months, destroying thousands of square miles of rainforest and smothering much of Southeast Asia under a thick blanket of smoke.

CÔTE D'AZUR
FIRE, SOUTH OF FRANCE, 1985
GAZETTEER P.134 – SITE NO. 111

EACH YEAR SEVERAL THOUSAND fires break out in the forests and scrubland of France. Due to the decline of traditional family farms, the number of fires has increased because grass and scrub, once grazed by sheep and goats, is now left to grow tall. Consequently, in the south of France, where summers are hot and dry, the ground is covered with tinder-dry vegetation, which can be ignited by lightning or a spark from a campfire.

On July 31, 1985, firefighters on the Côte d'Azur were on high alert as the region filled up with tourists. When a small fire started at 12:30 pm in the Estérel mountains, volunteer firefighters were on the scene quickly, but the squally northerly wind that the French call the "mistral" was exceptionally strong that day and 50-mph (80-kph) gusts whipped up the blaze. The flames ignited nearby trees, and the fire soon began to burn out of control, forcing the evacuation of three nearby campsites.

By 4 pm clouds of smoke had cut off the Cannes-to-Adrets motorway, and ash from the fire was falling on Mandelieu. Helicopters flew in reinforcements to help the local firefighters, and planes bombed the flames with water. Five firefighters were killed fighting the blaze, and 20 more suffered serious burns. In the evening, the wind died down and the fire was brought under control on the outskirts of Cannes.

That afternoon, another 1,000 firefighters had to be drafted to tackle a massive forest fire that threatened the towns of Callas and

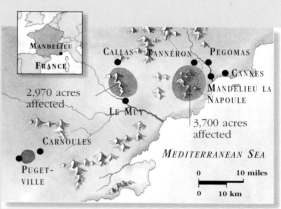

WILDFIRES IN SOUTHERN FRANCE
The fires that began on July 31, 1985 destroyed more than 6,670 acres (2,700 hectacres) of the Côte d'Azur. Thousands of firefighters, five of whom died, battled to control the blazes.

Le Muy. Although the gusting winds died down at about 5 pm, it took firefighters until daybreak to put out the blaze. Resources on the Côte d'Azur were stretched further by yet another forest fire that broke out near Carnoules at 8 pm.

Since 1985, France's investment in improving the spotting and fighting of wildfires has enabled them to extinguish fires more quickly. Without more rain in the area, however, the threat that a fire could rage out of control still remains.

MOUNTAIN ON FIRE
The fire that started in the Estérel mountains swept across the Massif du Tannéron (left), burning up 3,700 acres (1,500 hectares) of countryside. Local firefighters (above) were joined by professional firefighters and troops who, together, managed to prevent the fire from reaching Cannes.

YANGTZE RIVER

FLOOD, CHINA, 1991

GAZETTEER P.137 – SITE NO.95

IN 1991, PARTS OF CHINA SUFFERED A MONSOON season that began early, lasted much longer than usual, and brought exceptionally heavy rains. About 220 million people, one-fifth of China's population, were affected by flooding. The most devastation occurred when Tai Hu, a lake near the mouth of the Yangtze River, swelled to cover a vital industrial and agricultural region between Shanghai and Nanjing.

SUMMER FLOODS IN CHINA
Crops, homes, factories, and transportation were destroyed across much of central China in 1991, when heavy rains caused the Yangtze and other rivers to overflow. It is estimated that 20 percent of China's summer harvest was ruined.

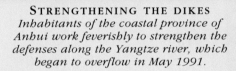

STRENGTHENING THE DIKES
Inhabitants of the coastal province of Anhui work feverishly to strengthen the defenses along the Yangtze river, which began to overflow in May 1991.

The reform of the Chinese economy that began in 1978 brought rapid development to the provinces of Anhui and Jiangsu. Anhui became China's main grain-producing region, and Jiangsu topped the national league tables for industrial and agricultural output for seven years in a row. However, the drive to increase production meant that less money was being spent on flood defenses.

While the defenses were able to cope with the typical monsoon floods that occur in July and August, they could not cope with the torrential rains that deluged large parts of China in 1991. The rains began in May, two months early, and were much heavier than usual. A weather system that normally brought heavy rain to the southern tip of China, moved 190 miles (300 kilometers) to the north, leaving drought in the southernmost region of China, and producing downpours in central China that unleashed about 15.7 inches

FLOODING IN JIANGSU
In the summer of 1991, floodwater inundated much of the province of Jiangsu, including the city of Xinghua (above). The army helped to evacuate millions of people from their flood-damaged homes (left).

(40 centimeters) of rain in two days. Floodwaters draining down from the upper reaches of the Yangtze flowed downstream and caused serious flooding along the length of the river.

By mid-July, 1,780 people had been drowned or killed in landslides triggered by heavy rainfall. Worst affected was Anhui, in which up to 80 percent of the population was affected by the floods, and much of the provincial capital of Hefei was under more than 3 feet (1 meter) of water. Floodwater swept away nearly a million houses in Anhui and killed 337 people, some of whom were electrocuted as they tried to salvage their belongings from their wrecked homes.

In Jiangsu, 500 rural families were marooned on a narrow dike for a week before finally being rescued, and 198 people drowned. The cities of Wuxi and Nanjing were also badly damaged.

During the floods, up to 10 million people were evacuated from the worst-hit areas in order to stop the spread of disease. After the water receded in September, the government started a major flood-control program to prevent such severe floods from ever happening again.

FLOODS

Creating firm boundaries around land seems to be the only way humans can live peacefully on this crowded planet. We also attempt to impose boundaries on nature. Time and time again, flood disasters demonstrate that the natural boundary between water and dry land is made up of a large area that is neither. Such areas, called floodplains, can be dry or covered with water, depending on the weather, the tides, and many other factors. Because floodplains contain some of the most fertile environments on Earth, they are heavily populated and intensively farmed. As a result, when the waters rise, the effect of the flood is usually disastrous.

RIVER FLOODS

It is no accident that fertile farmland lines the banks of flood-prone rivers. Floods make the land fertile by irrigating the soil and leaving behind nutrients as the floodwater slowly recedes. Many ancient civilizations, such as the Egyptians, were dependent on annual river

RIVER FLOOD IN TEXAS
This couple waded to safety with their dog and grandchild after heavy rain soaked the Southwest in 1994, causing the San Jacinto River to burst its banks.

floods. Population pressures since then have meant that dams, dikes, overflow channels, and reservoirs have been built to control the flow of water. It has not, however, proved possible to totally protect crops and buildings from flooding. Exceptionally heavy rain or snow sometimes swell a river so dramatically that the volume of water overwhelms our defenses.

SEASONAL HAZARD
During the 1983 monsoon season, floodwater swamped Varanasi in India, after torrential rains caused the Ganges River to overflow.

MISSISSIPPI RIVER

FLOOD, MIDWEST US, 1993

GAZETTEER P.129 – SITE NO.97

IN THE SUMMER OF 1993, floodwater inundated scores of cities and thousands of farms along the banks of the Mississippi River and its upper tributaries. Water levels reached record heights along a 1,000-mile (1,600-kilometer) stretch of the Mississippi and Missouri Rivers and overwhelmed hundreds of flood defenses. The resulting floods claimed the lives of 50 people, left 70,000 homeless, and disrupted the lives of hundreds of thousands more in nine midwestern states. About 20 million acres (8 million hectares) of farmland was waterlogged and unproductive throughout the growing season, and the total cost of the disaster was estimated to have reached $12 billion.

THE GREAT FLOOD OF 1993
Following months of record rainfall over much of the United States and Canada, more than 31,000 sq miles (80,000 sq km) of the American Midwest was flooded when the Mississippi and many other rivers in the region overflowed.

ROAD LINKS SEVERED
This bridge over the Mississippi was closed on July 16, 1993, when floods swamped Quincy, Illinois. Land 7 miles (11 km) from the river was affected.

Unusually heavy rain began to fall across much of North America in September 1992. A shift in high-altitude winds caused an endless succession of low-pressure weather systems to move up from the Gulf of Mexico and empty their clouds over the central United States.

By June 1993, some areas had been drenched by three times the expected annual rainfall in only eight months. The ground became saturated and there was nowhere left for the rainwater to go but into the web of rivers and streams that flowed into the Mississippi. On June 20, the flow became so great that a dam on the Black River in Wisconsin burst, submerging 100 houses and pouring floodwater into the Mississippi.

Then, in July, one-third of the catchment area of the Mississippi was swamped by more than four times as much rain as usual. By July 14, more than 100 rivers in the area had overflowed. As the waters continued to rise, residents, helped by units of the military reserve, used more than 26 million sandbags to strengthen and increase the height of the flood defenses. Known as levees, these defenses were designed only to

RAIN STOPS PLAY
Months of heavy rain caused the Mississippi to overflow in 1993. This stadium in Davenport, Iowa, was one of the many sports facilities to be temporarily put out of action by floodwater.

FIGHTING THE FLOODS
Residents of Des Moines, Iowa, pile up thousands of sandbags in an attempt to contain floodwater from the Des Moines River after it overflowed in 1993.

FLOODS NEAR ST. LOUIS
Photographed in July 1993, this satellite image shows, in red, the extent of the floods at the confluence of the Mississippi and Missouri Rivers, located just north of St. Louis.

RESCUED BY BOAT
These two residents of Ursa, Illinois, are finally rescued by boat after being stranded on the roof of their home, which was inundated by more than 3 feet (1 meter) of floodwater.

hold back the floodwater for a few days but, because the rivers were flooded for months on end, 150 of the levees gave way. Residents and soldiers worked around the clock in an attempt to rescue belongings from flooded homes and to evacuate millions of farm animals that were threatened.

Some of the worst flooding occurred at the confluence of the Mississippi and Missouri Rivers, where a vast expanse of land was completely submerged. By the beginning of August, the water surging through St. Louis was 49 feet (15 meters) deep, which was more than 20 feet (6 meters) above flood levels. Because the city was protected by a floodwall that could cope with crests of up to 52 feet (16 meters), it escaped being flooded. The raging torrent caused severe flooding downstream, however, and the Mississippi's level remained dangerously high until the end of August.

Many people believed that the 1993 floods would not have been so destructive, and would not have lasted as long, if the defenses had been designed to allow the controlled release of water, rather than to hold it back. Others argued that the economic loss would have been much greater if no protective measures had been taken. No one disputed, however, that living on a floodplain was dangerous, and everyone agreed that further floods in the area were inevitable.

NORTH SEA

FLOOD, NORTHERN EUROPE, 1953

—————— GAZETTEER P.134 – SITE NO. 95 ——————

SOME OF THE MOST fertile farmland in England and the Low Countries of northern Europe lies below sea level and is only protected from the stormy North Sea by dikes or sand dunes.

When a vicious gale began moving across Britain on January 31, 1953, weather forecasters predicted that these sea defenses were about to be severely tested. An exceptionally high spring tide was due, and it was feared that the storm's low atmospheric pressure and hurricane-force winds would raise sea levels further and drive enormous waves against coasts around the North Sea. Radio broadcasts advised people living in threatened areas to move themselves and their livestock to high ground. However, most people on the flat coastal plains found that they were too far from safe areas to reach them in time.

As the storm tore across the North Sea in the early hours of February 1, floods ravaged the English, Dutch, and Belgian coastlines. The most destruction occurred at the southern end of the North Sea, where the sea level was 18 feet (5.5 meters) higher than normal. By 4 am hundreds of dikes across the Netherlands were broken apart by

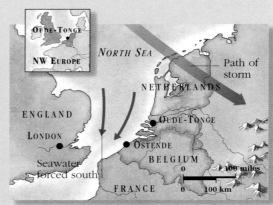

THE NORTH SEA OVERFLOWS
A severe gale coupled with exceptionally high tides caused the North Sea to breach English, Dutch, and Belgian coastal defenses. The floods killed more than 2,100 people.

monstrous waves. Whole communities were wrecked as walls of seawater surged inland. Hundreds of people drowned in their homes as the sea swept past and rushed 37 miles (60 kilometers) inland. Some coastal districts were submerged under 33 feet (10 meters) of water. High tides continued to damage coastal areas until the sea defenses were repaired a year later.

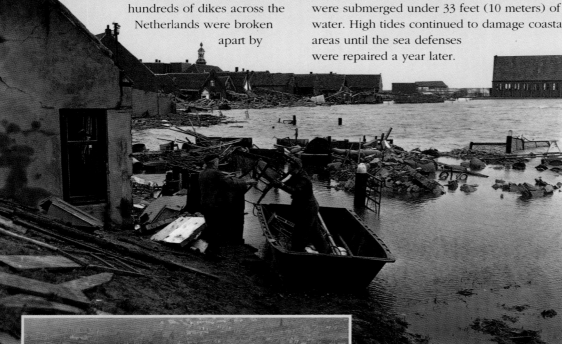

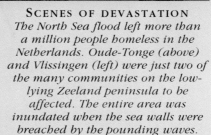

SCENES OF DEVASTATION
The North Sea flood left more than a million people homeless in the Netherlands. Oude-Tonge (above) and Vlissingen (left) were just two of the many communities on the low-lying Zeeland peninsula to be affected. The entire area was inundated when the sea walls were breached by the pounding waves.

SEA FLOODS

Coastal areas experience floods twice daily as the rotation of the Moon around the Earth causes sea levels to rise and fall, creating tides. By building dikes and walls to hold the sea back at high tide, humans have turned salt marshes into farmland and have built towns on flood-prone land. The predictability of the daily tides can give a false sense of security, however, since coastal defenses often fail to hold the sea back during violent storms. The low barometric pressure of these storms causes the sea level to rise well beyond the normal high-tide mark and, if the storm's winds blow toward the shore, large waves propel seawater even farther onto the land.

Climate change has caused sea levels to rise and fall many times in the history of the Earth. Global warming is currently causing the polar ice caps to shrink, making sea levels rise by about 0.08 inch (2 millimeters) per year. Low-lying areas, such as the Netherlands, are therefore more at risk of sea floods. Coral islands, such as the Maldives, are in danger of disappearing altogether.

The problem of rising sea levels is made worse in areas where coastlines are sinking into the sea. This is occurring because large areas of land are still readjusting to the effects of the Last Ice Age. A mere 18,000 years ago, much of North America and northern Europe was weighed down by a thick ice sheet. When the ice retreated, the land began to regain its shape. In some northern areas, the land is still rising and is causing areas to the south to tilt downward and sink slowly into the sea.

SEA-FLOOD PROTECTION
The massive Thames Barrier was built near the mouth of the Thames River in England to protect London from tidal surges and storm floods.

POLE POSITION
After waves flooded the resort of Palm Beach in Florida, a man who had taken refuge up a pole was stranded as more huge waves swept inland.

AVALANCHES AND LANDSLIDES

Extreme climatic conditions can cause disasters in mountainous regions. High rainfall often triggers landslides by saturating the soil and dislodging rocks. Heavy snowfalls increase the risk of avalanches by depositing unstable masses of snow on steep slopes. As the snow accumulates, fragile bonds form between ice particles that hold the mass of snow together and keep it clinging to the sides of mountains.

ROARING SNOW

A large avalanche cascades down a mountain in Antarctica. Such falls travel at great speeds and make a roaring noise because the weight of the snow blasts air out of the front of the avalanche.

When the snow begins to thaw, these bonds become brittle and can be fractured by a loud noise, a gust of wind, or any movement that disturbs the snow. Once loosened, the snow cascades down the mountain, sweeping up rock, gravel, and other debris.

The most lethal avalanches of the twentieth century occurred during World War I in the northern Italian Alps, where thousands of

VICTIM OF THE AVALANCHE WARS
Artillery fire in the Italian Alps during World War I precipitated avalanches that killed many Austrian and Italian troops. Rescuers recover the frozen corpse of one of their fellow soldiers.

Austrian and Italian troops were engaged in battle. After an avalanche killed 253 soldiers in December 1916, both sides resorted to firing shells at the snow-laden slopes to destabilize the snow. Over the next two winters, more than 40,000 young men died beneath the many avalanches that were triggered.

As an avalanche or landslide accelerates down a slope, air becomes trapped under the leading edge and lifts it off the ground. Escape is impossible because the snow or rock flies down the slope at up to 200 mph (320 kph), carrying away everything in its path.

GÖMEÇ

AVALANCHE, TURKEY, 1992

— GAZETTEER P.135 – SITE NO. 117 —

THE MOUNTAINOUS TERRAIN of northern Iraq and eastern Turkey is the home of the Kurdish people. It is relatively isolated from the more populated and developed parts of both Turkey and Iraq and is an area that many Kurds believe should become an independent state. To combat Kurdish unrest, the Turkish government placed military outposts in the area. Even without the military tension, life is very hard in this region, especially in the winter, and conditions were particularly severe at the start of 1992. Following heavy snowfalls, parts of eastern Turkey were buried under more than 30 feet (9 meters) of snow. The buildup of snow on the steep mountain slopes created the severe hazard of dangerous avalanches.

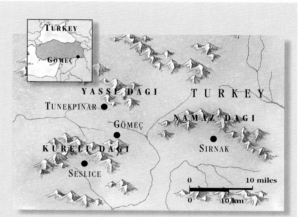

DEATH IN THE TURKISH MOUNTAINS
The deadliest avalanches in recent times occurred in eastern Turkey early in 1992. Snowslides engulfed several villages, including Gömeç, killing hundreds of people in the area.

WHITE DEATH
When rescue workers eventually reached the Gömeç area, they were faced with the grim task of having to dig out of the snow hundreds of victims who had been buried by the avalanches.

WINTER TERROR
Avalanches began to roar down Mount Gabar and other mountains in the region on Friday, January 31. The first places to be hit were the villages of Gömeç and Tunekpinar. More avalanches followed over the weekend, smothering other villages and destroying a Turkish military outpost. Strong blizzards prevented rescuers from reaching the stricken villages. Two helicopters carrying rescue and medical workers were forced back twice by high winds

and blinding snow. On Sunday the weather had cleared enough to allow Turkish Red Crescent doctors to reach Gömeç. They found that the village had virtually disappeared under the snow and more than half of its population of 250 was either dead or missing. In the Turkish military outpost, 132 soldiers had been killed.

For the next week, the death toll continued to rise because most of the people buried by the avalanches died before rescuers could reach them, and some of those pulled out alive from the snow died of hypothermia before reaching hospital. The avalanches also blocked roads, cutting off many villages from supplies of food and fuel. An even greater tragedy was averted by American troops, who flew blankets, medical supplies, and food to 110 villages in the region.

Although conditions remained difficult for the Kurdish people, the success of the American relief mission led to proposals for a permanent, worldwide rescue force to be set up.

THE LAST ICE AGE

FREEZE, GLOBAL, 114,000 – 12,000 YEARS AGO

GAZETTEER P.129 – SITE NO. 5

DURING THE PLEISTOCENE EPOCH, which began 1.6 million years ago, the Earth suffered some of the most unstable climatic conditions of its long history. Over a cycle about 100,000 years long, the polar ice caps repeatedly grew larger then retreated to cause a succession of long ice ages and briefer periods of relative warmth.

The most recent of these ice ages, known as the Last Ice Age, began 114,000 years ago, but it took 40,000 years for the ice sheets to become fully established. At this stage, the mean global temperature was about 9°F (5°C) lower than it is today, and massive thick sheets of ice covered much of North America and northern Eurasia, making them uninhabitable. Ice-age conditions continued for more than 60,000 years despite fluctuations in temperature. When the ice sheets were thickest and most widespread, 18,000 years ago, so much water was locked up as ice that the oceans were around five percent smaller than they are today. The ice sheets began to

THE LAST ICE AGE
The most recent ice age began about 114,000 years ago. The ice sheets reached their farthest extent 18,000 years ago and caused sea levels to drop by more than 330 ft (100 m).

melt rapidly 12,000 years ago. The release of water caused vast floods that killed far more species than the ice age itself. Much of North America was swamped by meltwater as the ice retreated and huge areas of coastal land were submerged by the returning seas.

Surviving through the unstable conditions of the Pleistocene Ice Epoch forced species to evolve very rapidly. The unique mental ability of human beings evolved during this time.

ANIMALS FROM THE LAST ICE AGE
The woolly mammoth (left) disappeared at the end of the Last Ice Age, possibly hunted to extinction by our ancestors. However, many of the species painted on cave walls in Lascaux, France, 30,000 years ago (below) survived.

MASS EXTINCTIONS

The millions of species that inhabit the Earth today are only a tiny proportion of the life that has ever existed. Competition between species and environmental changes are continually causing some species to disappear and others to evolve. In the Earth's history, however, there have been five mass extinctions in which more than half the animal and plant species died out over a relatively short time period. The dinosaurs disappeared 65 million years ago in the most recent mass extinction. Earlier extinctions were equally dramatic. More than 70 percent of animals died out toward the end of the Devonian period and, at the end of Permian period (see p.100), more than 90 percent of species became extinct.

ICE EPOCHS

Many species die out during periods of climatic instability known as ice epochs, of which there have been at least five in the last billion years. Ice epochs last several million years; the most recent began around two million years ago. They occur when the position of the continents prevents ocean currents from warming one or

LONDON FREEZES OVER
This painting of an ice fair on the Thames in 1814 shows that England's climate was colder than than it is today. The cold phase ended in 1850 and was known as the Little Ice Age.

both poles, allowing ice to collect and become a thick ice cap. During ice epochs, the world climate is sensitive to slight variations in the Earth's orbit. The average global temperature fluctuates by several degrees over a cycle of about 100,000 years, and the ice caps grow and shrink. We are now in a period of relative warmth and stability between ice ages.

MOUNTAIN GLACIER
Ice not only accumulates at the poles, but also builds up in mountainous regions, where snow compacts to form glaciers. Gorner Glacier in the Swiss Alps is one of the largest in Europe.

EVIDENCE OF CLIMATIC CHANGE
Scientists in Antarctica drill the ice cap for core samples, which reveal how much carbon dioxide was in the atmosphere at the time the ice formed.

CRETACEOUS EXTINCTION

MASS EXTINCTION, GLOBAL, 65 MILLION YEARS AGO

GAZETTEER P.130 – SITE NO.1

KILLER CRATER
Geophysical evidence suggests that a 125-mile (200-km) wide crater found under the Yucatan Peninsula was created when a meteorite struck the Earth 65 million years ago and blasted out 30,000 sq miles (80,000 sq km) of rock.

THE FOSSIL RECORDS SHOW that dinosaurs lived on Earth for about 160 million years. Then, 65 million years ago at the end of the geological period known as the Cretaceous, they, and about 70 percent of other species, disappeared. The rocks that formed around the time are now providing clues to the causes of this global catastrophe.

COLOR-ENHANCED SCAN OF CHICXULUB CRATER

After the dinosaurs appeared, around 225 million years ago, they quickly came to dominate the land, leaving mammals, which emerged about 10 million years later, little room for development. There also existed many marine reptiles, and an array of gigantic flying reptiles that dominated the skies.

During the reign of the reptiles, the climate remained warmer and more stable than it is now. Even so, dinosaurs had to adapt to shifts in the amount of rainfall, brought about by the merging and splitting apart of the supercontinent, Pangaea, as well as a series of mass extinctions, and the emergence of flowering plants 120 million years ago. By the end of the Cretaceous, many well-known dinosaur species had died out, including most of the huge plant-eating sauropods. A wide range of dinosaurs, including the flesh-eating *Tyrannosaurus rex*, still thrived, however.

At the time of the mass extinction, the Earth was hit by a 6-mile (10-kilometer) wide meteorite, which gouged out a huge crater in the Gulf of Mexico. Much of North America and the Caribbean was showered by molten

EXTINCTION VICTIMS
Fossils show that an order of mollusks known as ammonites (right) and all dinosaur species, including Edmontosaurus *(below), died out. It is still not possible to tell, however, if the upheaval happened over millennia or in an instant.*

rock, and the blast also triggered huge fires and tsunamis. Rocks formed at the time show that the entire planet was sprinkled by dust containing what may be the meteorite's pulverized remains. This led a number of scientists to speculate that enough dust was blasted into the atmosphere to block out the Sun's rays for months on end. The resulting cold and darkness prevented green plants from growing, causing the food chain to collapse and millions of species to die out. Advocates of this theory point out that among the surviving species were insects, which fed off the carcasses of the larger animals; mammals and birds, which fed on the insects; and green plants, which were able to produce seeds that germinated when sunlight returned.

Many other scientists do not agree that the meteorite impact was responsible for the global upheaval, however. Other events, such as massive lava eruptions in India, falling sea levels, and marked climatic change has also been blamed for this extinction.

In the rocks that formed after the Cretaceous, there is no trace left of the dinosaurs. There is, however, evidence that, after a few million years, surviving mammal species began to diversify and take over the complex role that dinosaurs once performed.

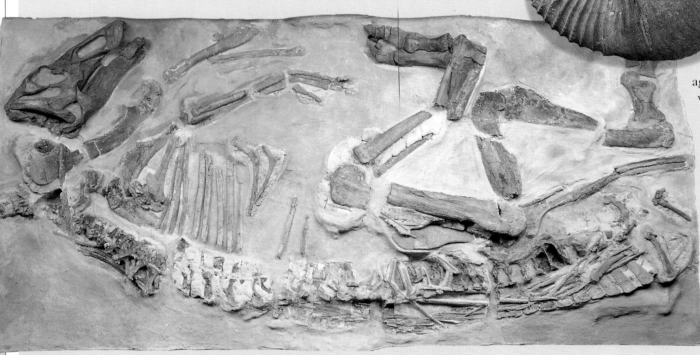

COMET ALERT
Comets are huge chunks of dirty ice that go around the Sun in highly elliptical orbits. Halley's Comet can be seen clearly with the naked eye from Earth every 76 years when its icy form evaporates to create a vast tail as it passes through the center of the Solar System.

THREAT FROM SPACE

Some scientists believe that the cause of many of the Earth's worst upheavals lies beyond our planet. The rotation of the Galaxy takes the Solar System through regions of space where there is a greater density of interstellar dust and gas. Passage through these interstellar clouds could partially block out the Sun's rays and increase the risk of the Earth being struck by cosmic debris. The Solar System is currently passing through a clear region of the Galaxy, but the Earth is still bombarded by a constant rain of interplanetary debris.

Most of this falling debris vaporizes in the atmosphere, to become short-lived shooting stars, without ever hitting the Earth. However, in 1908, a 200-foot (60-meter) wide meteor exploded over Tunguska, Siberia, Trees were flattened over a 31-mile (50-kilometer) wide area and a huge plume of fire blasted 13 miles (20 kilometers) up into the air. Also, geologists have located at least 150 impact craters on Earth. Some scientists have linked 12 of these to large extinctions, including three of the five biggest mass extinctions: the Cretaceous (see *opposite*), the end of Triassic extinction around 210 million years ago, and the mass extinction 367 million years ago in the Devonian period. In all of these events, the meteorite that struck would need to have been at least 2 miles (3 kilometers) wide, and would have left a crater ten times its width as vaporized rock and other debris blasted out at 50 times the speed of sound. It is argued that the dust hurled into the atmosphere could have blocked out the Sun's rays, causing darkness, sub-zero temperatures, and global windstorms.

By no means every scientist agrees that meteorites have a global effect; some believe that the damage is localized. Extensive impact damage last occurred about 50,000 years ago when a big meteorite hit the United States and Arizona's now-famous 3,960-foot (1,200-meter) wide Meteor Crater was created.

METEORITE REMAINS
The 34-ton Ahnighto meteorite (right) is one of the largest intact meteorites on Earth. The meteorite that created Meteor Crater (below) was larger, but shattered into tiny pieces on impact.

MOUNTAINS OF LAVA
The Deccan Traps were formed by massive lava flows that occurred about 65 million years ago, covering 200,000 sq miles (500,000 sq km) of western India.

THREAT FROM WITHIN

In addition to suffering the upheavals caused by meteorite strikes, the Earth has been threatened by events triggered from beneath the ground. At intervals of tens of millions of years, plumes of exceptionally hot molten rock rise through the Earth's mantle with such force that they

FOUNTAINS OF LAVA IN ICELAND
The streams of lava that periodically spurt out of rifts in Iceland are mere dribbles when compared to the awesome eruptions that have threatened life on this planet in prehistoric times.

burst through the crust, causing huge volcanic eruptions. Evidence of these events can be seen in India, Siberia, Africa, and the Americas, where vast plateaus of lava have been formed by repeated eruptions that devastated these areas over a period of about a million years.

When the rock of the Deccan Traps in India gushed from the ground 65 million years ago, each eruption spewed out about 240 cubic miles (1,000 cubic kilometers) of lava over a 3,900-square mile (10,000-square kilometer) area. The largest similar eruption in historical times began in Iceland in 1783 and lasted for a

year. The eruption produced a mere four cubic miles (15 cubic kilometers) of lava, but the gases emitted killed 75 percent of Iceland's livestock. Gases emitted during the much larger prehistoric eruptions temporarily altered the composition of the Earth's atmosphere and affected the climate on a global scale.

Movements in the Earth's mantle also affect the climate by causing landmasses to shift. Ice epochs occur when the continents block the flow of warm ocean currents to the poles. When the continents collide, mountains are thrown up, which alters weather patterns.

PERMIAN EXTINCTION
MASS EXTINCTION, GLOBAL, 250 MILLION YEARS AGO
GAZETTEER P.138 – SITE NO. 1

THE LARGEST EXTINCTION in the Earth's history occurred around 250 million years ago, at the end of the Permian period. At this time, movement of the Earth's crust was causing the continents to join together around a large, shallow sea to form one huge landmass. The oceans contained many species of fish, and a wonderful array of invertebrates such as trilobites, corals, and beautiful flowerlike animals called sea lilies. There was also a diverse and complex ecosystem on land that contained a variety of amphibians, reptiles, insects, and plants. The largest animal was a herbivorous mammal-like reptile, known as *Moschops*, which grew up to 16 feet (5 meters) in length. It and other herbivores were hunted by a wide variety of carnivorous reptilian creatures.

At the beginning of the Permian, the Earth was experiencing ice age conditions, but as the continents congregated on the tropics there was a rapid rise in temperature. At the time of the mass extinction, crustal movements caused the continents and the shallow sea they encircled to buckle upward and dry out. The same crustal movements also caused the surrounding ocean basins to deepen. As sea levels dropped, many

MARINE EXTINCTIONS
When the oceans ran short of oxygen at the end of the Permian, trilobites, along with around 90 percent of the other marine invertebrates, became extinct.

rich marine habitats were decimated and the continents were left high and dry. There was also a series of huge volcanic eruptions in Siberia. Over a period of 600,000 years, there were at least 45 eruptions, which covered more than 600,000 square miles (1.5 million square kilometers) of land in up to 12,100 feet (3,700 meters) of intensely hot lava. In addition to smothering all life in the area, the lava would have caused huge fires, and shot vast amounts of metals, gases, and other matter from the Earth's mantle high into the atmosphere.

It is thought that carbon dioxide released by the volcanic eruptions, combined with shifts in the Earth's crust, changed the composition of the atmosphere and dangerously reduced oxygen supplies in the oceans. The burned and rotting corpses of millions of creatures

LAVA FLOWS IN SIBERIA
The Central Siberian Plateau was formed by the vast quantities of lava erupted at the end of the Permian Period and engulfed more than 600,000 sq miles (1.5 million sq km) of land.

would have further polluted the environment and there may have been several waves of extinction, during which the Earth was virtually uninhabitable for tens of thousands of years.

As few as four percent of species survived the Permian event. Land and sea creatures were affected equally; and insects, which have fared comparatively well in other mass extinctions, were decimated. Of the larger land animals, only a few survived, probably by lying torpid in their burrows in the scorching hot summers. After the extinction the climate continued to stay warm, which helped cold-blooded reptiles to thrive and subsequently led to the emergence of the dinosaurs.

SURVIVORS OF THE MASS EXTINCTION
This 6.6-ft (2-m) long skeleton belongs to one of the Permian's largest surviving species, the flesh-eating amphibian, Eryops. Mammals later evolved due to the survival of Lystrosaurus, a pig-sized mammal-like reptile.

ICE AGE OR HOTHOUSE?

Climatic fluctuations have caused droughts, floods, and freezes that have been responsible for some of the most tragic disasters in human history. Yet, throughout the few thousand years covered by human history, the Earth's climate has been remarkably stable. For the last eight or nine thousand years, the average global temperature has fluctuated by less than 2°F (1°C). No one yet knows when this period of stability will end, but end it most surely will. For most of the last two million years the Earth has been in the grip of a series of ice ages, during which the mean temperature was about 9°F (5°C) lower and subject to much more extreme fluctuations than it is today.

These unstable ice ages have been punctuated by brief interglacial periods when, like today, the climate was relatively warm and stable. Each of these interglacial periods has lasted on average for about 10,000 years.

This suggests that in less than a thousand years the Earth's climate will become unstable and temperatures will drop again. However, this pattern may already have been seriously disrupted by recent human activity.

CHANGING ATMOSPHERE

Since the beginning of the Industrial Revolution about 200 years ago, the burning of coal, oil, and gas has slowly increased the amount of carbon dioxide in the Earth's atmosphere. Carbon dioxide is a normal and essential component of the atmosphere that is constantly being absorbed by plants and released by animals. Its presence in air helps to trap the Sun's energy in the lowest levels of the atmosphere and stops the Earth from turning

TINDER-DRY CONDITIONS
As California discovered in the 1990s, dry weather equals fires. Both deforestation and smoke pollution contribute to higher carbon dioxide levels.

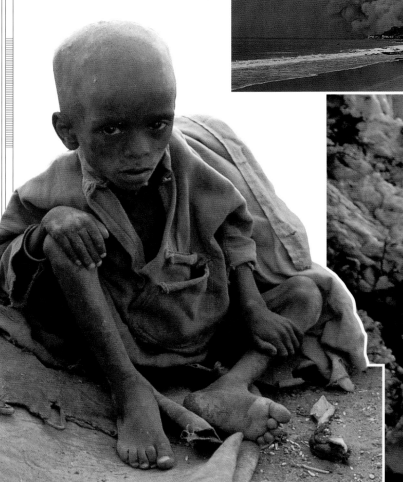

WAITING FOR RAIN
In the 1980s and early 1990s, poor rains in much of Africa left millions of people facing starvation. To prevent further famine, scientists recommend urgent research into drought-resistant crops.

into a frozen wasteland. Carbon dioxide is, however, only a minor ingredient of air, and consequently the amounts emitted by our burning of fossil fuels have caused a significant rise in global levels. In just 20 years, from 1970 to 1990, the level of carbon dioxide in the atmosphere increased by 10 percent. How this sudden increase will affect the Earth's climate is hard to predict, but rises in average global temperatures of between 2.7 and 8°F (1.5 and 4.5°C) are often forecast.

Even the smallest predicted rise would cause large sections of the polar ice caps and many glaciers to melt, leading to a sudden rise in sea levels. Around the world, low-lying coastal land, particularly in Bangladesh, China, and the Netherlands, would be even more exposed to sea floods. Coral islands, such as the Maldives and the Cook Islands, could disappear without trace.

EL NIÑO FLOODS
Some scientists believe that the increasing carbon dioxide levels are making the El Niño climate fluctuation more severe, causing the western Americas to suffer heavier rainfall and worse floods.

CURRENT CONCERNS

Studies of the rapid climatic fluctuations that occurred during the Last Ice Age suggest that they were triggered by immense flotillas of icebergs breaking off the Canadian ice sheet and surging into the Atlantic Ocean. When the icebergs melted, they disrupted the circulation of currents in the ocean by making the cold waters of the North Atlantic less dense than the warm Gulf Stream waters flowing up from the tropics.

Some scientists fear that, if global warming melts enough ice at the North Pole, the Gulf Stream would grind to a halt again. This, they believe, would cause the temperature of northwest Europe, which is warmed by the Gulf Stream, to drop suddenly by more than 9°F (5°C).

Most scientists are reluctant to say when this will happen because never before in the history of the Earth have conditions been such as they are today. Global temperatures are rising, carbon dioxide levels are high and rising; and this is all happening during an ice epoch, when the climate is known to be particularly unstable. To make matters worse, scientists also predict that rising sea levels will spark off a marked increase in volcanic activity, further polluting the atmosphere.

SHRINKING ICE CAPS
Arctic ice cliffs crash into Disenchantment Bay in Alaska. Global warming is causing the ice caps to shrink, which results in rising sea levels and threatens to disrupt ocean currents.

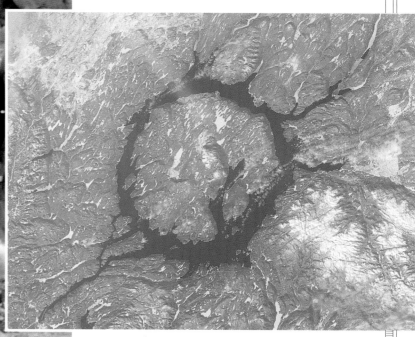

ANCIENT IMPACT CRATER
We have yet to experience the effects of a large meteorite impact. The 62-mile (100-km) wide Manicouagan Crater, visible after 210 million years was created at the end of the Triassic .

COMPETITION FOR LIFE

WE HUMANS IMAGINE ourselves to be the dominant species, but like all living things we must fight for our survival. The greatest threat to this survival comes from the billions of tiny creatures that live all around us. Insects and a wide variety of microorganisms have caused widespread famines by consuming, rotting, and poisoning our food supplies. The microbes that attack our bodies directly have been even more deadly. History has been shaped by a series of epidemics that have swept through whole populations, upending the social order. Both the civilizations of ancient Greece and Rome were overwhelmed by terrible outbreaks of disease. The Mongolian empire, which once stretched across much of Southeast Asia, collapsed after plague swept across Eurasia in the fourteenth century. The Europeans' rapid colonization of the Americas was made possible only by the infections that they brought with them. In the last 150 years we have learned far more about the causes of such outbreaks but, as the global spread of AIDS reveals, humans are far from safe from infectious disease.

THE POTATO FAMINE ②
More than a million Irish people died of starvation in the 1840s when a fungal infection destroyed potato crops across the country three years in a row.

① THE AMERICAN EPIDEMIC
Between 1492 and 1900, up to 90 percent of the Native American population died from European infections that the Spanish and other settlers introduced into the continent.

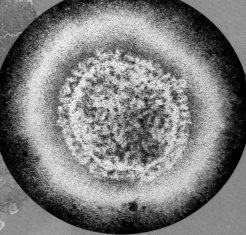

INFLUENZA VIRUS
Influenza viruses, such as the 1993 Beijing Flu virus, which is shown here at 160,000 times its actual size, are transmitted from infected people in water droplets when they cough or sneeze.

DEATH FROM CONTAMINATED WATER
During the 1990s, refugees from the fighting in Rwanda were forced to live in appalling conditions and to drink water contaminated with their own body waste. Many disease-causing microorganisms, among the most dangerous of which is the bacterium *Vibrio cholerae*, thrive in these sorts of conditions.

③ SPANISH FLU
The deadliest influenza pandemic broke out in 1918 and spread to the trenches of Flanders. By June 1919, it had killed more than 22 million people around the world, despite the use of masks to check the spread of the disease.

⑥ CHOLERA
An outbreak of cholera that began in northwest India in 1826 spread around the world by 1834, claiming millions of lives.

PLAGUE POMANDER
In times of plague, containers like this were filled with aromatic herbs to help prevent the wearer from catching the disease, which was thought to be spread by bad air.

⑤ THE BLACK DEATH
The plague pandemic which rampaged across Asia in the fourteenth century arrived in Europe in 1346, where it killed up to one-third of the population in less than six years.

④ AIDS
Since AIDS was first recognized in the 1980s, billions of dollars have been spent on medical research to find a way of curing or preventing the disease. Despite these efforts, the number of cases is rising alarmingly.

RAT INFESTATIONS
Rats live off human food supplies, which encourages them to live among people. The fleas living off rats can transmit diseases such as plague to us. Although antibiotics can cure plague, the infection multiplies so quickly that it can still cause death if not treated in time.

PESTS AND PLAGUES

HUMAN LIFE IS CONSTANTLY UNDER THREAT FROM UNSEEN ENEMIES: microorganisms that compete for our food and prey on our bodies. Only in the last 150 years has the cause of epidemics and crop diseases been understood, but this knowledge has not always provided us with protection from the tiny but deadly predators that are all around us. Neither can we control the ravages that larger pests, such as insects, can inflict on us and on our food supply.

OUR ENEMIES

Lions, tigers, wolves, and bears, ferocious predators that our ancestors used to fear, are now endangered species. We protect them and donate money in the hope of saving them from extinction. Yet no one mourns the passing of smallpox. The eradication of the disease and containment of the virus, in 1979, is regarded as a remarkable achievement. Our attitude to these two different types of killers reflects our awareness that viruses are the deadlier predators. It is easier to protect ourselves from a pack of wolves than a swarm of insects. It is even more difficult to escape the hordes of unseen viruses, bacteria, fungi, and other microorganisms that surround us.

The fundamental fact of life is that all living things must compete for the Earth's resources. We see ourselves as being at the top of the food chain, but in reality we are providing sustenance for a host of other living things. Farming was a development that enabled us to produce more food, but we must still compete

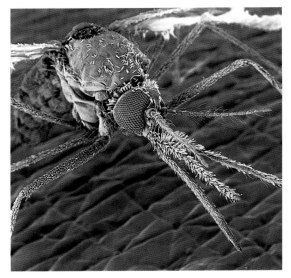

DISEASE CARRIER
Female Anopheles *mosquitoes infect humans with malaria while feeding on their blood. Other types of mosquitoes also carry deadly infections, such as yellow fever, dengue, and Rift Valley fever.*

for our share of that food with plant-eating insects and microorganisms, as well as larger pests such as rats, mice, and birds.

An unforeseen side-effect of farming was the opportunities that it gave disease-causing microorganisms to infect humans. The bacteria that cause leprosy and tuberculosis are closely related to soil bacteria and these diseases were probably first contracted by our ancestors soon after they began to cultivate the soil. Humans also share about 300 diseases with animals that they have domesticated. Many of the infectious diseases that have caused epidemics are thought to have originated in domesticated animals. The virus that causes smallpox in humans, for instance, is related to the virus that causes cowpox, and the measles virus is probably related to the virus that causes distemper in dogs.

Throughout the centuries, human ingenuity has been pitted against pests and plagues. This has led to the development of condoms, mosquito nets, sewage treatment, hygiene codes, pasteurization, antibiotics, vaccines, pesticides, and many other means of keeping ahead of our many minute competitors. It will never be possible, however, to gain more than a temporary advantage over the microbes that surround us. Our rivals may lack our ability to think up new ways of competing with us, but they are far more numerous and can reproduce far more quickly. This allows them to evolve new, more efficient weapons and defenses with astonishing speed, so that when they get the upper hand, even for a short while, the whole of humanity is at severe risk.

MAIN INFECTIONS OF THE 1990S
Infectious diseases currently kill about 17 million people every year. This map shows the three most commonly contracted infections in nine regions of the world and also gives the average number of reported cases per year for each of the diseases.

EUROPE		NORTH ASIA AND JAPAN		NORTH AMERICA	
TUBERCULOSIS	194,891	TUBERCULOSIS	159,605	AIDS	41,231
MALARIA	90,317	MEASLES	8,334	TUBERCULOSIS	22,860
MEASLES	71,489	MALARIA	2,923	MEASLES	2,666

MIDDLE EAST		SOUTHEAST ASIA		CENTRAL AMERICA	
MALARIA	211,666	MALARIA	4,696,895	MALARIA	172,258
TUBERCULOSIS	83,368	TUBERCULOSIS	1,865,493	TUBERCULOSIS	32,717
MEASLES	10,930	LEPROSY	666,091	LEPROSY	8,308

AFRICA		SOUTH PACIFIC		SOUTH AMERICA	
MALARIA	27,315,759	MALARIA	765,677	MALARIA	937,946
TUBERCULOSIS	478,574	TUBERCULOSIS	9,978	TUBERCULOSIS	182,519
MEASLES	333,053	MEASLES	4,967	LEPROSY	152,710

LOCUST SWARMS IN AFRICA
In 1992, massive areas of African farmland were laid waste by what has been described as "the largest plagues of locusts in history."

The red menace

Today, measles mostly infects children, producing chills, fever, and a distinct red rash. When it was first introduced into the Americas, it killed millions of people.

PESTS AND BLIGHT

Food is plentiful in some parts of the world but, globally, food production is struggling to keep up with the world's growing population. Our efforts to increase food production have meant that more and more land is required to come under the plow. Areas that were once rainforest, marshland, and desert are now farmed, which has led to the decline and extinction of many species and encouraged the proliferation of pests. Every year pests destroy about 35 percent of the world's crops

FEEDING OFF HUMANS
Rats not only eat our food supplies but also pollute them with the viruses and bacteria they spray in their urine. These black rats were linked to an outbreak of plague in India in 1994.

COLORADO BEETLE
Originating from the United States, the Colorado beetle is now found across much of Europe and Asia. The insect, which is highly resistant to insecticides, destroys potato and tomato crops by eating the leaves.

and, after the food is harvested, consume a further 10 to 20 percent of food stores. The presence of large pests such as pigeons and rats is obvious, but insects and microorganisms such as fungi actually cause far more damage.

Insect pests are highly efficient breeding machines when food is plentiful. The most destructive pests can survive hard times and then reproduce rapidly when they have ample food. A female aphid with a good food supply clones herself continually, producing thousands of eggs that rapidly develop into more female aphids. These also clone themselves and the cycle continues until the food supply is used up. In this way, one single aphid can produce 600 billion descendants in one year.

Only by using pesticides is the human population able to produce enough food to support itself, but each new pesticide provides only temporary protection. Because pests reproduce rapidly, they can rapidly evolve the

TACKLING LOCUST SWARMS
Airplanes are used to spray swarms of locusts with pesticides. The sheer size of these swarms, which may contain over a billion locusts, makes them hard to control once they are in flight.

ability to tolerate toxic chemicals. DDT, the first widely used insecticide, was developed in the 1940s but, by 1947, DDT-resistant house-flies began to appear, first in Italy, and then in many other countries. Soon after, mosquitoes and lice also became resistant. Many non-pest species were vulnerable to DDT because they could not evolve resistance as quickly. Birds of prey developed no resistance at all because they breed slowly, and their numbers declined severely while the chemical was in use. DDT made very little long-term impact on insect populations, however, and they remain a threat.

CROP DISEASES

Even though insects are directly responsible for a great deal of crop damage, they probably cause more damage indirectly, by providing a means for microorganisms to infect the plants and cause disease. Worldwide, more than 80,000 plant diseases have been identified. Bacteria and viruses are responsible for some of these diseases, but the majority are caused by a group of organisms known as fungi.

Some fungi have evolved specialized means of infiltrating and living as parasites within certain species of plants, and it is these strains that devastate crops. Like most other fungi, they reproduce by releasing billions of spores, which are spread over a wide area by the wind. The fungus *Phytophthora infestans*, which infects potato plants, was responsible for the deaths of millions of people in Europe (see right).

Some fungi kill more directly by producing a toxin that contaminates the plants that they attack. During World War I, about 70,000 German troops died from food poisoning after being given bread made from rye that had been infected with ergot fungus.

THE POTATO FAMINE
POTATO BLIGHT, IRELAND, 1845–1848
GAZETTEER P.134 – SITE NO. 65

THE SPANISH BROUGHT THE FIRST potatoes to Europe in the 16th century. The crops grew well in European soil, which contained none of the microorganisms that had infected the plant in its native Peru. By the 19th century, potatoes were the staple diet all over Europe, but especially in Ireland, where peasant farmers had to sell most of the grain and livestock that they produced to pay rent to their landlords.

Potato blight first appeared in crops in the United States in the early 1840s and arrived in Europe in 1845. The spores of the fungus that causes the disease, *Phytophthora infestans*, were probably transported across oceans on trading ships and once on land, were spread from field to field by the wind.

The summer of 1845, being unusually wet, created ideal conditions for the fungus to grow. Overnight, it turned healthy potato plants into a mass of stinking black slime. By the end of the summer the blight had spread throughout Europe, and the Potato Famine had begun. The threat of starvation grew worse over the next two years because the weather remained wet and the potato crops failed. By the winter

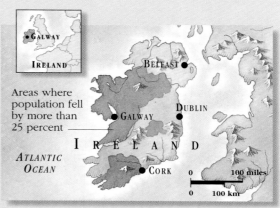

THE DEPOPULATION OF IRELAND
When potato blight struck in 1845, Ireland's population was nine million. One-and-a-half million people died during the ensuing famine, and an additional 1,600,000 emigrated.

of 1847–48, millions of people across Europe were affected by the famine. In Ireland almost the entire population was starving. People ate grass, garbage, and sawdust to fill their stomachs, and the gnawing hunger set off food riots and looting. Typhus and dysentery spread quickly, decimating the already weakened population, most of whom had no money for food or fuel.

RIOTS IN GALWAY
Driven by starvation, residents of Galway in western Ireland storm a grocery store to seize its stock of potatoes. More than a million Irish people died during the famine.

FAMINE AND EVICTION
During the famine, some Irish farmers became too weak to tend their land, and many were evicted. Because many of the landlords were from England, the evictions led to calls for an Irish Free State, which was established in 1922.

DISEASES

No volcano, earthquake, storm, or flood has devastated human populations on the same scale as infectious disease. A plague outbreak known as the Black Death killed roughly one-third of the populations of Europe and Asia in the Middle Ages (see *p.112*). In the years following the colonization of Central America by Europeans, as much as 90 percent of the native population died of infectious diseases (see *p.114*). Because the victims of these disasters could neither see the cause of, nor find a way of preventing, their suffering, these diseases spread both death and terror.

It was not until the 1860s that the French scientist Louis Pasteur carried out research that established microscopic living organisms as the cause of infectious diseases. Since then, many diseases have been linked to specific bacteria, viruses, and other microbes; and the work must continue because microbes evolve rapidly and new disease-causing strains keep emerging. HIV, the virus that causes AIDS, was not identified until 1984 (see *p.121*). Research is also linking microbes to a number of diseases that were not previously thought to be associated with infection. Stomach ulcers and arterial damage in heart disease have been linked to bacterial infections, and a number of cancers and rare neurological diseases have been linked to viral infections.

Only a tiny proportion of the microbes that surround us are harmful, but those that cause disease represent almost the entire range of microscopic life. These killer microbes have a diverse range of carriers. Malaria, which is the

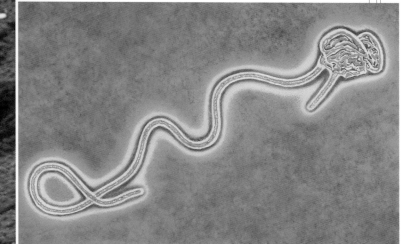

DYING OF EBOLA
The Ebola virus (above), seen here at 13,500 times actual size, causes hemorrhaging. Because the virus often kills those it infects within a week, people who handle Ebola victims wear protective clothing to avoid contracting the disease (left).

THE BLACK DEATH

PLAGUE, EURASIA AND NORTH AFRICA, 1346–1352

GAZETTEER P.135 – SITE NO.26

BUBONIC PLAGUE, a disease that is caused by the bacterium *Yersinia pestis*, is prevalent among wild rodents and the fleas that live off their blood. However, in 1331 rats became infected by the disease and their fleas began feeding on people living in the Chinese province of Hopei. By 1332, northern China was in the grip of a deadly plague epidemic that spread west across Asia, reaching the shores of the Black Sea in 1346. Here, the plague was contracted by Genoese traders in Kaffa, who carried it to Europe.

The people of medieval Europe were all too familiar with infectious disease and untimely death, but they had experienced nothing like the horror of this plague pandemic. It killed the old, young, healthy, and sick alike. When the disease raged through the cities, hundreds of bodies had to be disposed of every day. In some smaller villages every single person died. The first sign that a person was infected with plague was the appearance of swellings (buboes) in the groin or armpits. The disease also destroyed the blood

THE GREAT DYING
Plague broke out in China, reaching Europe in 1346. Here it spread quickly, killing up to one-third of the population. The loss of life in North Africa and the Middle East was also horrific.

vessels and earned the title of "Black Death" because of the dark swellings this caused. Reports written at the time also record "the unbearable stench" of victims' breath and "all the matter which exuded from their bodies."

Some victims became delirious, others went into a coma. Most of them died within a few days of the buboes appearing, but sometimes the buboes burst open, releasing their poison. In these cases, there was a chance of recovery. Some of the victims caught a pneumonic form of plague, which infected their lungs and caused them to cough up blood. This form of the disease was almost always fatal. Reports told of people falling ill and dying within a few hours.

Because *Yersinia pestis* kills quickly and is unable to survive once its host is dead, the Black Death did not last long. Plague epidemics continued to break out again in Europe until the end of the seventeenth century, and an outbreak in Hong Kong in 1894 went on to kill more than 10 million people in Asia.

TRIUMPH OF DEATH
The specter of death dominated European art for over a century after the Black Death killed up to 30 million people in Europe.

PLAGUE MINIMIZED IN INDIA
During an outbreak of plague in India in 1994, residents of Surat were told to burn all trash immediately so that rats, which helped spread the disease, would be deprived of food.

most deadly infectious disease in the world, is caused by highly complex microbes called protozoa, which are transported from victim to victim by mosquitoes.

Bacteria are much simpler and smaller single-celled organisms. The effect they have on the body varies enormously from species to species. For example, *Yersinia pestis*, the bacterium responsible for plague, reproduces so rapidly that it can overwhelm the immune system and kill within days or even hours of infection. *Mycobacterium tuberculosis*, on the other hand, is a slow-growing organism with a waxy coat that protects it from the immune system. Few people infected with this microbe develop tuberculosis immediately, but clusters of it can lie dormant for years and become active if the body's resistance is lowered by poor nutrition, stress, or another disease.

Viruses are smaller than bacteria and consist of a small number of genes surrounded by a protein coat, which allows the virus to stick to certain cells and insert its genes. These genes

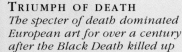

DISEASE-CARRYING TICK
The deer tick, shown here at almost 50 times its actual size, carries a bacterium that causes Lyme disease in humans. The disease can lead to arthritis and brain or heart disorders.

commandeer the cell's biochemical machinery. Some viruses, such as the wart virus, integrate with the genes of the host cell and cause the cell to grow abnormally. However, the viruses more commonly associated with infectious disease, influenza viruses for example, cause the cell to manufacture many copies of the virus that burst out and infect more cells.

EPIDEMICS

During an epidemic, disease spreads rapidly, infecting a large proportion of a population. It kills healthy people as well as the infirm and causes a great deal of economic and social upheaval.

In most circumstances, the human body is protected from disease because antibodies in the immune system recognize and destroy invading infectious microbes. However, people are vulnerable to infection

MICROBE-HUNTER
Robert Koch (1843–1910) isolated the bacilli that cause cholera and tuberculosis, and proved the link between microbes and disease.

when a new and virulent microbe appears, or when the immune system is run down. Epidemics often occur when a microbe that previously infected another species mutates and begins to infect humans, or when a microbe develops a way of evading the human immune system. Influenza epidemics occur every few years

because the virus responsible, which infects poultry and pigs as well as humans, changes in each host and becomes unrecognizable to the immune systems of the other species. One strain of influenza, known as Spanish Flu, killed more than 22 million people (see *p.118*).

Sometimes relatively nonvirulent microbes, such as the bacterium that causes tuberculosis, can trigger an epidemic by getting a foothold

BLOOD CELLS UNDER ATTACK
Malaria protozoa invade red blood cells and multiply inside them. The blood cells eventually burst, allowing the protozoa to spread.

THE AMERICAN EPIDEMIC

OLD WORLD DISEASES, THE AMERICAS, 1492–1900

GAZETTEER P.130 – SITE NO.5

FOR MANY YEARS historians believed that, prior to the arrival of Christopher Columbus in 1492, there were only eight to 12 million people living in North and South America. New estimates, based on a closer examination of the records, suggest that in Mexico alone, 25 to 30 million people lived under the control of the Aztec Empire. Eighty years after Columbus landed, the population had fallen to three million. Very few of these lives were lost fighting the Spanish Conquistadors. Most Aztecs died fighting germs.

GOLDEN PROMISES
To coerce the disease-weakened inhabitants of Central and South America into giving up their gold, the Spanish told them that they were suffering from a disease that only gold could cure.

For 11,000 years there had been almost no contact between the native peoples of America and the Old World civilizations of Europe, North Africa, and Asia. During that time, the Native Americans had escaped all of the epidemics of measles, smallpox, and other infectious diseases. These diseases are now thought to be caused by microbes that originally occurred only in domesticated animals but have evolved to attack humans. Unlike Old World inhabitants, who had

SMALLPOX REACHES AMERICA
Spanish troops infected Hispaniola with smallpox in 1518 before carrying the disease to Mexico, where it spread like wildfire, reaching the Incas in Peru long before the Spanish arrived there.

been in contact with domesticated animals for thousands of years, Native Americans kept few domesticated animals, obtaining most food by hunting and by cultivating crops. As a result, they had no immunity from the diseases that settlers from the Old World brought with them.

The role of infectious diseases in the shaping of American history cannot be underestimated. In 1521, the Spanish general Hernán Cortés won an extraordinary victory to capture the Aztec capital, Tenochtitlan. The defeat of one-and-a-half-million people by his tiny army was possible only because an epidemic of smallpox killed most of the Aztec leaders, half of their warriors, and left the survivors scarred and demoralized. No one could understand why only the Aztecs fell ill, so both sides assumed that it was divine retribution.

The same tragic pattern of infection occurred in North America when the English and French settlers arrived 90 years later. It has now been estimated that between 1492 and 1900, the native population of America dropped from 100 million to less than 10 million.

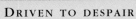

DRIVEN TO DESPAIR
Infections from the Old World decimated the Aztec population and enabled the Spanish to subjugate the survivors (above). Contemporary sketches of smallpox victims (right) shows the terrible suffering that the disease caused.

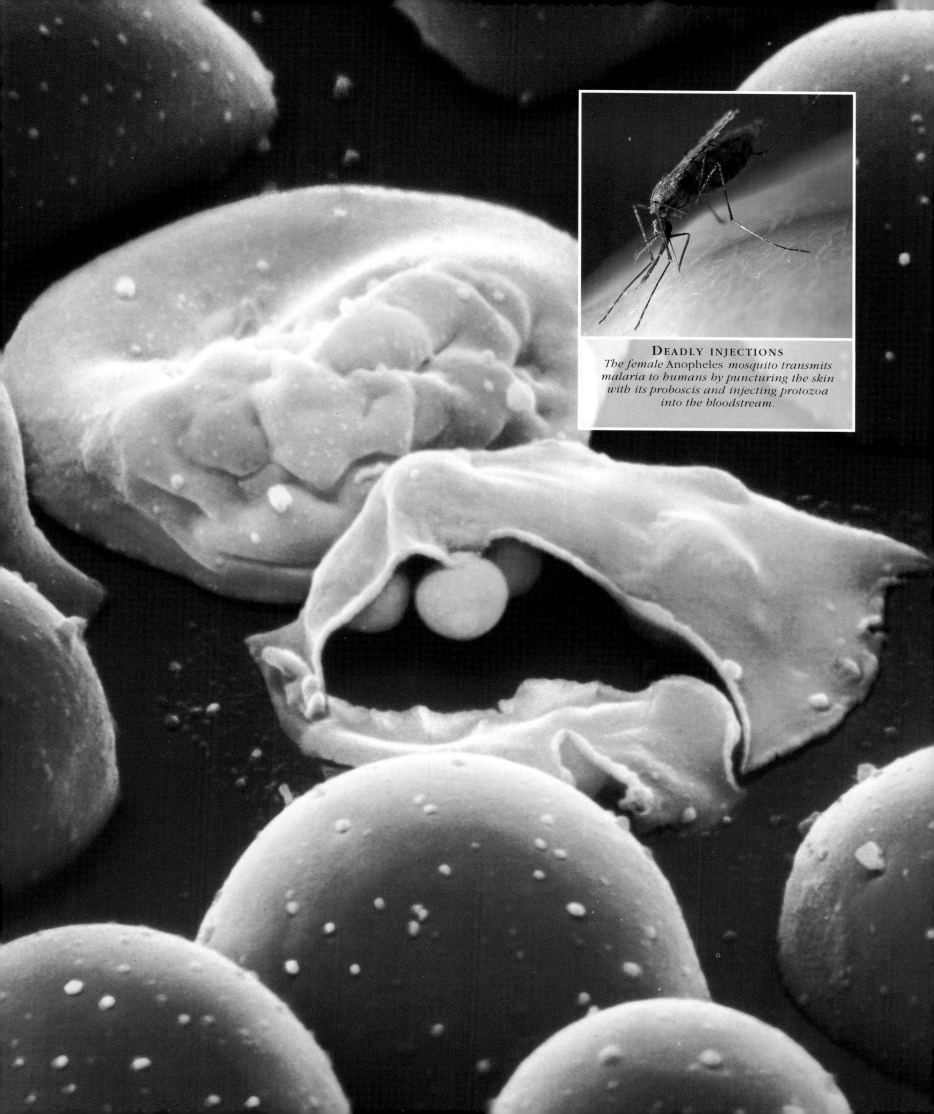

DEADLY INJECTIONS
The female Anopheles mosquito transmits malaria to humans by puncturing the skin with its proboscis and injecting protozoa into the bloodstream.

in a population that is made more vulnerable to disease by overcrowding, poor sanitary conditions, and inadequate nutrition.

Since agriculture was developed and people began settling in large communities, human history has been punctuated by numerous epidemics. The risk of widespread infection increased as villages grew into towns, and towns expanded into cities. Traders, soldiers, and explorers then spread disease from city to city and from continent to continent. In AD 166, Roman troops fighting in Syria caught an unspecified infection and brought it back to Italy. From there, the contagion raged throughout Europe, killing up to one-third of the population.

Epidemics have conquered many armies and destroyed civilizations. The Russian winter is usually credited with bringing about the collapse of Napoleon's invasion of the country in 1812, but dirty water drunk by the French army was probably their real nemesis. As many as 380,000 of the 500,000 troops who set out on the march to Moscow died after contracting typhus or dysentery. The Aztec and Inca civilizations, which collapsed in the early sixteenth century, were both victims of the bacteria and viruses carried to the New World by the Spanish conquistadors (see *p.114*).

CHOLERA AND WAR
Refugees from the bloody civil war in Rwanda, Africa, sought safety in makeshift camps, where many lost their lives in a cholera epidemic that was caused by the unsanitary conditions.

FILTERING OUT GERMS
Water filters such as this one became common in the nineteenth century after Dr. John Snow established a link between cholera and polluted water.

CHOLERA
THE SECOND PANDEMIC, GLOBAL, 1826–1834
GAZETTEER P.136 – SITE NO. 21

THE ORIGINAL HABITAT of *Vibrio cholerae*, the bacterium that causes cholera, was the waters of the Ganges delta in northeast India. Villagers in the region sometimes caught cholera, but it only became a mass killer when residents in Calcutta first became infected in 1817. Ingesting a small number of *Vibrio cholerae* seldom causes illness because the bacteria are killed by stomach acid, but in higher concentrations they can pass into the intestines, where they reproduce rapidly. In the crowded streets of Calcutta, billions of the bacteria were expelled in victims' feces, making the spread of cholera more likely. Within five years, it had spread across Southeast Asia, the Arabian peninsula, and into eastern Africa.

In 1826, cholera once again tore out of Calcutta, and moved north across India, Afghanistan, Persia, and Russia. The disease reached Moscow in 1830, where it

killed 50 percent of the people that it infected. Panicking Muscovites headed west, spreading the disease to Central Europe. In the summer of 1831, cholera killed at least 100,000 people in Hungary, and the peasants, believing that they were being poisoned, began massacring doctors and officials who tried to impose health restrictions. In the meantime, Muslim pilgrims spread cholera to the Middle East and North Africa. In 1832, cholera arrived in northern Europe, where it decimated the populations of the major cities. About 10,000 people died of the disease in both Stockholm and Paris, and a further 7,000 in London. Terrified citizens rioted, calling for quarantines and travel restrictions. Although they were imposed, they did no good. At the end of 1832,

CHOLERA IN FRANCE
When cholera struck Paris in 1832, it killed 10,000 people. Some died within hours of contracting it.

SCOURGE OF THE NINETEENTH CENTURY
The cholera pandemic that broke out in 1826 was the first to cover the entire world. The disease is spread when its victims' feces contaminates water supplies, bedclothes, fruit, and flies.

European emigrants took cholera to the Americas, where it claimed 50,000 lives in New York alone. During the nineteenth century, millions of people died of cholera, which became more feared than any other disease because the death it brought was quick and horrible. This fear prompted the industrialized countries to improve water sanitation, but cholera still occurs today where the water supplies are polluted.

SPANISH FLU

INFLUENZA PANDEMIC, GLOBAL, 1918–1919

GAZETTEER P.134 – SITE NO.84

IN THE AUTUMN OF 1918, soldiers fighting in World War I began to fall victim to a vicious new form of influenza. It was so contagious that entire units of men fell ill at once. Most of them recovered, but many developed fatal complications. Following the armistice in November, troops returning home took the virus with them, spreading flu around the globe. Half of the world's population fell sick and by mid-1919, 22 million people had died as a result of this infection.

GLOBAL IMPACT OF THE KILLER FLU
More than 22 million people died from a deadly strain of flu in 1918 and 1919. English speakers labeled it "Spanish Flu." In Spain it was called "Naples Soldier," in Japan "Wrestler's Fever," and in Germany "Blitz Kattarrh" (lightning cold).

PITS OF INFECTION
Spanish Flu spread quickly in the crowded, dirty, and damp trenches of northern Europe, after its arrival in the autumn of 1918.

At the time, World War I was the deadliest conflict in history, and its ending was a time of great rejoicing. However, as the troops came home, they brought death with them. In a few months, the 1918–1919 Spanish Flu pandemic killed more people than four years of fighting in Europe.

Before this lethal strain of influenza struck, people regarded flu much as we do today, as a highly contagious infection that makes its victims feel dreadful but is only life-threatening in the weak and elderly. Spanish Flu was different, however; more than 80 percent of those who died after catching the disease were between the ages of 17 and 40. The sudden deaths of millions of men and women who were of working age, many of whom were parents, was not only a tragedy but also a great economic blow to a society that had just lost many of its young men fighting on the battlefields of Europe.

The 1918 strain of flu was particularly deadly because it damaged the lungs, making its victims extremely vulnerable to more serious bacterial infections. Antibiotics had yet to be developed

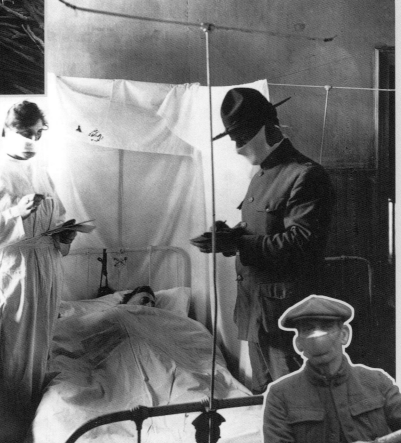

FIGHTING THE FLU
In London and many other European cities, public buildings, buses, and trains were regularly sprayed with disinfectants in an attempt to halt the spread of the disease.

INFLUENZA IN AMERICA
A flu epidemic broke out in the US in the spring of 1918, where it infected numerous servicemen. It has been suggested that American troops sent to the war in Europe introduced the killer virus into the trenches.

and doctors were only able to watch as people sickened and died. Victims' lungs often became so clogged with fluid that it gushed from their mouths and nostrils. Violent nosebleeds were another common symptom.

Reports exist of victims being so violently stricken by the flu disease that they dropped dead in the street or crashed their cars. When Spanish Flu infected the crews of a convoy of warships sailing off the Irish coast, they became so ill that they could no longer keep the vessels on course. As a result, two of the ships collided and sank with the loss of 431 lives. Much publicity was given to odd remedies such as inhaling eucalyptus, sulfur, or garlic. Some victims took scalding baths or drank alcohol to help them sweat, since this was considered a sign of recovery. Spanish Flu died down only after nearly everyone in the world had become immune to that form of the influenza virus. New strains soon developed, however, and there have been many flu epidemics since. It is not known when or if a strain will develop that is as virulent as the one that struck between 1918 and 1919.

MEDICINE AND ITS LIMITS

People have been immunizing their children for hundreds of years by exposing them to infectious diseases while they are still young. When smallpox was common, children were inoculated with the scab tissue of someone with a mild case of the disease. Usually, they too caught a mild case and gained lifelong immunity. Modern immunization uses vaccines designed to provide immunity without causing the disease. Vaccines are of limited use with diseases such as influenza because the microbes

MEDICINE ON THE FRONTLINE

Perhaps the main limitation to medicine is its cost. Hospitals like this one in Hergeisa, Somalia, lack the funds to provide the latest drugs and vaccines to all those in the region needing care.

that cause them have found ways to avoid the immune system's defenses.

The cure of infectious diseases made an enormous leap forward following the development of antibiotics in the 1940s. Antibiotics are chemicals that are much more toxic to bacteria than to animals. The majority of these drugs are able to cure bacterial infections without causing serious damage to the patient. However, some of these drugs, such as mefloquine, which is used in the treatment of malaria, can have serious side effects. Drugs to combat viral infections are

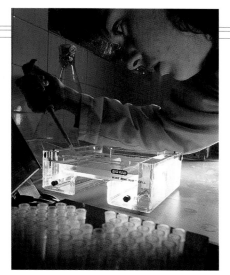

TESTING MICROBES

Cultures of infectious agents are grown in laboratories and tested by scientists to find out how they spread disease.

more difficult to develop because viruses reproduce by using the biochemical machinery of our cells. As a result, drugs that interfere with the reproduction of viruses may also harm the patient. Another limitation of using drugs to destroy invading microbes is that the microbes evolve resistance to them. A half-century of antibiotic treatment has produced a number of microbes that are resistant to most antibiotics.

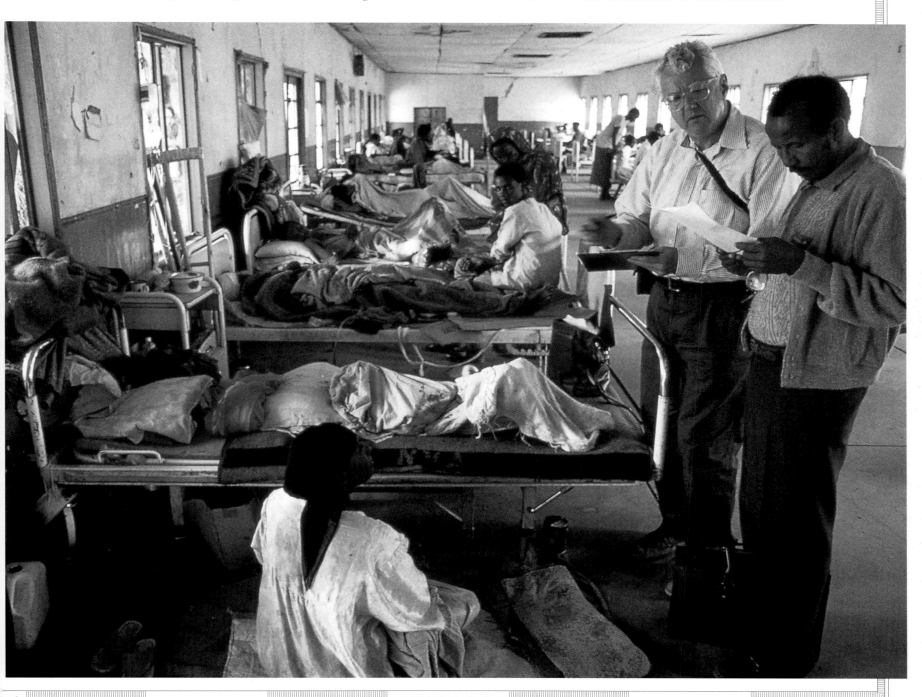

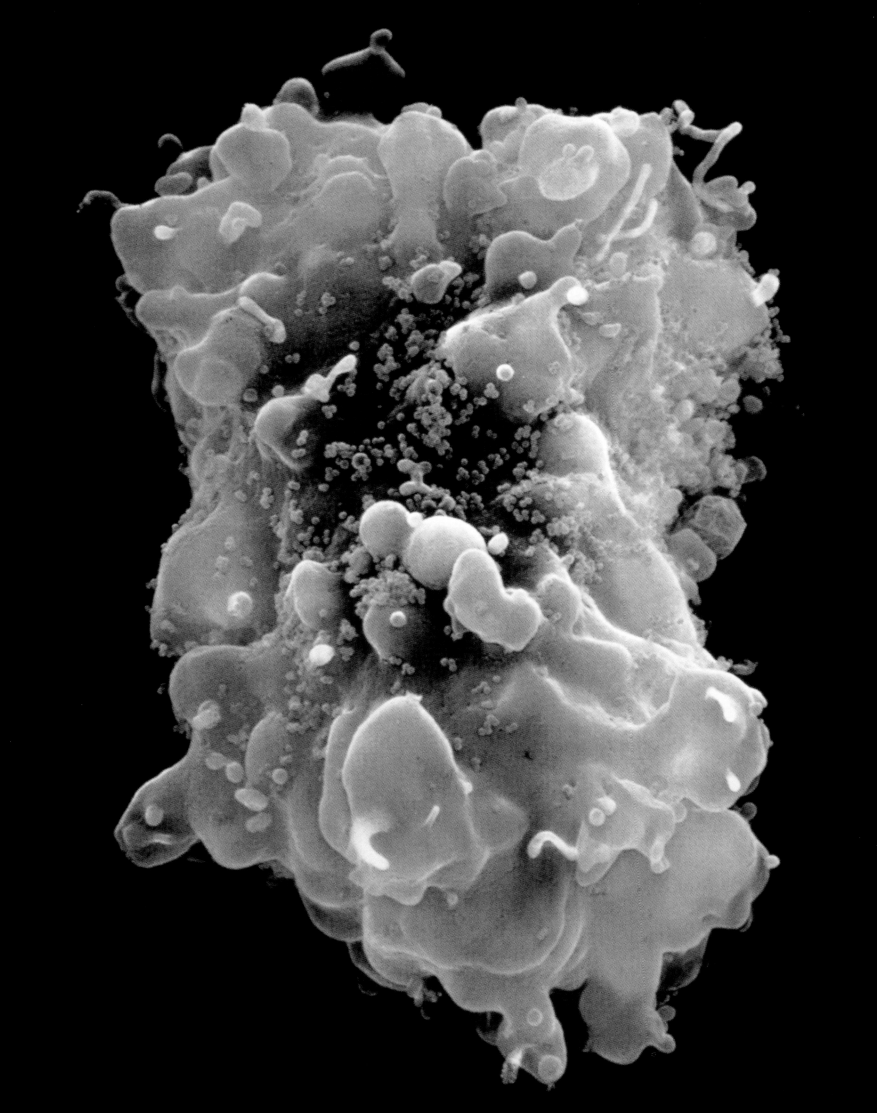

AIDS

EPIDEMIC, GLOBAL, 1959 TO PRESENT DAY

GAZETTEER P.133 – SITE NO.25

A MODERN PLAGUE
Evidence that a virus similar to HIV was present in Africa in the 1950s has convinced many scientists that AIDS originated here around this time. This map shows how the disease may have spread around the world from Africa.

THE GLOBAL SPREAD OF AIDS (Acquired Immunodeficiency Syndrome) has terrified a world that thought that modern medicine had conquered disease epidemics. By 1997, about 30 million people had become infected with HIV, the virus that causes AIDS; and, in the United States alone, more than 350,000 people had died of the disease. The virus is passed on in body fluids such as semen, blood, and breast milk; it can also pass from a woman to her unborn child. It kills by slowly destroying the body's immune system. Drugs to combat AIDS have been developed but they can only slow the progress of the disease.

The first official report about AIDS appeared in an American medical journal in 1981. Doctors in New York and California, however, had been describing symptoms that are now closely linked with the disease since the 1970s. They had noticed that a growing number of healthy young men were developing various infections previously seen only in very old people, or in those whose immune systems had been badly damaged by medical treatment. Once AIDS was recognized, researchers took a further two years to isolate the virus responsible for this disease, which was named the Human Immunodeficiency Virus (HIV) because it attacks the cells of the immune system. HIV was soon found to be present on every continent. A large proportion of people infected with the virus appeared to be healthy, but many of them have since developed AIDS symptoms and died.

A SLOW AND SILENT KILLER
When people initially become infected with HIV they experience mild flulike symptoms but then seem to recover as their immune system destroys the viruses. HIV cannot be killed off completely, however, because the viruses mutate rapidly, producing different forms of the virus, which the body's immune system has to equip itself to

T-CELL UNDER ATTACK
Shown at 40,000 times its actual size is a human immune system cell, known as a T-cell, whose surface is covered by HIV (blue). HIV destroys T-cells and thereby weakens the immune system.

VICTIMS REMEMBERED
This quilt was begun in 1986 by the friends and families of people who died of AIDS. Each panel is dedicated to the memory of one victim.

destroy. The battle between the viruses and the immune system usually goes on for six to ten years, until the immune system is worn down. Once this occurs, the body becomes vulnerable to many infections. Because people infected with HIV are free of AIDS symptoms for such a long time, the spread of the disease is hard to trace and even harder to stop. Many of those infected do not know that they have the disease and therefore unknowingly pass on the virus to their sexual partners.

A connection was made in the 1980s between AIDS and people who had many sexual partners or had injected drugs. This led to strong moral criticism, by certain segments of society, of those who had contracted AIDS, and delayed a concerted effort to combat the disease for a decade. In this time it had spread and become a global plague that medical science is still not able to cure.

THE FINAL STAGES
In its final stages, once HIV has destroyed the immune system, AIDS frequently causes severe wasting. Death may occur from the effects of other infections, a collapse of the central nervous system, or starvation.

NEW THREATS

Soon after the isolation in the 1980s of HIV, the virus which causes AIDS, rumors began circulating that it had been developed in germ-warfare laboratories and accidentally, or perhaps deliberately, released. Some people even thought that it was produced by a group that wanted to punish sexual promiscuity and drug abuse. It seemed to be designed to spread death and misery as widely as possible. The long incubation meant that victims could pass on the disease for years without knowing that they were infected. The resistance of HIV to every weapon in modern medicine's arsenal convinced many people that it could not have emerged by accident. However, history shows that new diseases readily emerge with no help at all. The Earth is the ultimate genetic laboratory. Living things compete to develop extraordinary new weapons and survival techniques.

It is human nature to explore new ways of using and exploiting the environment, but by doing so we unwittingly make ourselves vulnerable to new diseases. It is impossible to predict when or how we will give microbes a new chance to attack us. Air conditioning, for example, gave a previously harmless bacterium the opportunity to infect human lungs. The infection, which became known as Legionnaire's disease, was only recognized when 180 American legionnaires attending a convention in July 1976 suddenly became ill and died. Since then, ways have been found to prevent and cure Legionnaire's disease, but it is not always so easy.

Changes in food production and handling have increased the risk of food being a carrier of infectious disease. Industrial-scale food processing allows pathogens in some raw materials to be spread throughout a large batch of produce, which may then be shipped around the world.

The introduction of animal brains and offal into the feed of farm animals drastically transformed the diet of cattle. This change was responsible for a major outbreak of bovine spongiform encephalopathy (BSE) in the United Kingdom. BSE is a brain disease in cattle that is spread by a prion, an infectious protein particle. Studies suggest that the consumption of cattle produce infected with BSE is linked to the emergence of a new variant of Creutzfeldt-Jakob Disease (nvCJD), a degenerative brain condition in humans. To date, few cases of new variant CJD have been recorded, but it has a

A NEW TERROR IN AFRICA
The bodies of those who died of Ebola in Zaire in 1995 had to be disposed of carefully since the virus that caused this hemorrhagic fever killed more than 80 percent of the people it infected.

PLAGUE IN INDIA
The 1994 outbreak of plague in India caused widespread alarm. The disease claimed few lives, however, because it can now be treated with antibiotics.

NEW FLU IN HONG KONG
Millions of chickens were killed in Hong Kong since they were thought to be the source of a new strain of flu virus that began to infect people in 1997.

DRUG-RESISTANT BACTERIA
MRSA strains of staphylococcus, seen here at 15,000 actual size, are resistant to most antibiotic drugs. They cause suppurative infections, internal abscesses, and boils.

lengthy dormancy period so it is not yet possible to tell how many people it has infected. Epidemics of smallpox and many other deadly diseases began when microbes that had previously infected only other animals began spreading in human populations. Many of the most lethal new infections, such as Ebola, are also caused by microbes that primarily infect other animals. So far, there have only been sporadic outbreaks of Ebola, but a chance mutation in the virus may cause the disease to become more infectious.

THE RISK OF MUTATION

Doctors are especially concerned that one particular family of viruses could change its pattern of infection. Known as hantaviruses, they are named after the Hantaan River in Korea where, during the Korean War in the 1950s, several thousand United Nations troops fell sick and 400 of them died. The symptoms included fever, internal bleeding, kidney failure, and shock. When the virus responsible was eventually isolated in 1976, it was found to infect wild rodents in the area. Since then, hantaviruses have been discovered in rodents all over the world, and their presence is thought to be linked to strange new human diseases that have killed many thousands of people. Outbreaks of hantavirus remain sporadic, however, because the infection can occur only in people who come into direct contact with rodents or rodent feces. However, a mutation could produce a strain that is able to pass from human to human as efficiently as it spreads among rodent populations and cause a worldwide epidemic of a disease to which we have developed no immunity.

MAD COW
British cattle are thought to have first contracted BSE in 1985 after sheep brains infected with scrapie were introduced into their feed.

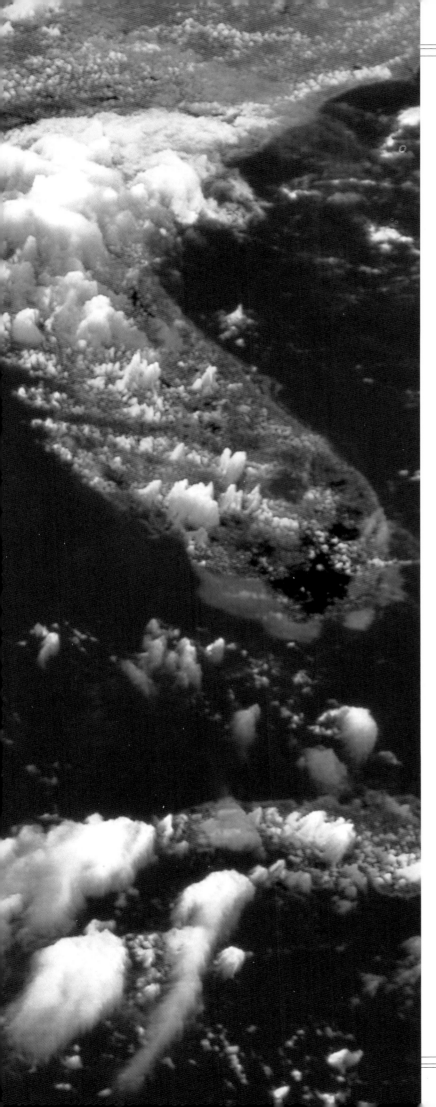

PART TWO

THE GAZETTEER

"There is nothing exempt from the peril of mutation; the earth, heavens, and whole world is thereunto subject."

SIR WALTER RALEIGH (1552-1618)

UNDERSTANDING NATURAL DISASTERS is far easier with a map at your side because the kinds of disasters experienced in a particular area are highly influenced by the geography and geology of that area. The pattern of earthquakes and volcanoes occurring on the surface of the Earth provides vital clues to the movements within it that cause the continents to drift and the oceans to grow and shrink. Plotting the position of storms on a map provides an insight into the circulation of air in the atmosphere and water in the oceans. The human geography of an area also affects the consequences of disasters. In wealthier areas, disasters cost far more money. In poorer areas, they cost many more lives.

STORM MENACES THE UNITED STATES
This computer-generated perspective of Hurricane Andrew reveals the vast size of the tropical cyclone that inflicted $27 billion worth of damage across the southeastern United States in August 1992.

GAZETTEER

THE FOLLOWING PAGES (128–139) contain the 8 gazetteer maps, on which are plotted more than 550 natural disaster sites. Each disaster site is given a number, which corresponds to an entry in the gazetteer listings, found on pages 140–153, and a visual key defines at a glance the category of disaster. The map below shows the areas covered by these maps and the pages on which they can be found. The gazetteer listings themselves give detailed information on each site and are grouped chronologically by region. Each entry is allocated a number corresponding to a site on the relevant map, which in turn is located by a grid reference, shown as a letter and a number. Each entry goes on to define the type of disaster and the year or years in which the disaster took place. Following these details is specific information about the location. Where relevant, this gives the contemporary name for a town, city, or country, followed in brackets by the modern name. The entry then gives a full account of the disaster, including, where possible, the extent of damage and the death toll.

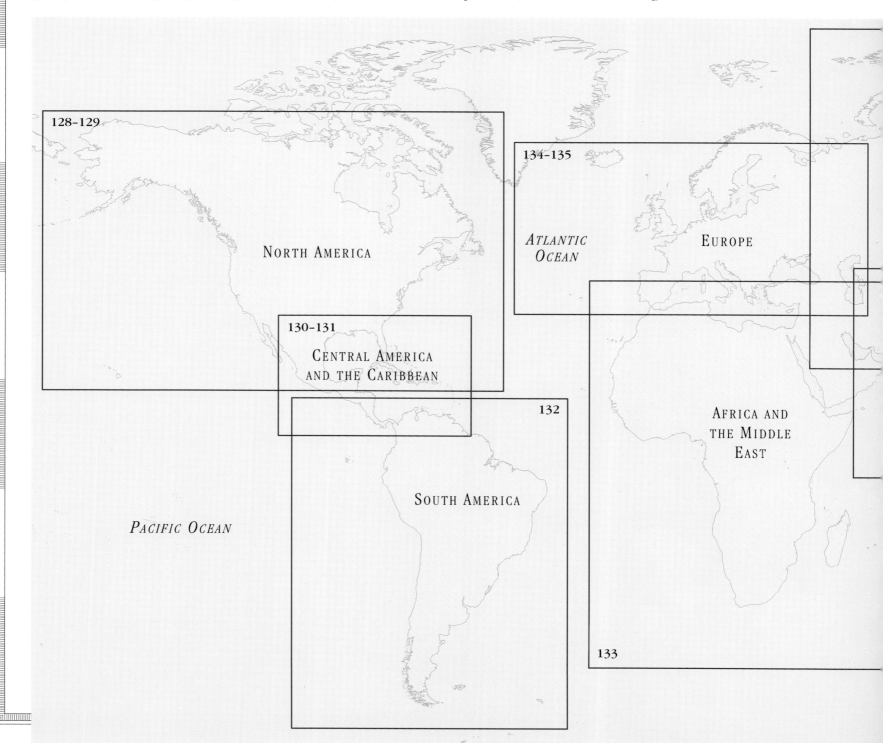

128–129

134–135

ATLANTIC OCEAN

EUROPE

NORTH AMERICA

130–131

CENTRAL AMERICA AND THE CARIBBEAN

132

AFRICA AND THE MIDDLE EAST

SOUTH AMERICA

PACIFIC OCEAN

133

THE MAP SECTION

The world map below shows the area covered by each of the 8 maps in this section of the book. Each box refers to a map that is spread over one or two pages. The key box in the bottom right-hand corner of this page gives the title of every map and the pages on which it can be found with the relevant listings. Each map carries the following information:

● The locations of up to 121 disaster sites.

● A short introduction, which outlines the main tectonic and climatic features of each region and the incidence of disease. Page numbers at the end of these introductions refer the reader to the relevant gazetteer listings pages.

● A globe at the side of each introductory paragraph to indicate the area covered by the map in relation to the rest of the globe.

● A colour-coded key on each double page to indicate the different types of disaster.

● Arrows at the sides of the maps to indicate the page numbers of adjacent geographical areas covered by other maps in the section.

THE LISTINGS SECTION

For each map there is a corresponding listing, which provides information about each of the disaster sites plotted on that map. The key box below shows the pages on which each of the listings can be found. Disasters that have been covered in detail in Part One of the book are featured in the listings and are plotted on the maps, but no details are given. Intead, the reader is referred to the full account of the disaster in Part One. The listings give the following information on each of the disasters not featured in Part One:

● A grid reference to locate the site on the relevant map.

● The name of the disaster site, or, in the case of volcanic eruptions, the name of the volcano.

● The type of disaster and its date or duration.

● The geographical location of the disaster.

● A detailed account of the disaster, including the sequence of events, the damage caused, and the death toll.

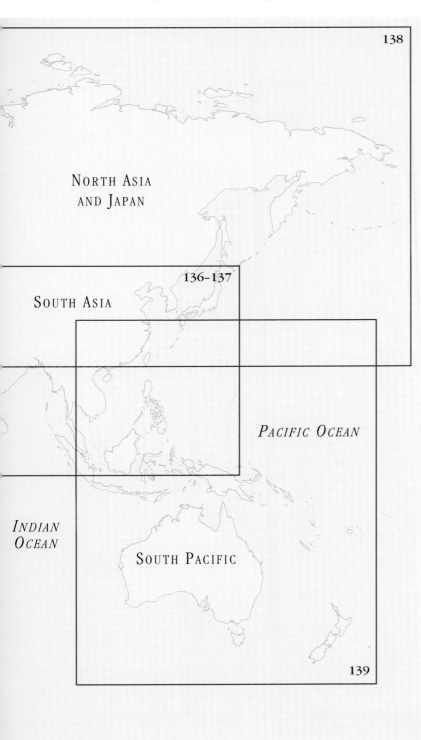

KEY TO MAPS AND LISTINGS

GEOGRAPHICAL AREA	MAPS	LISTINGS
NORTH AMERICA	128–129	140–142
CENTRAL AMERICA AND THE CARIBBEAN	130–131	142–144
SOUTH AMERICA	132	144–145
AFRICA AND THE MIDDLE EAST	133	145–146
EUROPE	134–135	146–149
SOUTH ASIA	136–137	149–151
NORTH ASIA AND JAPAN	138	152
SOUTH PACIFIC	139	153

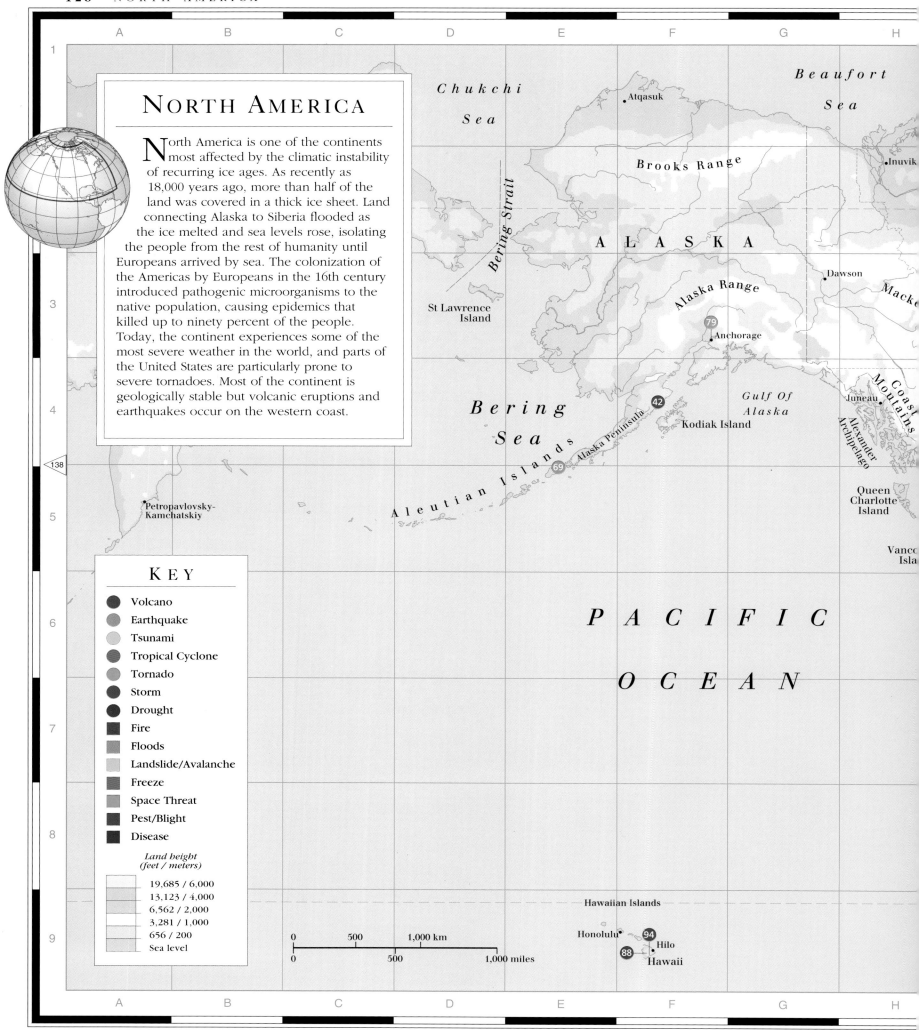

NORTH AMERICA

North America is one of the continents most affected by the climatic instability of recurring ice ages. As recently as 18,000 years ago, more than half of the land was covered in a thick ice sheet. Land connecting Alaska to Siberia flooded as the ice melted and sea levels rose, isolating the people from the rest of humanity until Europeans arrived by sea. The colonization of the Americas by Europeans in the 16th century introduced pathogenic microorganisms to the native population, causing epidemics that killed up to ninety percent of the people. Today, the continent experiences some of the most severe weather in the world, and parts of the United States are particularly prone to severe tornadoes. Most of the continent is geologically stable but volcanic eruptions and earthquakes occur on the western coast.

KEY

- Volcano
- Earthquake
- Tsunami
- Tropical Cyclone
- Tornado
- Storm
- Drought
- Fire
- Floods
- Landslide/Avalanche
- Freeze
- Space Threat
- Pest/Blight
- Disease

Land height (feet / meters)

	19,685 / 6,000
	13,123 / 4,000
	6,562 / 2,000
	3,281 / 1,000
	656 / 200
	Sea level

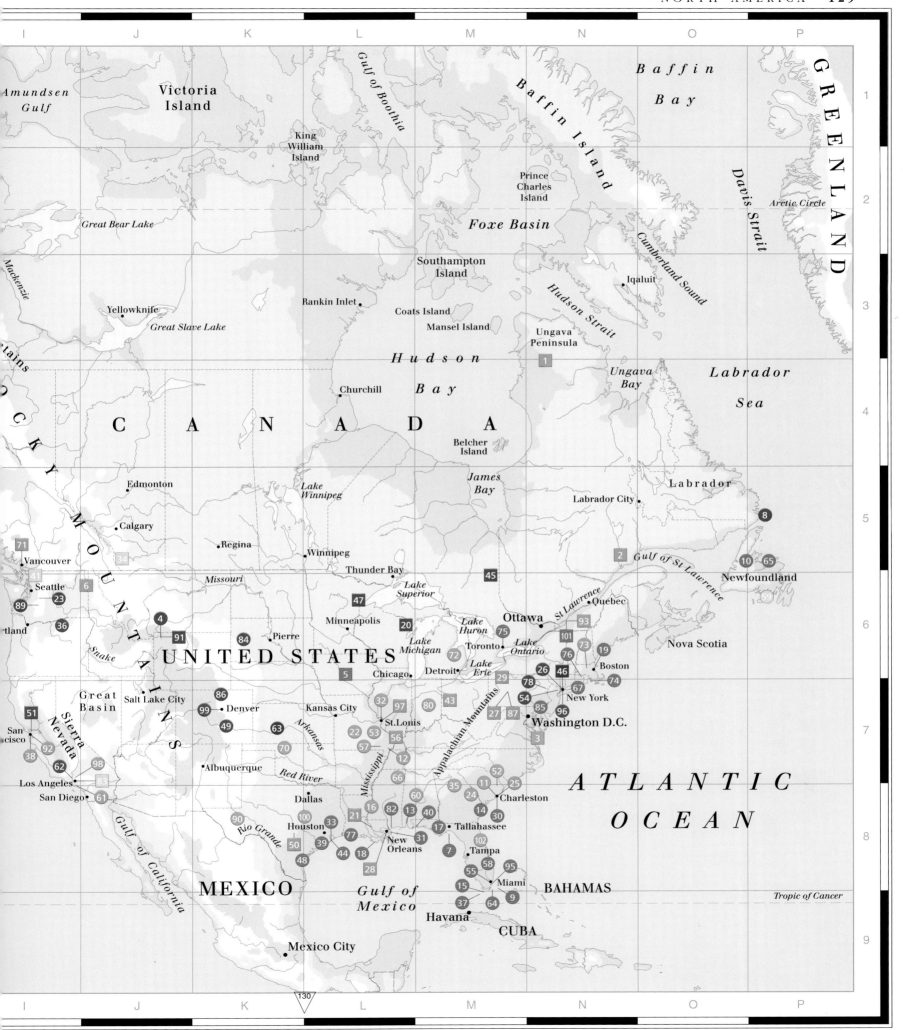

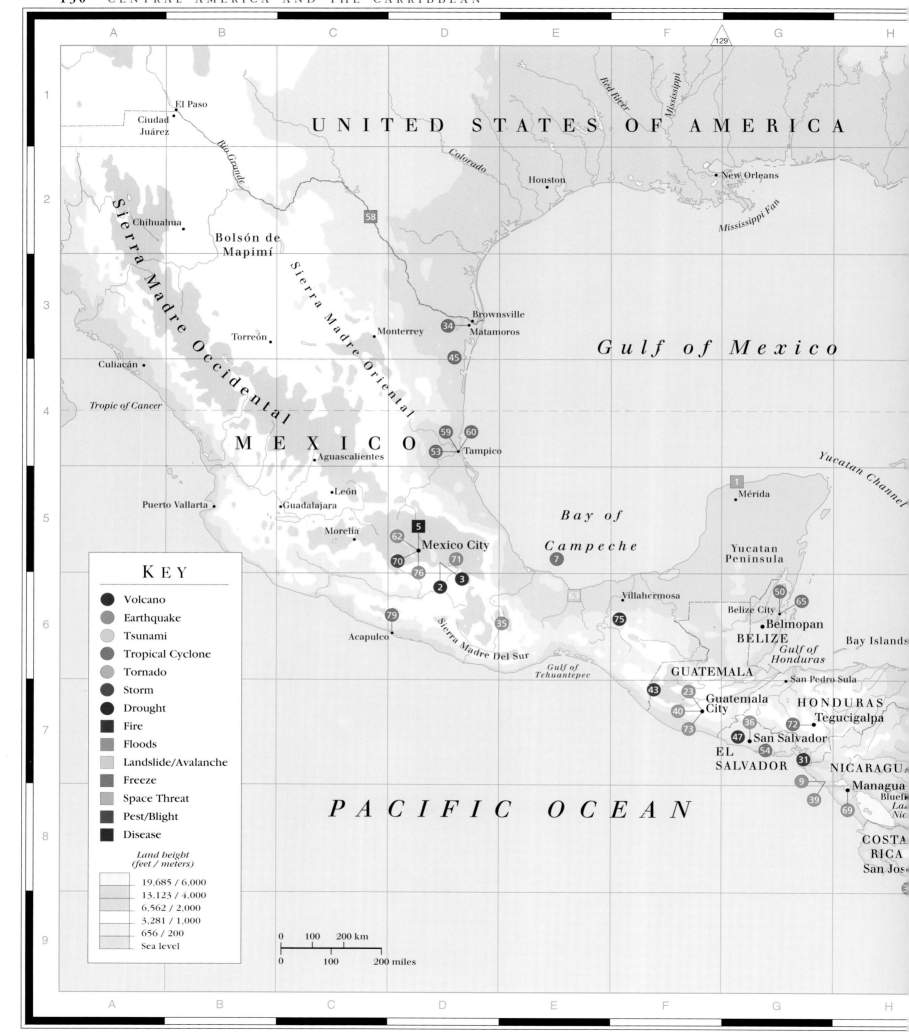

KEY

- ● Volcano
- ● Earthquake
- ● Tsunami
- ◐ Tropical Cyclone
- ● Tornado
- ● Storm
- ● Drought
- ■ Fire
- ▨ Floods
- ▨ Landslide/Avalanche
- ▨ Freeze
- ▨ Space Threat
- ■ Pest/Blight
- ■ Disease

*Land height
(feet / meters)*

19,685 / 6,000
13,123 / 4,000
6,562 / 2,000
3,281 / 1,000
656 / 200
Sea level

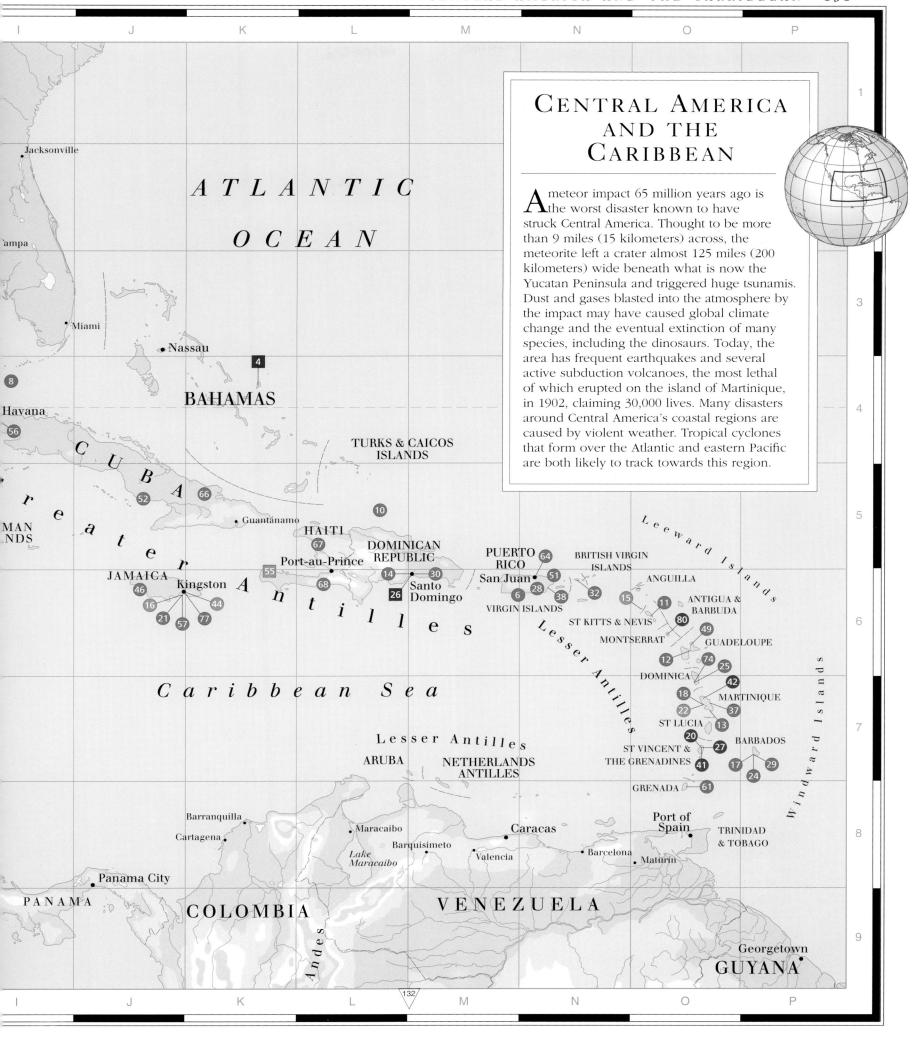

ATLANTIC

OCEAN

CENTRAL AMERICA AND THE CARIBBEAN

A meteor impact 65 million years ago is the worst disaster known to have struck Central America. Thought to be more than 9 miles (15 kilometers) across, the meteorite left a crater almost 125 miles (200 kilometers) wide beneath what is now the Yucatan Peninsula and triggered huge tsunamis. Dust and gases blasted into the atmosphere by the impact may have caused global climate change and the eventual extinction of many species, including the dinosaurs. Today, the area has frequent earthquakes and several active subduction volcanoes, the most lethal of which erupted on the island of Martinique, in 1902, claiming 30,000 lives. Many disasters around Central America's coastal regions are caused by violent weather. Tropical cyclones that form over the Atlantic and eastern Pacific are both likely to track towards this region.

Jacksonville

Tampa

Miami

Havana

Nassau

BAHAMAS

TURKS & CAICOS ISLANDS

CUBA

Guantánamo

HAITI

Port-au-Prince

DOMINICAN REPUBLIC

Santo Domingo

PUERTO RICO

San Juan

BRITISH VIRGIN ISLANDS

Leeward Islands

ANGUILLA

ANTIGUA & BARBUDA

ST KITTS & NEVIS

MONTSERRAT

GUADELOUPE

DOMINICA

MARTINIQUE

VIRGIN ISLANDS

JAMAICA

Kingston

Greater Antilles

Caribbean Sea

Lesser Antilles

ARUBA

NETHERLANDS ANTILLES

ST LUCIA

BARBADOS

ST VINCENT & THE GRENADINES

GRENADA

Windward Islands

Barranquilla

Cartagena

Maracaibo

Barquisimeto

Lake Maracaibo

Caracas

Valencia

Barcelona

Maturín

Port of Spain

TRINIDAD & TOBAGO

Panama City

PANAMA

COLOMBIA

Andes

VENEZUELA

Georgetown

GUYANA

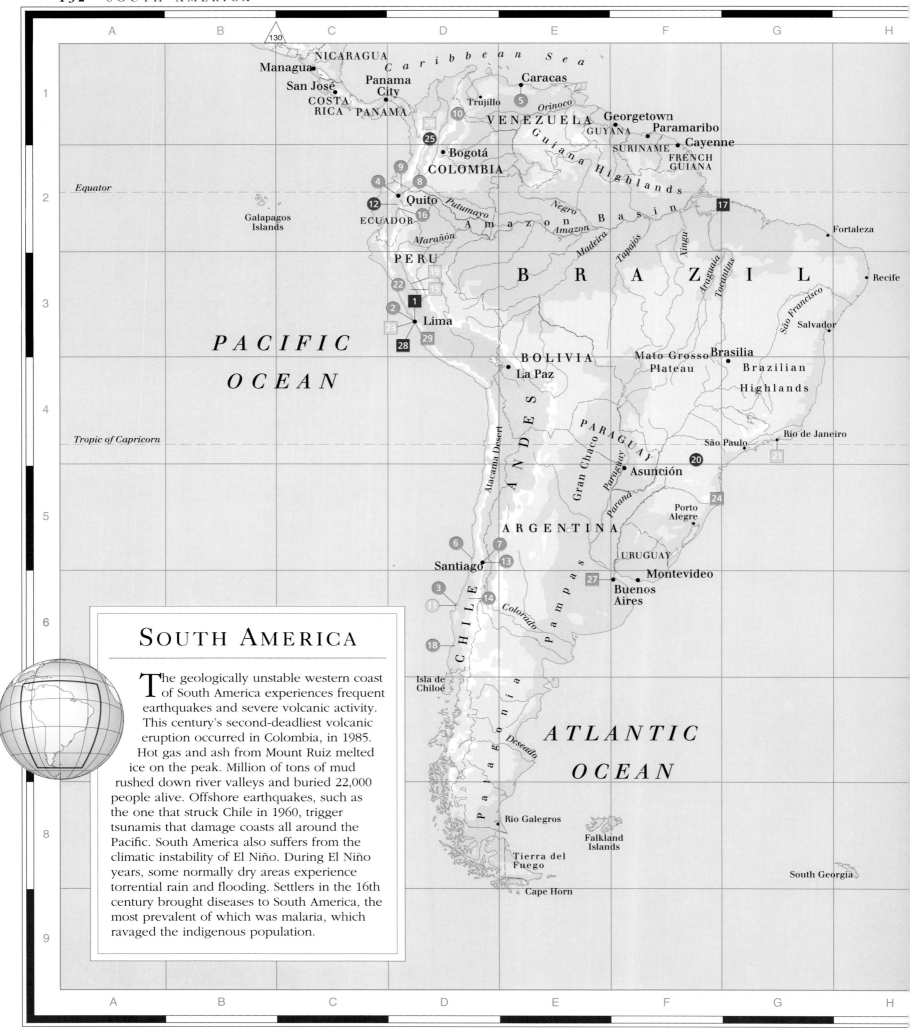

SOUTH AMERICA

The geologically unstable western coast of South America experiences frequent earthquakes and severe volcanic activity. This century's second-deadliest volcanic eruption occurred in Colombia, in 1985. Hot gas and ash from Mount Ruiz melted ice on the peak. Million of tons of mud rushed down river valleys and buried 22,000 people alive. Offshore earthquakes, such as the one that struck Chile in 1960, trigger tsunamis that damage coasts all around the Pacific. South America also suffers from the climatic instability of El Niño. During El Niño years, some normally dry areas experience torrential rain and flooding. Settlers in the 16th century brought diseases to South America, the most prevalent of which was malaria, which ravaged the indigenous population.

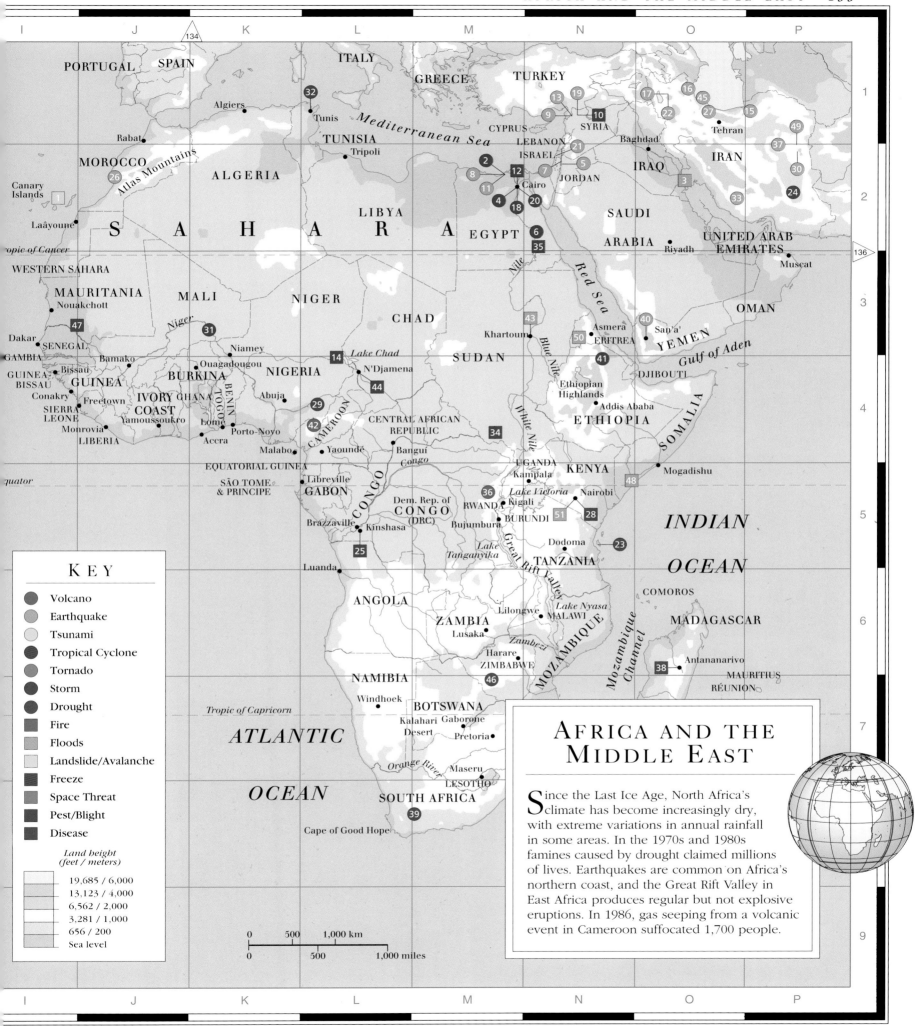

134

136

KEY

- Volcano
- Earthquake
- Tsunami
- Tropical Cyclone
- Tornado
- Storm
- Drought
- Fire
- Floods
- Landslide/Avalanche
- Freeze
- Space Threat
- Pest/Blight
- Disease

Land height (feet / meters)

19,685 / 6,000	
13,123 / 4,000	
6,562 / 2,000	
3,281 / 1,000	
656 / 200	
Sea level	

0 500 1,000 km

0 500 1,000 miles

AFRICA AND THE MIDDLE EAST

Since the Last Ice Age, North Africa's climate has become increasingly dry, with extreme variations in annual rainfall in some areas. In the 1970s and 1980s famines caused by drought claimed millions of lives. Earthquakes are common on Africa's northern coast, and the Great Rift Valley in East Africa produces regular but not explosive eruptions. In 1986, gas seeping from a volcanic event in Cameroon suffocated 1,700 people.

EUROPE

The history of some parts of Europe has been recorded for thousands of years, and ancient mythology includes accounts of many disasters. Archaeologists and geologists have added a new dimension to stories of the destruction of Atlantis and Noah's flood by uncovering evidence of catastrophic damage that ancient civilizations suffered at the hands of nature. The varied climate has produced years of flood and drought, that have resulted in the destruction of crops and spread of famine. Epidemics have swept the continent several times. Bubonic plague was the biggest killer, but measles, tuberculosis, typhus, cholera, and syphilis have also taken their toll. Mediterranean islands and coasts are geologically unstable, suffering repeated volcanic eruptions and earthquakes, which are common in the Caucasus Mountains. The mountains running across the southern central part of the continent have heavy snow, and avalanches are a regular occurrence. The most severe storms occur in the northwest.

KEY

- ● Volcano
- ● Earthquake
- ● Tsunami
- ● Tropical Cyclone
- ● Tornado
- ● Storm
- ● Drought
- ■ Fire
- ■ Floods
- ■ Landslide/Avalanche
- ■ Freeze
- ■ Space Threat
- ■ Pest/Blight
- ■ Disease

Land height (feet / meters)

	19,685 / 6,000
	13,123 / 4,000
	6,562 / 2,000
	3,281 / 1,000
	656 / 200
	Sea level

ICELAND

Reykjavík

Heimaey

118
58
93
28
106
108

Norwegian Sea

Arctic Circle

Faeroe Islands

Shetland Islands

40
Orkney Islands

Outer Hebrides

Nort Sea

71
107 Edinburgh

UNITED
17
KINGDOM

25 Belfast

REPUBLIC OF IRELAND

65 51 Dublin
Manchester

60
19
24 5
35 31
41 94 47 18 30
London 112 95
15
66
45
77 52 109 *Channel* BELG
English Channel 97
Channel Islands 27
70

A T L A N T I C

O C E A N

Bay of Biscay Bordeaux

Nantes

F R A N C

Toulouse

A Coruña

Bilbao *Pyrénées*

ANDORRA

Ebro
99
Porto Madrid Barce

Valencia Majorca Mer
PORTUGAL *Tagus* Ibiza Bale isla

79
Lisbon 56 120 S P A I N
36 76
Seville 33
75 Malaga M e d
GIBRALTAR

Rabat

Azores

0	200	400 km
0	200	400 miles

129

I J K L M N O P

1
2
138
3
4
5
6
7
8
136
9

White Sea

Arkhangel'sk

Severnaya Dvina

Troudheim

ORWAY

SWEDEN

Oslo

Uppsala

Stockholm

Vänern

Vättern

stiansand

Ålborg

Gothenburg

Gotland

DENMARK

Copenhagen

Baltic Sea

HERLANDS

Hamburg

Elbe

Berlin

GERMANY

Frankfurt
am Main

Prague

**CZECH
REPUBLIC**

sburg

Munich

Vienna

Z.

AUSTRIA

Alps

Milan

ITALY

Venice

**SAN
MARINO**

Kemi

Vaasa

FINLAND

Turku

Helsinki

St Petersburg

Tallinn

ESTONIA

Lake Peipus

Riga

LATVIA

LITHUANIA

**RUSSIAN FEDERATION
(KALININGRAD)**

Gdansk

Wisla

Vilnius

Minsk

BELARUS

POLAND

Warsaw

SLOVAKIA

Bratislava

Budapest

HUNGARY

Carpathian Mountains

SLOVENIA

CROATIA

**BOSNIA &
HERZEGOVINA**

Sarajevo

Adriatic Sea

YUGOSLAVIA

Belgrade

**Lake
Ladoga**

**Lake
Onega**

RUSSIAN

FEDERATION

North European Plain

Moscow

UKRAINE

Kiev

MOLDOVA

Timisoara

ROMANIA

Bucharest

Danube

Dnieper

Odessa

Don

Aktyubinsk

Voronezh

Saratov

Volgograd

Rostov-na-Donu

Volga

*Sea of
Azov*

Black Sea

Caucasus

GEORGIA

Tbilisi

*Caspian
Sea*

Rome

San Marino

Naples

*Tyrrhenian
Sea*

Palermo

Tunis

TUNISIA

MALTA

Sicily

*Ionian
Sea*

ranean

Sea

Skopje

MACEDONIA

ALBANIA

Tirana

BULGARIA

Sofia

Varna

GREECE

*Aegean
Sea*

Athens

Crete

Istanbul

Bursa

TURKEY

Ankara

Konya

Nicosia

CYPRUS

SYRIA

IRAQ

Yerevan

ARMENIA

AZERBAIJAN

AZERBAIJAN

Baku

IRAN

64

63

38

85

121

89

72

96

61

83

54

42

102

101

98

11

105

119

82

10

110

12

34

32

92

46

59

11

21

43

57

69

20

4

80

49

81

55

87

50

9

16

5

6

104

3

8

68

13

23

74

88

90

115

113

48

117

136

1

2

14

67

26

91

103

86

133

Corsica

dinia

nia

I J K L M N O P

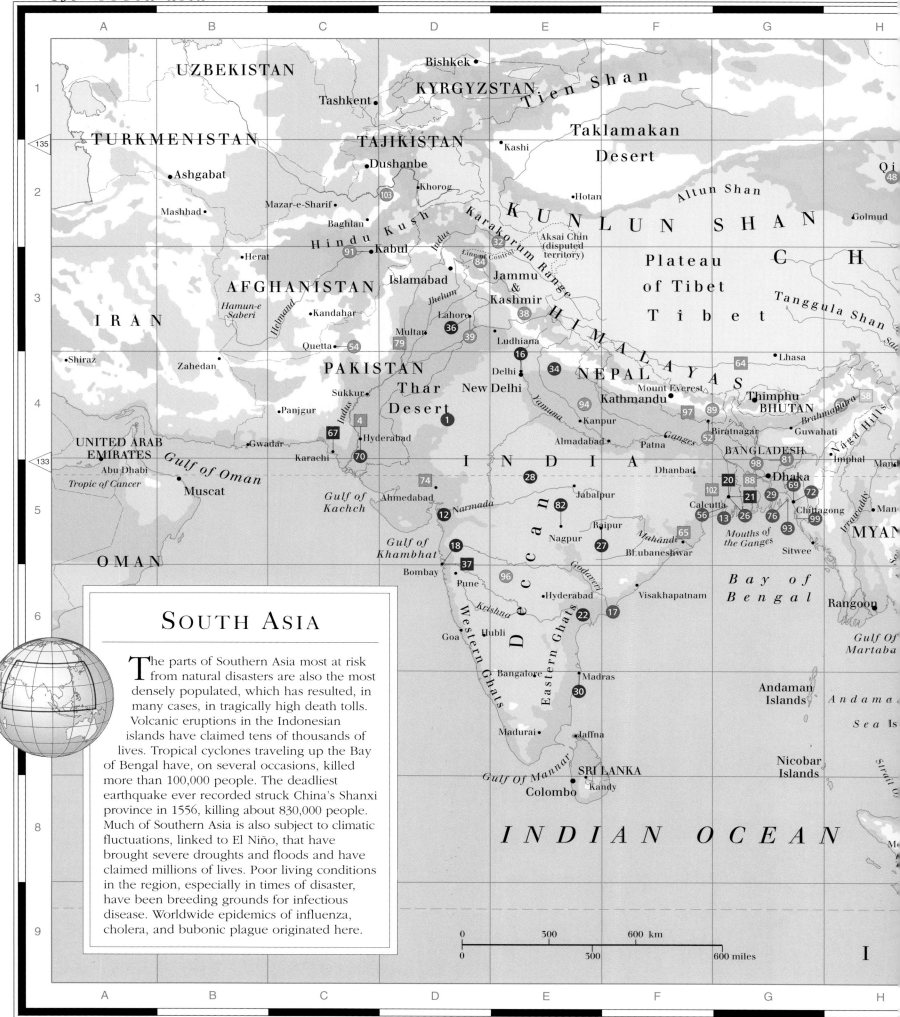

SOUTH ASIA

The parts of Southern Asia most at risk from natural disasters are also the most densely populated, which has resulted, in many cases, in tragically high death tolls. Volcanic eruptions in the Indonesian islands have claimed tens of thousands of lives. Tropical cyclones traveling up the Bay of Bengal have, on several occasions, killed more than 100,000 people. The deadliest earthquake ever recorded struck China's Shanxi province in 1556, killing about 830,000 people. Much of Southern Asia is also subject to climatic fluctuations, linked to El Niño, that have brought severe droughts and floods and have claimed millions of lives. Poor living conditions in the region, especially in times of disaster, have been breeding grounds for infectious disease. Worldwide epidemics of influenza, cholera, and bubonic plague originated here.

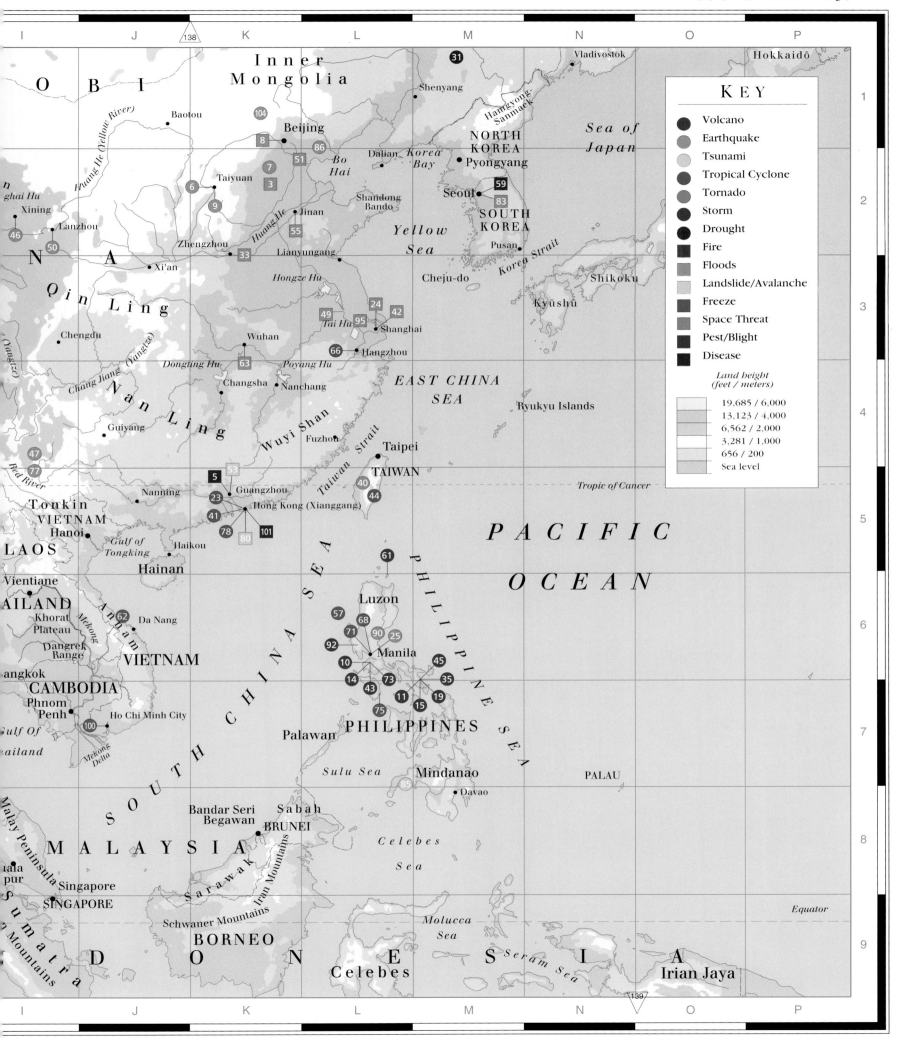

O B I

Inner
Mongolia

Shenyang •

Vladivostok •

Hokkaidō

Huang He (Yellow River)

Baotou •

104

Beijing •

8

Dalian •

Korea
Bay

NORTH
KOREA

Sea of
Japan

Hamgyong-
Sanmaek

Taiyuan •

86

51

7

3

Bo
Hai

Pyongyang •

ghai Hu

Xining •

6

Huang He

Jinan •

Shandong
Bando

Seoul •

59

83

SOUTH
KOREA

N A

46

Lanzhou •

50

9

55

Zhengzhou •

Yellow
Sea

Pusan •

Q i n   L i n g

33

Lianyungang •

Korea Strait

Cheju-do

Shikoku

Xi'an •

Hongze Hu

Chengdu •

Wuhan •

49

24

42

Kyūshū

(Yangtze)

Tai Hu

95

Shanghai •

N a n   L i n g

Dongting Hu

63

Poyang Hu

66

Hangzhou •

EAST CHINA
SEA

Chang Jiang (Yangtze)

Changsha •

Nanchang •

Ryukyu Islands

Guiyang •

Wuyi Shan

Fuzhou •

47

77

Red River

Taiwan Strait

Taipei •

TAIWAN

Tropic of Cancer

Tonkin

5

53

VIETNAM

23

Guangzhou •

40

Hanoi •

41

Hong Kong (Xianggang)

44

LAOS

Gulf of
Tongking

78

80

101

Haikou •

Nanning •

Hainan

Vientiane •

61

AILAND

62

Da Nang •

Luzon

PACIFIC

OCEAN

Khorat
Plateau

Annam

57

68

Dangrek
Range

VIETNAM

71

90

25

ngkok

92

Manila •

45

CAMBODIA

10

Phnom
Penh •

Ho Chi Minh City •

14

73

35

43

ulf Of

11

19

ailand

100

75

15

Mekong
Delta

PHILIPPINES

Palawan

SOUTH CHINA SEA

PHILIPPINE SEA

Sulu Sea

Mindanao

PALAU

85

Davao •

Bandar Seri
Begawan •

Sabah

Celebes

BRUNEI

Sea

MALAYSIA

Sarawak

Iran Mountains

Molucca

pur

Singapore •

Sea

Equator

SINGAPORE

Schwaner Mountains

BORNEO

N E S

Seram Sea

I A

Celebes

Irian Jaya

KEY

● Volcano
● Earthquake
● Tsunami
● Tropical Cyclone
● Tornado
● Storm
● Drought
■ Fire
■ Floods
■ Landslide/Avalanche
■ Freeze
■ Space Threat
■ Pest/Blight
■ Disease

*Land height
(feet / meters)*

19,685 / 6,000
13,123 / 4,000
6,562 / 2,000
3,281 / 1,000
656 / 200
Sea level

Malay Peninsula

Sumatra

n Mountains

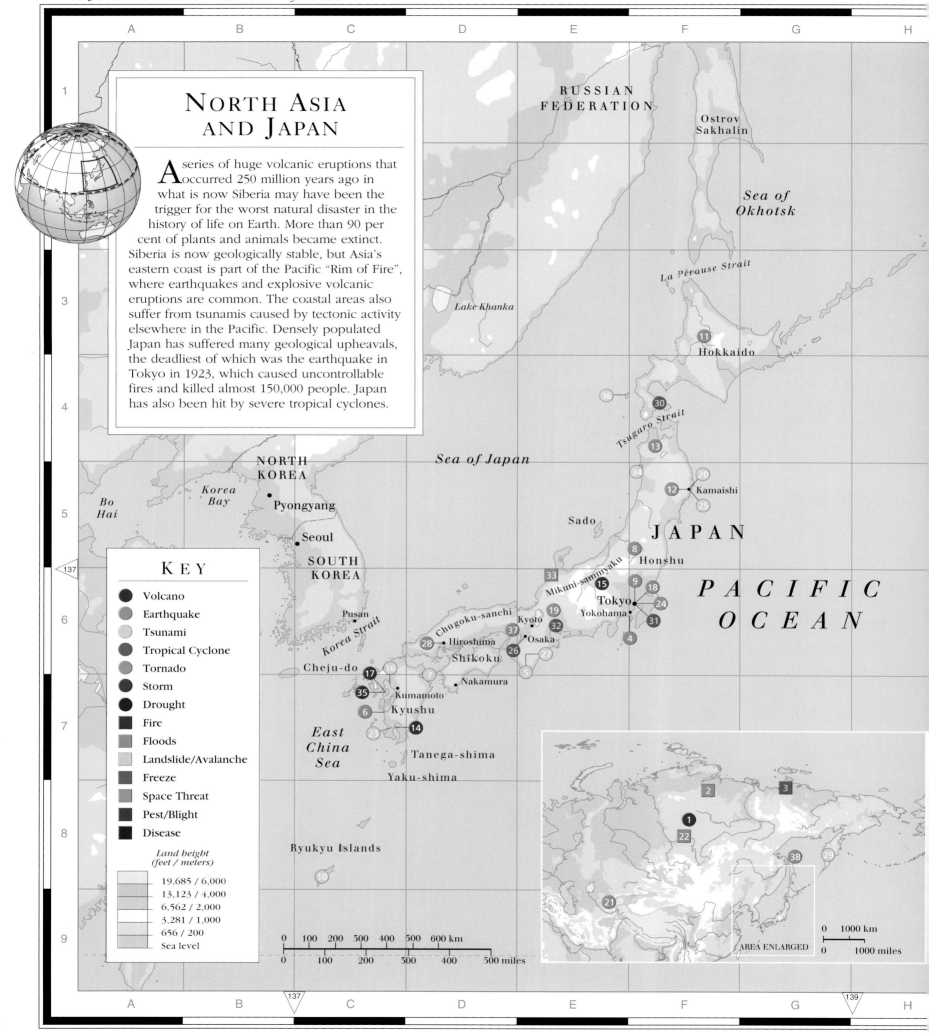

NORTH ASIA AND JAPAN

A series of huge volcanic eruptions that occurred 250 million years ago in what is now Siberia may have been the trigger for the worst natural disaster in the history of life on Earth. More than 90 per cent of plants and animals became extinct. Siberia is now geologically stable, but Asia's eastern coast is part of the Pacific "Rim of Fire", where earthquakes and explosive volcanic eruptions are common. The coastal areas also suffer from tsunamis caused by tectonic activity elsewhere in the Pacific. Densely populated Japan has suffered many geological upheavals, the deadliest of which was the earthquake in Tokyo in 1923, which caused uncontrollable fires and killed almost 150,000 people. Japan has also been hit by severe tropical cyclones.

KEY

- Volcano
- Earthquake
- Tsunami
- Tropical Cyclone
- Tornado
- Storm
- Drought
- Fire
- Floods
- Landslide/Avalanche
- Freeze
- Space Threat
- Pest/Blight
- Disease

Land height (feet / meters)

- 19,685 / 6,000
- 13,123 / 4,000
- 6,562 / 2,000
- 3,281 / 1,000
- 656 / 200
- Sea level

RUSSIAN FEDERATION

Ostrov Sakhalin

Sea of Okhotsk

La Pérouse Strait

Lake Khanka

Hokkaido

Tsugaro Strait

NORTH KOREA

Korea Bay

Pyongyang

Bo Hai

Seoul

SOUTH KOREA

Sea of Japan

Sado

JAPAN

Honshu

Kamaishi

Mikuni-sammyaku

Tokyo

Yokohama

PACIFIC OCEAN

Pusan

Korea Strait

Chugoku-sanchi

Kyoto

Osaka

Hiroshima

Shikoku

Nakamura

Cheju-do

Kumamoto

Kyushu

East China Sea

Tanega-shima

Yaku-shima

Ryukyu Islands

AREA ENLARGED

| 0 100 200 300 400 500 600 km |
| 0 100 200 300 400 500 miles |

0 1000 km
0 1000 miles

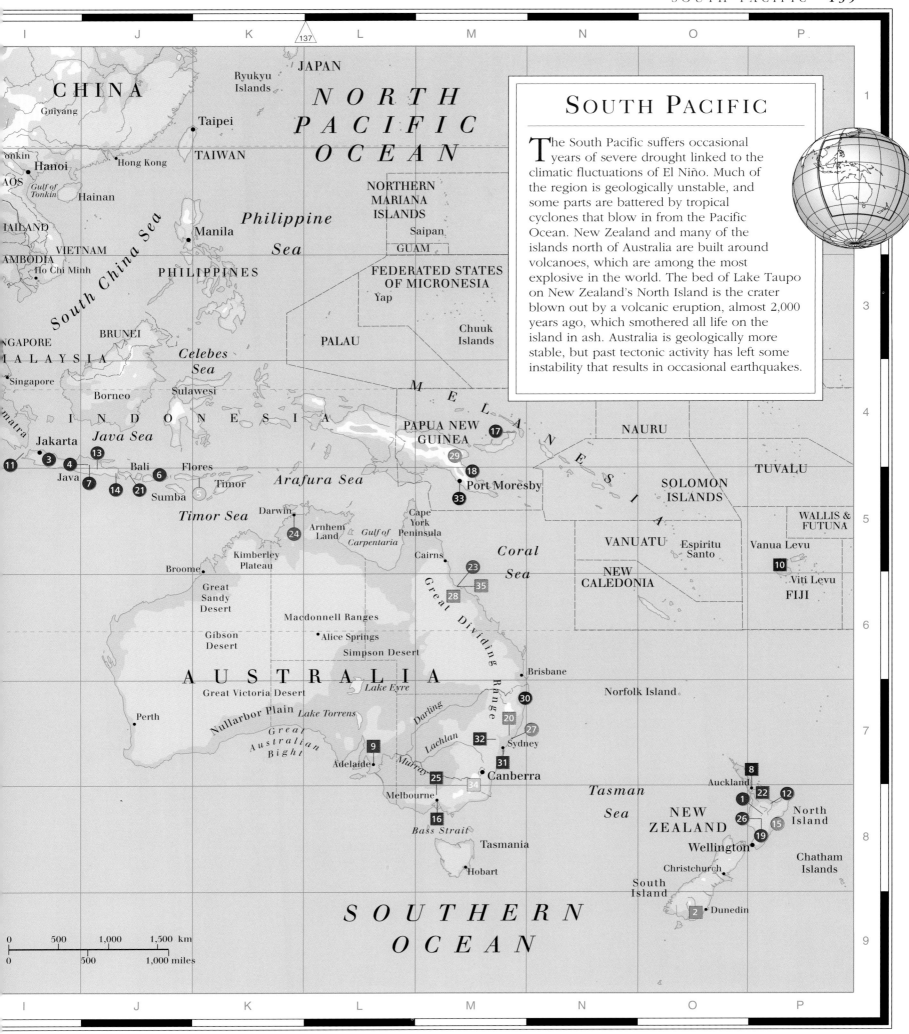

SOUTH PACIFIC

The South Pacific suffers occasional years of severe drought linked to the climatic fluctuations of El Niño. Much of the region is geologically unstable, and some parts are battered by tropical cyclones that blow in from the Pacific Ocean. New Zealand and many of the islands north of Australia are built around volcanoes, which are among the most explosive in the world. The bed of Lake Taupo on New Zealand's North Island is the crater blown out by a volcanic eruption, almost 2,000 years ago, which smothered all life on the island in ash. Australia is geologically more stable, but past tectonic activity has left some instability that results in occasional earthquakes.

THE LISTINGS

The listings in this section correspond to sites plotted on the maps of the preceding pages (128–139). After each number in the listings a map reference is given. The page number of the relevant map is given under the title of each section.

NORTH AMERICA

The map for these listings is on pp.128–129.

1 N4 LAC COUTURE
SPACE THREAT 425 MILLION YEARS AGO
LOCATION: Quebec, Canada
NOTES: A meteor strike left a 6 mile (10-km) wide crater, which filled with water, creating Lac Couture. The impact may have contributed to heavy loss of marine life, including brachiopods and trilobites, that occurred around this time.

2 N5 QUEBEC
SPACE THREAT C. 210 MILLION YEARS AGO
LOCATION: Manicouagan Crater, Canada
NOTES: A meteor strike is thought to have contributed to the loss of many marine and terrestrial species at the end of the Triassic Period. The impact created a 63-mile (100-km) wide crater lake.

3 N7 CHESAPEAKE BAY
SPACE THREAT 35 MILLION YEARS AGO
LOCATION: Maryland/Delaware, US
NOTES: A meteor strike scattered cosmic debris across the southeastern US and left a huge crater at the bottom of Chesapeake Bay. It is thought that the impact killed off some species of giant birds and mammals that lived during the Eocene Epoch.

4 J6 YELLOWSTONE
VOLCANO 2 MILLION YEARS AGO
LOCATION: Wyoming, US
NOTES: This eruption was 250 times more powerful than that of Pinatubo in 1991. It had a dramatic global impact and may have triggered the Pleistocene Ice Age.

5 L6 DES MOINES
FREEZE 114,000-12,000 YEARS AGO
LOCATION: Iowa, US
NOTES: See pp.96–97.

6 J6 SPOKANE
FLOOD C. 10,000 YEARS AGO
LOCATION: Scabland, Washington, US
NOTES: Vast floods were unleashed over Montana and the Washington Scabland when the ice dam holding back Lake Missoula gave way.

7 M8 APALACHEE BAY
TROPICAL CYCLONE 1528
LOCATION: Gulf of Mexico, US
NOTES: The Spanish ships of the Narvaez expedition were sunk in the bay. Only 20 of the 400 sailors and soldiers on board survived.

8 P5 BELLE ISLE
STORM 1711
LOCATION: Labrador, Canada
NOTES: An English armada of 61 ships was caught in a heavy storm while on its way to attack Quebec. Eight transport ships were wrecked on Belle Isle's rocky shoals, and all 1,342 servicemen and their families on board were lost.

9 M8 STRAITS OF FLORIDA
TROPICAL CYCLONE 1715
LOCATION: off Miami, Florida, US
NOTES: All but one of the 11 ships of the Spanish Flota were destroyed as they sailed from Havana to Spain laden with 14 million gold and silver pesos, gems, and gold bars. About 1,000 sailors were drowned.

10 O5 ISLAND OF NEWFOUNDLAND
TROPICAL CYCLONE 1775
LOCATION: Canada
NOTES: The storm developed over warm waters in the mid-Atlantic then swept north to strike the island. Hundreds of fishing boats foundered off the coast, and almost all the fisherman aboard drowned. In all, 4,000 lives were lost.

11 M8 CHARLESTON
TORNADO 1811
LOCATION: South Carolina, US
NOTES: Huge areas of the city were destroyed, and more than 500 people lost their lives, in one of the worst tornadoes on record in the US.

12 L7 NEW MADRID
EARTHQUAKES 1811-1812
LOCATION: Missouri, US
NOTES: Despite lying more than 1,000 miles (1,600 km) from the nearest plate boundary, the area was hit by three huge tremors. Few lives were lost, but major land upheavals caused the Mississippi River to change course, eroding the banks and destroying New Madrid.

13 L8 MOBILE
TROPICAL CYCLONE 1819
LOCATION: Alabama, US
NOTES: The small but powerful tropical cyclone wrecked many buildings in the town and surrounding areas and sank several ships in the bay. More than 200 lives were lost.

14 M8 ST. SIMONS ISLAND
TROPICAL CYCLONE 1824
LOCATION: Georgia, US
NOTES: Buildings were toppled and the island's plantations were swamped by floodwater. Almost all of the 83 people killed were slaves working in the fields.

15 M9 KEY WEST
TROPICAL CYCLONE 1835
LOCATION: Florida Keys, US
NOTES: Many small villages were wiped out, and several vessels were wrecked on the reefs at Cape Canaveral. The area was so sparsely populated that the exact death toll was unknown. About 100 people were thought to have died.

16 L8 NATCHEZ
TORNADO 1840
LOCATION: Mississippi, US
NOTES: More that 300 people died and around 100 were injured in the most destructive tornado in the US to that date. Damage was estimated at $1 million.

17 M8 ST. JO
TROPICAL CYCLONE 1841
LOCATION: Near Apalachicola, Florida, US
NOTES: This boom town was obliterated, and its entire population of 4,000 wiped out, as water surged across the bayou on which it stood. Local preachers had long been predicting the destruction of this "hellhole" by divine retribution.

18 L8 DERNIÈRES ISLAND
TROPICAL CYCLONE 1856
LOCATION: Louisiana, US
NOTES: Every building was destroyed and 137 people died when the island was totally submerged. Survivors swam to a steamer anchored in the bay, the Star, which was the only sign that there had ever been an island on that spot.

19 N6 BOSTON
TROPICAL CYCLONE 1869
LOCATION: Massachusetts, US
NOTES: The storm caused havoc along the length of the Northeast seaboard, but Massachusetts was hardest hit. All along the coast, vessels at anchor were wrecked and around 50 lives were lost.

20 L6 PESHTIGO
FIRE 1871
LOCATION: Wisconsin, US
NOTES: Logging fires, whipped up by ferocious winds, created the greatest wildfire in the US to that date. The town of Peshtigo and almost all its inhabitants were consumed by the fire, which spread over 4.25 million acres (1.72 million hectacres). A total of 1,500 people were killed by the flames.

21 L8 BATON ROUGE
FLOOD 1874
LOCATION: Louisiana, US
NOTES: In the first accurately recorded flood of the Mississippi, spring rain and thawing snow caused the river to burst its banks throughout the Mississippi Valley. Tens of thousands of acres of mostly rural land were under water, and around 250 people drowned.

22 L7 MARSHFIELD
TORNADOES 1880
LOCATION: Missouri, US
NOTES: A series of 24 tornadoes leveled the city and wreaked havoc from Arkansas to Wisconsin. Damage was in the region of $2 million, and more than 100 people were killed.

23 I6 MOUNT RAINIER
VOLCANO 1882
LOCATION: Cascade Mountains, US
NOTES: The eruption caused major lahars that engulfed vast areas. Potentially the most dangerous volcano in the Cascade Mountains, it is expected to erupt again soon, threatening to bury valleys and towns as far away as Puget Sound beneath hundreds of tons of mud.

24 M8 DAVISBORO
TORNADO 1884
LOCATION: Georgia, US
NOTES: The town was obliterated and 800 people were killed when more than 60 tornadoes spiraled across the southern states in a single day.

25 M8 CHARLESTON
EARTHQUAKE 1886
LOCATION: South Carolina, US
NOTES: In one of the most widely felt earthquakes in the US, buildings in the city were extensively damaged and 100 people died. Shocks were felt in New York to the north, Alabama to the south, and Nebraska to the west.

26 N7 NEW YORK CITY
STORM (BLIZZARD) 1888
LOCATION: New York, US
NOTES: Following a weather forecast for "fair and colder" weather, the blizzard brought the city to a standstill, snapping telegraph wires, breaking gas and water pipes, and freezing 400 people to death.

27 M7 JOHNSTOWN
FLOOD 1889
LOCATION: Pennsylvania, US
NOTES: The South Fork reservoir dam, the largest earth dam in the world at the time, gave way, sending a wall of water 38 m (125 ft) high thundering down the Johnstown valley. Johnstown and many neighbouring towns were washed away. An estimated 7,000 people were killed.

28 L8 NEW ORLEANS
FLOOD 1890
LOCATION: Illinois, US
NOTES: At least 100 people drowned and 50,000 more were left homeless when the Mississippi River, swollen by heavy rains and thaws, burst its banks.

29 M6 OIL CITY
FLOOD 1892
LOCATION: Pennsylvania, US
NOTES: The city was flooded, and the surface of the water was covered in a thick layer of oil from broken pipelines. The oil caught fire, creating a blazing river that ran through the city, burning every building down to the waterline and killing 130 people, many of whom were struggling to survive in the water.

30 M8 CHARLESTON
TROPICAL CYCLONE 1893
LOCATION: South Carolina, US
NOTES: There was widespread damage to towns and cities along the Georgia and South Carolina coasts. Dozens of islands were totally submerged by floodwater, and more than 1,000 lives were lost. Damage was estimated at $10 million.

31 M8 PORT EADS, NEW ORLEANS
TROPICAL CYCLONE 1893
LOCATION: Louisiana, US
NOTES: The storm sent a 13-ft (4-m) high wave crashing on to the town, catching the residents unawares and killing 2,000. The storm went on to cause severe damage across the southeastern US.

32 L7 ST. LOUIS
TORNADO 1896
LOCATION: Missouri, US
NOTES: A densely populated part of St. Louis was destroyed in 20 minutes by the tornado. More than 306 people were killed and around 2,500 were injured.

33 L8 GALVESTON
TROPICAL CYCLONE 1900
LOCATION: Texas, US
NOTES: See p.70.

34 J5 FRANK
LANDSLIDE 1903
LOCATION: Alberta, Canada
NOTES: The town was pulverized and 70 of its inhabitants were killed when

a gargantuan slab of Turtle Mountain sheared off and thundered down into the valley below.

35 M7 GAINESVILLE

TORNADO 1903
LOCATION: Georgia, US
NOTES: More than 200 people were killed and almost 1,000 were injured when the tornado ripped through the town. Scores of people were killed when a cotton mill collapsed on its 750 workers.

36 I6 HEPPNER

STORM (FLASH FLOOD) 1903
LOCATION: Oregon, US
NOTES: A sudden cloudburst in the Blue Mountains caused Willow Creek to flash flood. Within an hour, one-third of the town had been washed away and more than 325 people were dead.

37 M9 FLORIDA KEYS

TROPICAL CYCLONE 1906
LOCATION: Florida, US
NOTES: A hurricane struck during the construction of a road- and rail-link across the Florida keys. The construction survived, but 124 workmen living on Sandy Key were drowned when their houseboats were broken apart.

38 I7 SAN FRANCISCO

EARTHQUAKE 1906
LOCATION: California, US
NOTES: See pp.36–37.

39 L8 BAY CITY

TROPICAL CYCLONE 1909
LOCATION: Texas, US
NOTES: The storm pummelled towns and cities along the Texas coast, including Galveston, Velasco, and Bay City. A total of 41 lives were lost.

40 M8 WARRINGTON

TROPICAL CYCLONE 1909
LOCATION: Florida, US
NOTES: The town was wrecked as the storm raged across four southern states. New Orleans was deluged as dykes at the mouth of the Mississippi River gave way. Around 350 people were killed and damage was estimated at $5 million.

41 I6 WELLINGTON

AVALANCHE 1910
LOCATION: Cascade Mountains, US
NOTES: Tons of snow hurtled down the mountains, engulfing the town's railway station and sweeping three passenger trains into a 150-ft (45-m) gorge. The avalanche, known as the "Wellington Snowslide", killed 100 people and is the worst in US history.

42 F4 KATMAI

VOLCANO 1912
LOCATION: Alaska, US
NOTES: The major eruption produced a loud explosion that was heard 930 miles (1,500 km) away. Further explosions produced an ash cloud so dense that much of Alaska was as dark as night for up to 60 hours. A layer of pumice thick enough to walk on clogged the sea.

43 M7 DAYTON

FLOOD 1913
LOCATION: Ohio, US
NOTES: Prolonged rains caused severe flooding across three states. Many cities and towns were inundated, including Dayton, which was submerged beneath 13 ft (4 m) of water. More than 500 people died and hundreds more were missing. Damage exceeded $47 million.

44 L8 GALVESTON

TROPICAL CYCLONE 1915
LOCATION: Texas, US
NOTES: A new stormwall erected after the disastrous Galveston Hurricane of 1900 was breached by 6-m (20-ft) high waves in the course of the storm. Damage to the city was in excess of $50 million, and 275 residents died, many of whom had ignored storm warnings.

45 M6 MATHESON

FIRE 1916
LOCATION: Northern Ontario, Canada
NOTES: The town of Matheson and 184 of its inhabitants were consumed by a massive forest fire.

46 N7 NEW YORK CITY

DISEASE (POLIO) 1916
LOCATION: New York, US
NOTES: In New York City, 9,000 people, mostly children, contracted polio in the 1916 outbreak, and 2,500 of them died. Throughout the eastern and midwestern US, 27,000 people contracted the disease, 6,000 of whom died.

47 L6 CLOQUET

FIRE 1918
LOCATION: Minnesota, US
NOTES: Following an exceptionally dry summer, vast tracts of brush burst into flames, engulfing 26 towns and villages. More than 800 people lost their lives in the conflagrations, and the damage was estimated at $175 million.

48 K8 CORPUS CHRISTI

TROPICAL CYCLONE 1919
LOCATION: Texas, US
NOTES: The town was so badly damaged by the force of the storm that it took several days to recover the bodies of the 284 victims. The liner, Valbanera, and its 488 passengers and crew, disappeared in the Florida straits.

49 K7 PUEBLO

STORM (FLASH FLOOD) 1921
LOCATION: Colorado, US
NOTES: Heavy rain caused the Arkansas River to burst its banks and swamp the town and surrounding area. Many people were caught unawares by the sudden flood, and 120 were drowned.

50 K8 SAN ANTONIO

FLOOD 1921
LOCATION: Texas, US
NOTES: During what is claimed by Texans to be the largest single rainfall in US history, 51 people were drowned when nine streams overflowed and the city of San Antonio was deluged in minutes.

51 I7 BERKELEY

FIRE 1923
LOCATION: California, US
NOTES: A grassfire on the outskirts of Berkeley was turned into an inferno by high winds. Much of the city was razed to the ground and at least 24 people perished in their homes. Volunteers fought the blaze with buckets of water because the local water company had not provided enough hydrants to fight such a huge fire.

52 M7 FLORENCE

TORNADOES 1924
LOCATION: South Carolina, US
NOTES: The town was devastated by ferocious winds when a series of 22 tornadoes spun across seven states, causing widespread damage and the deaths of 115 people.

53 L7 ANNAPOLIS

TRI-STATE TORNADO 1925
LOCATION: Missouri, US
NOTES: See pp.58–59.

54 N7 LAKE DENMARK

STORM (LIGHTNING) 1926
LOCATION: Near Dover, New Jersey, US
NOTES: Towns and villages around a US naval ammunition dump were blown up when lightning struck the dump during a violent storm. Shells and bullets rained down, killing thirty people and seriously injuring a further 400.

55 M8 MIAMI

TROPICAL CYCLONE 1926
LOCATION: Florida, US
NOTES: Miami, built up a year earlier in a land boom, was almost wiped out in one of the century's most destructive storms. In Miami alone, 115 people died and damage was estimated at $76 million. Across the state, the final death toll was 450, and damage exceeded $100 million.

56 L7 CAIRO

FLOOD (MISSISSIPPI RIVER) 1927
LOCATION: Illinois, US
NOTES: In the river's greatest flood to that date, many of the banks and levees broke, leaving around 17 million acres (7 million hectares) of farmland under water. Around 300 people were drowned, and damage of an incredible $300 million was incurred.

57 L7 POPLAR BLUFF

TORNADOES 1927
LOCATION: Missouri, US
NOTES: The town was decimated and 92 people were killed when a series of 36 tornadoes wreaked havoc across six states. In all, 142 lives were lost and damage was estimated at $8 million.

58 M8 LAKE OKEECHOBEE

TROPICAL CYCLONE 1928
LOCATION: Florida, US
NOTES: The storm devastated the state of Florida and the entire US Atlantic coast. The mud dykes around the lake were flattened and more than 2,500 people died in the ensuing floods.

59 P6 BURIN

TSUNAMI 1929
LOCATION: Burin Peninsula, Canada
NOTES: The tsunami, the result of a large earthquake, drowned 27 people when it smashed across the peninsula.

60 M8 MARION

TORNADOES 1932
LOCATION: Alabama, US
NOTES: A dozen or so tornadoes whipped along the "tornado belt" and left seven states in utter chaos. Marion was the first town to be hit. More than 8,000 people were left homeless and 268 people died.

61 I7 LONG BEACH

EARTHQUAKE 1933
LOCATION: California, US
NOTES: Poorly constructed buildings collapsed in the moderate 6.3-magnitude earthquake, causing widespread panic and 120 deaths.

62 I7 GLENDALE

STORM (FLASH FLOOD) 1934
LOCATION: California, US
NOTES: Heavy rains caused the Verdugo Creek to overflow into La Canada valley. The flash flood carried rocks, mud, and debris through the town, wrecking 500 homes and killing 40 people.

63 K7 DODGE CITY

DROUGHT ("DUST BOWL") 1935
LOCATION: Kansas, US
NOTES: See p.81.

64 M8 MATECUMBE KEY

LABOUR DAY HURRICANE 1935
LOCATION: Florida Keys, US
NOTES: The entire area was devastated, and the road- and rail-link, built across the Florida Keys 30 years earlier, was destroyed. More than 400 people were killed, including 121 army workers who were in the process of building a new government road.

65 P5 ISLAND OF NEWFOUNDLAND

TROPICAL CYCLONE 1935
LOCATION: Canada
NOTES: The savage storm, which had hit the West Indies seven days earlier, killed scores of people on Newfoundland and virtually wiped out whole fishing fleets in harbors across the island.

66 L7 TUPELO

TORNADO 1936
LOCATION: Mississippi, US
NOTES: The tornado cut a swathe 1,300 ft (400 m) wide through a residential section of Tupelo, killing 216 people and injuring 700.

67 N7 LONG ISLAND

TROPICAL CYCLONE 1938
LOCATION: New York State, US
NOTES: Long Island was torn apart, with 14,000 homes being destroyed. Around 500 people were killed and 100 more were missing. Damage, estimated at $400 million, was incurred along the length of the US Eastern Seaboard.

68 I5 COURTENAY

EARTHQUAKE 1946
LOCATION: Vancouver Island, Canada
NOTES: The 7.3-magnitude earthquake, which was felt as far away as Oregon, caused major damage across the island. A small boat capsized in the resulting tsunami, killing its occupant.

69 E5 UNIMAK ISLAND

EARTHQUAKE/TSUNAMI 1946
LOCATION: Aleutian Islands, Alaska, US
NOTES: The earthquake, which occurred in the northern Pacific, smashed the island, destroying its lighthouse and killing its five operators. The ensuing Pacific-wide tsunami submerged the city of Hilo in the Hawaiian Islands, killing 165 people.

70 K7 WOODWARD

TORNADO 1947
LOCATION: Oklahoma, US
NOTES: The tornado ripped through the centre of the town, reducing it to a ruin and killing 95 of its residents. Damage was estimated at more than $6 million.

71 I5 VANCOUVER

FLOOD 1948
LOCATION: British Columbia, Canada
NOTES: The Columbia river, swollen by spring thaws, caused severe flooding across the state. Washington and Oregon in the US were also swamped, and at least 15 people were killed.

72 M6 FLINT

TORNADOES 1953
LOCATION: Michigan, US
NOTES: Eight tornadoes cut a swathe through Ohio and Michigan. In Flint alone, 116 people died, 867 were injured, and damage exceeded $19 million.

73 N6 WORCESTER
TORNADO 1953
LOCATION: Massachusetts, US
NOTES: In Worcester alone, the tornado killed 62 people and injured a further 738. It was the worst tornado ever to strike a New England state and caused the highest amount of tornado damage ever recorded in the US – $52 million.

74 N7 NEWPORT
HURRICANE CAROL 1954
LOCATION: Rhode Island, US
NOTES: Across ten states Carol caused damage estimated at $461 million, which broke all previous records. Newport was hardest hit, and more than 200 homes being demolished. In all, 60 people died and a further thousand were injured.

75 M6 TORONTO
HURRICANE HAZEL 1954
LOCATION: Canada
NOTES: Originating in the Atlantic Ocean, Hurricane Hazel raged through the US and on into Canada, where it killed 56 people in Toronto. One of the most durable hurricanes ever, Hazel took a total of 411 lives and caused damage of a staggering $1 billion.

76 N6 PUTNAM
HURRICANES CONNIE AND DIANE 1955
LOCATION: Connecticut, US
NOTES: Following in the wake of Connie, the more powerful Hurricane Diane wrecked the town's magnesium plant. Barrels of burning magnesium floated along the flooded streets, exploding periodically, and shooting white-hot metal into the air. Six eastern states were declared disaster areas before the hurricanes finally dissipated. Damage exceeded $1.5 billion, and 310 people lost their lives.

77 L8 CAMERON
HURRICANE AUDREY 1957
LOCATION: Louisiana, US
NOTES: Hurricane Audrey destroyed the town and wreaked havoc along the Louisiana coast. The high death toll of 534 was due to many people ignoring US Weather Service warnings because Audrey was two months ahead of the hurricane season.

78 N7 ALLENTOWN
STORM (BLIZZARD) 1958
LOCATION: Pennsylvania, US
NOTES: The entire Northeast was affected by the worst snowfall in US history. Damage exceeded $500 million, and more than 500 people were killed.

79 F3 ANCHORAGE
EARTHQUAKE 1964
LOCATION: Prince William Sound, Alaska
NOTES: The 8.6-magnitude earthquake, the worst in US history, killed 118 people and caused damage estimated at $500 million. Tremors were felt as far south as California, where a 13-ft (4-m) tsunami hit Crescent City, killing six people.

80 M7 INDIANAPOLIS
TORNADOES 1965
LOCATION: Indiana, US
NOTES: A cluster of 37 tornadoes struck the Midwest on a single day. In nine hours, 271 people died, and damage was estimated at $300 million.

81 H4 SKEENA MOUNTAINS
AVALANCHE 1965
LOCATION: British Columbia, Canada
NOTES: The Leduc Camp copper mine was wrecked when tons of snow hurtled down Granduc Mountain, killing 27 of the mine's 154 workers.

82 L8 GULFPORT
HURRICANE CAMILLE 1969
LOCATION: Mississippi, US
NOTES: Hurricane Camille decimated the states of Mississippi and Louisiana, killing almost 300 people and making thousands more homeless.

83 I7 LOS ANGELES
LANDSLIDES 1969
LOCATION: California, US
NOTES: A subtropical storm blowing in from Hawaii brought heavy rains that persisted for nine days and caused massive landslides. Hundreds of homes on the hillsides around the city were destroyed and 95 people were killed.

84 K6 RAPID CITY
STORM (FLASH FLOOD) 1972
LOCATION: South Dakota, US
NOTES: Flash floods caused by heavy rains wrecked 1,200 homes, and killed 236 people. Damage was estimated at $100 million. The city was declared a disaster area.

85 N7 WILMINGTON
HURRICANE AGNES 1972
LOCATION: Delaware, US
NOTES: The hurricane swept across seven states, killing more than 100 people and leaving 200,000 homeless. Damage was in excess of $100 million.

86 K7 BIG THOMPSON RIVER
FLOOD 1976
LOCATION: Colorado, US
NOTES: See pp.56–57.

87 M7 JOHNSTOWN
FLOOD 1977
LOCATION: Pennsylvania, US
NOTES: Despite extensive preventive measures following a major flood in 1889, several small dams upriver burst, flooding the town. Damage was in the region of $200 million, and 80 people were killed.

88 F9 MAUNA LOA
VOLCANO 1984
LOCATION: Hawaii
NOTES: The eruption of the largest and most active volcano on Earth spewed lava to within 4 miles (6 km) of Hilo.

89 I6 MOUNT ST. HELENS
VOLCANO 1980
LOCATION: Cascade Mountains, US
NOTES: See pp.18–19.

90 K8 SARAGOSA
TORNADO 1987
LOCATION: Texas, US
NOTES: The triple-funnelled tornado, which cut through the centre of the town, destroyed more than 100 homes, killed 31 people, and injured 121 more.

91 J6 YELLOWSTONE
FIRE 1988
LOCATION: Wyoming, US
NOTES: In a programme of controlled burning, fires started by lightning were left to burn themselves out. But a dry winter followed by the driest summer since the 1930s meant that control was soon lost. By the autumn, more than 1.5 million acres (610,000 hectares) of forest had been consumed by the fire, which continued to burn until the September snows arrived.

92 I7 SAN FRANCISCO
EARTHQUAKE 1989
LOCATION: California, US
NOTES: Damage to buildings was limited, but the 6.9-magnitude quake collapsed the upper deck of the freeway, crushing drivers on the lower deck. In all, there were 275 deaths and 3,757 injuries.

93 N6 MONTREAL
SPACE THREAT (GEOMAGNETIC STORM) 1989
LOCATION: Quebec Province, Canada
NOTES: A massive solar storm plunged six million people into darkness for nine hours when hot, electrically charged gas from the Sun ploughed into the Earth, shutting down Quebec's power grid.

94 F9 KILAUEA
VOLCANO 1991
LOCATION: Hawaii
NOTES: Lava from an eruption, ongoing since 1983, invaded the southern coastal area, burying 8 miles (13 km) of road, 181 homes, and a visitor center.

95 M8 CORAL GABLES
HURRICANE ANDREW 1992
LOCATION: Florida, US
NOTES: See pp.64–67.

96 N7 NEW YORK CITY
"STORM OF THE CENTURY" 1993
LOCATION: New York, US
NOTES: See pp.72–73.

97 L7 ST. LOUIS
FLOOD 1993
LOCATION: Missouri, US
NOTES: See pp.90–91.

98 I7 NORTHRIDGE
EARTHQUAKE 1994
LOCATION: Los Angeles, California, US
NOTES: The 6.8-magnitude earthquake was the most expensive in US history because it was the first to occur directly under a metropolitan area. Nine raised highways and around 11,000 buildings were destroyed in just 30 seconds. The quake also killed around 60 people and caused the surrounding mountains to rise by one foot (30 cm).

99 K7 DENVER
STORM 1997
LOCATION: Colorado, US
NOTES: A state of emergency was declared when a blanket of snow buried the city, bringing it to a standstill and stranding 2,000 people at the new airport, specially designed to overcome blizzards.

100 L8 JARRELL
TORNADO 1997
LOCATION: Texas, US
NOTES: See pp.62–63.

101 N6 MONTREAL
FREEZE (ICE STORM) 1998
LOCATION: Canada
NOTES: Temperatures as low as –4°F (–20°C) splintered trees like matchwood and snapped pylons, leaving the homes of about two million people without electricity. A state of emergency was declared and at least 12,000 troops were deployed to clear up and restore power supplies. The death toll reached 17, and damage was estimated at $1 billion.

102 M8 SANFORD
TORNADOES 1998
LOCATION: Orlando, Florida, US
NOTES: A posse of tornadoes touched down in Florida, killing more than 38 people and injuring 260 others.

CENTRAL AMERICA & THE CARIBBEAN

The map for these listings is on pp.130–131.

1 G5 CHICXULUB
SPACE THREAT 65 MILLION YEARS AGO
LOCATION: Yucatan Peninsula, Mexico
NOTES: See pp.98–99.

2 D5 POPOCATEPÉTL
VOLCANO C. 400 BC
LOCATION: Lake Texcoco, Mexico
NOTES: A major eruption around this time may have created pyroclastic surges and lahars that laid waste to a 44-mile (70-km) wide area.

3 D5 POPOCATEPÉTL
VOLCANO AD 822
LOCATION: Lake Texcoco, Mexico
NOTES: Settlements around the lake were temporarily abandoned, possibly because lahars turned them and surrounding farmland into a muddy wasteland.

4 K4 SAN SALVADOR
DISEASE (EUROPEAN POXES) 1492-1513
LOCATION: Bahamas
NOTES: The native Lucayans were virtually wiped out after Columbus landed and brought disease. The few natives who did not succumb were sent into slavery.

5 D5 TENOCHTITLÁN
DISEASE (SMALLPOX/AMERICAN EPIDEMIC) 1521
LOCATION: (Now Mexico City), Mexico
NOTES: See pp.114–115.

6 M6 PONCE
TROPICAL CYCLONES 1533
LOCATION: Puerto Rico, Antilles
NOTES: Three tropical cyclones hit the Spanish settlement, decimating the sugarcane plantations, and killing 2,000 African slaves working on them.

7 E5 GULF OF MEXICO
TROPICAL CYCLONE 1553
LOCATION: Off Veracruz, Mexico
NOTES: Following the storm, only two Spanish ships from a fleet of 20 reached Havana. Their crews were subsequently killed by the native islanders.

8 I4 OFF HAVANA
TROPICAL CYCLONE 1591
LOCATION: Straits of Florida
NOTES: During a hurricane, the Spanish Grand Fleet lost 12 ships and 500 crew as it carried treasure back to Spain.

9 G7 LÉON
EARTHQUAKE 1609
LOCATION: Nicaragua
NOTES: There was great loss of life when the old capital was demolished by the earthquake. The subsequent eruption of the Momotombo volcano engulfed what remained of the city in lava.

10 L5 OFF HISPANIOLA
TROPICAL CYCLONE 1643
LOCATION: West Indies
NOTES: The flagship of the Spanish Silver Fleet sank during the violent storm, with the loss of 324 lives.

11 O6 BASSETERRE
TROPICAL CYCLONE 1650
LOCATION: St. Kitts-Nevis, Lesser Antilles
NOTES: Thousands of lives were lost when the storm devastated Basseterre and sank 28 ships in coastal waters.

12 O6 POINTE À PITRE
TROPICAL CYCLONE 1666
LOCATION: Guadeloupe, Lesser Antilles
NOTES: The storm, which also raged across Martinique and St. Kitts-Nevis, killed thousands of people, including 2,000 sailors who drowned when a fleet of 17 ships was sunk.

13 O7 CUL-DE-SAC DU MARIN BAY
TROPICAL CYCLONE 1680
LOCATION: Martinique, Lesser Antilles
NOTES: Thousands of people lost their lives when the storm decimated the island and sank 22 ships in the bay.

14 M6 SANTO DOMINGO
TROPICAL CYCLONE 1680
LOCATION: Dominican Republic, Antilles
NOTES: The entire Dominican Republic was devastated by the massive storm, and thousands of people died, including all hands on the 25 French ships that sank in Santo Domingo's harbor.

15 O6 ST. EUSTATIUS
EARTHQUAKE 1690
LOCATION: Lesser Antilles
NOTES: Hundreds of people were killed when the town of St. Eustatius was torn apart and thrown into the sea by the force of this powerful earthquake.

16 J6 PORT ROYAL
EARTHQUAKE/TSUNAMI 1692
LOCATION: Jamaica, West Indies
NOTES: Around 2,000 people died when huge fissures swallowed up most of the town, which was built on gravel and sand. The ensuing tsunami washed the few remaining buildings into the sea.

17 P7 CARLISLE BAY
TROPICAL CYCLONE 1694
LOCATION: Barbados, Lesser Antilles
NOTES: The storm tore across Barbados, sinking 26 British ships at anchor in the bay and killing 3,000 people.

18 O7 FORT DE FRANCE
TROPICAL CYCLONE 1695
LOCATION: Martinique, Lesser Antilles
NOTES: The capital of Martinique was decimated by the storm, and several hundred people were killed. A dozen French ships were wrecked off the west coast with great loss of life.

19 I4 HAVANA
TROPICAL CYCLONE 1705
LOCATION: Cuba
NOTES: The cyclone tore the city apart, killing hundreds of people, including the crews of four Spanish warships that foundered in the harbor.

20 O7 LA SOUFRIÈRE
VOLCANO 1718
LOCATION: St. Vincent Island, West Indies
NOTES: Hundreds of people died in the the volcano's first recorded eruption. The entire surrounding area was buried beneath a sea of ash.

21 J6 PORT ROYAL
TROPICAL CYCLONE 1722
LOCATION: Jamaica, West Indies
NOTES: Around 400 people were killed when the ferocious storm blew Port Royal apart and capsized 26 merchant vessels at anchor in the harbour.

22 O7 FORT DE FRANCE
EARTHQUAKE 1767
LOCATION: Martinique, Lesser Antilles
NOTES: In 1658, rather than surrender to the French, the native Caribs committed mass suicide, vowing that Mont Pelée volcano would avenge them, which it did some 250 years later. In the meantime, the island was struck by numerous large earthquakes, including this one in 1767, which killed 16,000 people and badly damaged Fort de France.

23 F7 ANTIGUA GUATEMALA
EARTHQUAKE 1773
LOCATION: Guatemala
NOTES: The old capital at the foot of the Acatenango, Feugo, and Agua volcanoes was relocated and renamed Guatemala City following this earthquake, which caused widespread devastation.

24 P7 BRIDGETOWN
TROPICAL CYCLONE 1780
LOCATION: Barbados, Lesser Antilles
NOTES: The "Great Hurricane" flattened every building on the island and wrecked the British fleet in nearby St. Lucia before it hit Martinique, wiping out 20 towns. It also hit St. Vincent, St. Eustatius, and Puerto Rico before finally dissipating. A total of 20,000 lives were lost.

25 O7 ROSEAU
TROPICAL CYCLONE 1806
LOCATION: Dominica, Leeward Islands
NOTES: The storm killed more than 100 people when it caused the Roseau River to overflow. The town disappeared under several metres of mud and sand.

26 M6 SANTO DOMINGO
DISEASE (YELLOW FEVER) 1806
LOCATION: Martinique, Lesser Antilles
NOTES: Of the 33,000 French soldiers sent to the city to suppress a rebellion, almost 95 percent died of yellow fever within months. Following this catastrophic loss, Napoleon curbed his ambitions in the New World and sold Louisiana Territory to the United States.

27 O7 LA SOUFRIÈRE
VOLCANO 1812
LOCATION: St. Vincent Island, West Indies
NOTES: A pall of smoke left the island in darkness for three days, and the ground was covered by several feet of ash. Vast rivers of lava ran down the side of the mountain, engulfing scores of villages and killing thousands of people.

28 N6 CAYEY
SANTA ANA HURRICANE 1825
LOCATION: Puerto Rico, Antilles
NOTES: One of the worst hurricanes in the island's history, Santa Ana destroyed 7,000 homes, killed 374 people, and injured a further 1,210.

29 P7 BRIDGETOWN
TROPICAL CYCLONE 1831
LOCATION: Barbados, Lesser Antilles
NOTES: The storm, one of the fiercest of the 19th century, caused widespread devastation in Barbados before it swept through the entire West Indies and on to Louisiana. It claimed 1,500 lives, and damage was estimated at $7.5 million.

30 M6 SANTO DOMINGO
TROPICAL CYCLONE 1834
LOCATION: Dominican Republic, Antilles
NOTES: The storm swept in from the island of Dominica and badly damaged Santo Domingo. Forests and crops along the Ozama River were laid waste, and thousands of people were killed.

31 G7 COSEGÜINA
VOLCANO 1835
LOCATION: Nicaragua
NOTES: The top of the mountain blew up and 300 people living below were killed by falling rocks and blasts of intense heat. The eruption was heard 800 miles (1,290 km) away by the superintendent of Belize, who mobilized his army in the belief that an invasion was under way.

32 N6 ST. THOMAS
TROPICAL CYCLONE/EARTHQUAKE 1837
LOCATION: Virgin Islands, Lesser Antilles
NOTES: The earthquake followed the vicious storm, destroying what little was left of St. Thomas. Every ship in the bay was sunk, at least 500 people died, and a further 2,000 were injured.

33 H8 CARTAGO
EARTHQUAKE 1841
LOCATION: Costa Rica
NOTES: Around 4,000 people died and more than 4,000 buildings, including all 600 of the city's government offices, were ruined by the quake. Aftershocks occurred for nearly two years afterward.

34 D3 MATAMOROS
TROPICAL CYCLONE 1844
LOCATION: Mexico
NOTES: The storm rampaged through the Rio Grande area, claiming 70 lives and leaving only the church and two other buildings standing in the town.

35 E6 OAXACA
EARTHQUAKE 1870
LOCATION: Mexico
NOTES: Half of the city was left in ruins, and more than 100 lives were lost, when the earthquake struck Oaxaca. Minor tremors were felt for the next 24 hours.

36 G7 SAN SALVADOR
EARTHQUAKE 1878
LOCATION: El Salvador
NOTES: The earthquake killed thousands of people and left San Salvador a ruin, along with Guadeloupe, Incuapa, and Santiago de Marie. Many villages around Incuapa disappeared entirely.

37 O7 LE ROBERT
TROPICAL CYCLONE 1881
LOCATION: Martinique, Lesser Antilles
NOTES: The storm lasted for only four hours, but killed more than 700 people on the island of Martinique and caused damage of $10 million.

38 N6 HUMACAO
SAN CIRIACO HURRICANE 1885
LOCATION: Puerto Rico, Antilles
NOTES: More than 3,000 people were killed when the hurricane raged over the island of Puerto Rico, decimating its coffee crop and hurling huge waves over the port at Humacao.

39 G7 LÉON
EARTHQUAKE 1885
LOCATION: Mexico
NOTES: The city, which was relocated following a catastrophic earthquake in 1609, was hit by a 7.5-magnitude tremor that caused great loss of life.

40 F7 GUATEMALA CITY
EARTHQUAKE/VOLCANO 1902
LOCATION: Guatemala
NOTES: The earthquake badly damaged the city and destroyed 18 other towns. Then the Santa Ana volcano spewed lava over the already decimated area. More than 12,000 people were killed and 80,000 were made homeless.

41 O7 LA SOUFRIÈRE
VOLCANO 1902
LOCATION: St. Vincent Island, West Indies
NOTES: The native Caribs were so transfixed by the clouds of ash and steam belching from the volcano that they made no attempt to escape. Rivers of lava surrounded several villages, trapping the natives and burning them alive. A total of 3,000 people died.

42 O7 MONT PELÉE
VOLCANO 1902
LOCATION: Martinique, Lesser Antilles
NOTES: See pp.22–23.

43 F7 TACANA
VOLCANO 1902
LOCATION: Retalhuleu, Guatemala
NOTES: Around 1,000 people were killed when Tacana was engulfed by lava and ash. Floating pumice clogged the bay of Champanico.

44 J6 KINGSTON
EARTHQUAKE 1907
LOCATION: Jamaica, West Indies
NOTES: A power station was destroyed and scores of live electricity cables hung down over the streets, causing fires and electrocuting people as they fled. More than 1,400 people lost their lives.

45 D3 MENDEZ
TROPICAL CYCLONE 1909
LOCATION: Mexico
NOTES: Beginning in the Windward Islands, the cyclone went on to devastate Puerto Rico, Haiti, and Cuba before surging across the northeastern provinces of Mexico, where it created flash floods and caused 1,500 deaths.

46 J6 BLACK RIVER
TROPICAL CYCLONE 1912
LOCATION: Jamaica, West Indies
NOTES: The storm swept massive tidal waves over the island, destroying Black River and causing 100 deaths, before it dissipated over eastern Cuba.

47 G7 BOQUERON
VOLCANO 1917
LOCATION: San Salvador, El Salvador
NOTES: The volcano's cone exploded, showering Boqueron with ash and engulfing it in molten lava. A torrent of scalding water from the lake inside the crater blew out, flooding a further 15 towns and leaving a total of 100,000 people homeless and 450 dead.

48 I4 HAVANA
TROPICAL CYCLONE 1926
LOCATION: Cuba
NOTES: The storm tore through Cuba, killing 650 people and leaving 10,000 more destitute. In Havana, 325 buildings were demolished in an hour.

49 O6 PORT-LOUIS
TROPICAL CYCLONE 1928
LOCATION: Guadeloupe, Lesser Antilles
NOTES: The storm ripped across the island, killing more than 600 people, before going on to ravage Puerto Rico, where it killed a further 300 people.

50 G6 BELIZE
TROPICAL CYCLONE 1931
LOCATION: British Honduras (now Belize)
NOTES: The storm passed across the Caribbean from Barbados. It hit Belize with such force that, within ten minutes, the city had been smashed by howling winds and then swamped by a huge wave. Around 1,500 lives were lost.

51 N6 CEIBA
SAN CIPRIAN HURRICANE 1932
LOCATION: Puerto Rico, Greater Antilles
NOTES: The hurricane killed 225 people throughout the island, injured a further 3,000, and destroyed 75,000 homes.

52 J5 SANTA CRUZ DEL SUR
TROPICAL CYCLONE 1932
LOCATION: Cuba
NOTES: The city was ruined, and 2,500 of the 4,000 inhabitants were killed, most of whom drowned in a massive wave that swept inland.

53 D4 TAMPICO
TROPICAL CYCLONE 1933
LOCATION: Mexico
NOTES: The second tropical cyclone to hit Tampico within ten days caused massive damage and widespread flooding. The exact death toll is uncertain because thousands of immigrants had come to the city to seek work; but it is thought that hundreds died.

54 G7 LEMPA RIVER
TROPICAL CYCLONE 1934
LOCATION: El Salvador
NOTES: The storm unleashed torrential rainfall that caused the river to flood. Many ships on the estuary were sunk and around 2,000 people were killed.

55 K6 JÉRÉMIE
FLOOD 1935
LOCATION: Haiti, Greater Antilles
NOTES: Around 2,000 people drowned, many of whom were swept out to sea, when the Roseau, Voldrogue, and Great Anse Rivers burst their banks, causing widespread flooding.

56 I4 HAVANA
TROPICAL CYCLONE 1944
LOCATION: Cuba
NOTES: Hundreds of Havana's buildings were ruined and 300 people were killed by the storm. Despite wartime shortages, every shop on the city's boulevard was reopened to tourists within 12 hours.

57 J6 PORT ROYAL
HURRICANE CHARLIE 1951
LOCATION: Jamaica, West Indies
NOTES: The hurricane swept in from the Antilles, sinking dozens of ships in the port and smashing every wooden structure to splinters. It raged across the island killing 154 people, injuring 2,000, and leaving 50,000 homeless.

58 C2 PIEDRAS NEGRAS
FLOODS 1954
LOCATION: Border of Mexico/Texas, US
NOTES: Heavy rains caused the Pecos and Devil's Rivers to swell, and the Rio Grande to burst its banks. The resulting floods drowned 185 people.

59 D4 TAMPICO
HURRICANE HILDA 1955
LOCATION: Mexico
NOTES: Hilda pounded Tampico and left 200 people dead. The Panuco River was at its highest level for thirty years and half of the city was underwater.

60 D4 TAMPICO
HURRICANE JANET 1955
LOCATION: Mexico
NOTES: The second major hurricane in a month destroyed what was left of the city. This ferocious storm killed 300 people and left 60,000 homeless.

61 O8 GRENVILLE
TROPICAL CYCLONE 1956
LOCATION: Grenada, Lesser Antilles
NOTES: In the course of the storm, more than 40,000 homes were wrecked and 230 lives were lost. The island's coconut and nutmeg plantations were decimated.

62 D5 MEXICO CITY
EARTHQUAKE 1957
LOCATION: Mexico
NOTES: The earthquake claimed the lives of 70 people and affected an area that stretched from Mexico City to Acapulco.

63 E6 MINATITLÁN
LANDSLIDES 1959
LOCATION: Mexico
NOTES: The landslides, caused by heavy rains, devastated dozens of towns along the Pacific coast and killed more than 5,000 people. In Minatitlán, 200 people died after being bitten by scorpions, snakes, and spiders that were dislodged from their nests in the hills.

64 N6 SAN JUAN
HURRICANE DONNA 1960
LOCATION: Puerto Rico, Greater Antilles
NOTES: The hurricane caused severe flooding across Puerto Rico. More than 100 people died and 600 were injured.

65 G6 BELIZE
HURRICANE HATTIE 1961
LOCATION: British Honduras (now Belize)
NOTES: Almost half of the city's buildings were destroyed and another third were badly damaged. Around 300 people died, but the death toll was greatly reduced by a warning system that was set up after a hurricane had destroyed the city of Belize thirty years earlier.

66 K5 HOLGUIN
HURRICANE FLORA 1963
LOCATION: Cuba
NOTES: The hurricane blew in from Tobago, wrecking Haiti before hurling itself at Cuba. Cuba's sugar crop was wiped out and 1,000 people died.

67 L5 GONAÏVES
HURRICANE CLEO 1964
LOCATION: Haiti, Greater Antilles
NOTES: For four days 100-mph (160-kph) winds whipped up massive storm waves that battered Haiti's coastline and killed more than a hundred people.

68 L6 JACMEL
HURRICANE INEZ 1966
LOCATION: Haiti, Greater Antilles
NOTES: Inez lashed the Caribbean for five days. Guadeloupe, the Dominican Republic, and Cuba were smashed, but hardest hit was Haiti, where there were 1,000 deaths in Jacmel alone. At least 1,100 more bodies piled up in a deep gorge, which became known as "the valley of death".

69 H8 MANAGUA
EARTHQUAKE 1972
LOCATION: Nicaragua
NOTES: The worst earthquake in the country's history caused the deaths of 7,000 of Managua's inhabitants and left 200,000 more homeless.

70 D5 MEXICO CITY
STORM 1972
LOCATION: Mexico
NOTES: Violent thunderstorms caused the San Buenaventura River to burst its banks and flood the city of eight million people. Strong winds, a mudslide, and a hailstorm brought the death toll to 37.

71 D5 CIUDAD SERDAN
EARTHQUAKE 1973
LOCATION: Mexico
NOTES: The powerful earthquake, which followed severe rains and flooding, decimated dozens of towns and villages in the Sierra Madre mountains. At least 700 people died and tens of thousands were left destitute.

72 G7 TEGUCIGALPA
HURRICANE FIFI 1974
LOCATION: Honduras
NOTES: Honduras was ravaged and around 5,000 people died when torrential rains produced a massive surge of water that triggered lethal lahars.

73 F7 GUATEMALA CITY
EARTHQUAKE 1976
LOCATION: Guatemala
NOTES: The 5.7-magnitude earthquake killed around 23,000 people and made a further 435,000 homeless.

74 O7 ROSEAU
HURRICANE DAVID 1979
LOCATION: Dominica, Lesser Antilles
NOTES: Hurricane David wiped out the island's entire banana crop, causing an economic disaster. More than 1,000 people were killed by the fierce storm and 60,000 were left homeless.

75 F6 EL CHICHON
VOLCANO 1982
LOCATION: Pichucalco, Mexico
NOTES: This volcano, not thought to pose a significant threat, killed at least 3,000 people when it erupted.

76 D5 MEXICO CITY
EARTHQUAKE 1985
LOCATION: Mexico
NOTES: See pp.32–33.

77 J6 KINGSTON
HURRICANE GILBERT 1988
LOCATION: Jamaica, West Indies
NOTES: Hurricane Gilbert raged across Jamaica for eight hours, badly damaging much of the island, including its airport.

78 H8 SAN JOSÉ
EARTHQUAKE 1991
LOCATION: Costa Rica
NOTES: The 7.5-magnitude earthquake severely damaged San Jose and claimed the lives of 80 people.

79 D6 ACAPULCO
HURRICANE PAULINE 1997
LOCATION: Mexico
NOTES: The hurricane, with winds of up to 120 mph (190 kph), wreaked havoc on Acapulco and caused severe floods across southwest Mexico. More than 400 people were killed, many of whom were buried in thick mud and debris.

80 O6 SOUFRIÈRE HILLS
VOLCANO 1997
LOCATION: Montserrat, Lesser Antilles
NOTES: A series of eruptions engulfed Plymouth, Montserrat's capital, and left two-thirds of the island uninhabitable. The eruptions killed 23 people and forced a further 8,000 to leave the island.

SOUTH AMERICA

The map for these listings is on p.132.

1 D3 LIMA
DISEASE 1526
LOCATION: Peru
NOTES: Smallpox and a host of other European diseases killed off the Inca king and his heirs, and civil war ensued. In the midst of the turmoil, the Spanish invaded and quickly conquered Peru.

2 D3 LIMA
EARTHQUAKE 1746
LOCATION: Peru
NOTES: The city and nearby Callao were devastated by the violent tremor. From a total of 3,000 homes, only 21 were left standing, and 18,000 lives were lost.

3 D6 CONCEPÇION
EARTHQUAKE/TSUNAMI 1757
LOCATION: Chile
NOTES: The earthquake created a tsunami that swept through the city, killing 5,000 people and injuring a further 10,000.

4 D2 QUITO
EARTHQUAKE 1797
LOCATION: Ecuador
NOTES: Violent tremors altered Ecuador's landscape in seconds. Mountains shifted and rivers changed their course. Almost the entire population of Quito, about 40,000 people, perished.

5 E1 CARACAS
EARTHQUAKE 1812
LOCATION: Venezuela
NOTES: Nine-tenths of the city was ruined and 10,000 residents were killed in one of Venezuela's worst ever quakes. The local barracks disappeared into a huge fissure, wiping out a whole regiment of soldiers. The death toll reached 20,000 through famine and disease.

6 D5 VALPARAISO
EARTHQUAKE 1822
LOCATION: Chile
NOTES: The quake killed 10,000 people in Valparaiso. Scores of other towns and villages were destroyed along the entire western coast, which was tilted up by the quake and left permanently raised.

7 D5 SANTIAGO
EARTHQUAKE/TSUNAMI 1835
LOCATION: Chile
NOTES: According to Charles Darwin, who was in Santiago at the time of the quake, the tsunami "broke into a fearful line of white breakers" 23 ft (7 m) high. About 5,000 people died during the disaster.

8 D2 QUITO
EARTHQUAKE 1859
LOCATION: Ecuador
NOTES: Within six minutes, about 5,000 people had been killed, and most of the city's buildings and historic monuments, including Quito's great cathedral, had been razed to the ground.

9 **D2 IBARRA**
EARTHQUAKE 1868
LOCATION: Ecuador
NOTES: The earthquake was felt over a distance of 1,400 miles (2,250 km), and 25,000 people perished. Ibarra was destroyed and almost all its inhabitants were buried in the rubble. The quake caused major floods, and the nearby town of Cotocachi disappeared under what is now a lake of the same name.

10 **D1 CUCUTA**
EARTHQUAKE/VOLCANO 1875
LOCATION: Colombia
NOTES: Molten lava rained down on Cucuta after the earthquake activated a nearby volcano. All across Colombia, towns and cities were shaken by the 45-second earthquake, and more than 16,000 people were killed.

11 **D6 CONCEPÇION**
TSUNAMI 1877
LOCATION: Chile
NOTES: The 75-ft (23-m) wave surged along the coast, wreaking havoc on the city and killing thousands of people.

12 **D2 COTOPAXI**
VOLCANO 1877
LOCATION: Ecuador
NOTES: More than 1,000 people were killed instantly when the eruption blew the side off the mountain, bombarding the villages in the valleys below with rocks and engulfing them in lava.

13 **D5 SANTIAGO**
EARTHQUAKE 1906
LOCATION: Chile
NOTES: Santiago was devastated and around 20,000 people were killed when the high-magnitude earthquake shook towns and cities along the entire length of Chile. In Valparaiso, 1,500 people were killed and 100,000 more were left homeless by the tremors.

14 **D6 CHILLÁN**
EARTHQUAKE 1939
LOCATION: Chile
NOTES: Within 3 minutes, the massive 8.3-magnitude tremor had killed 25,000 of the city's residents. A further 50,000 people perished in towns and cities all along Chile's western coast.

15 **D3 HUARAZ**
AVALANCHE 1941
LOCATION: Peru
NOTES: The avalanche engulfed Huaraz, which lies in the foothills of the Andes, and around 5,000 people perished.

16 **D2 AMBATO**
EARTHQUAKE 1949
LOCATION: Ecuador
NOTES: Around 6,000 people died and 20,000 were injured in the worst quake in Ecuador's history. At least 53 cities and towns along a 1,500-mile (2,400-km) stretch of the Andes were in ruins.

17 **G2 BELÉM**
DISEASE (OROPOUCHE) 1951
LOCATION: Brazil
NOTES: A flu-like epidemic afflicted 11,000 people in Belém. The virus that was responsible for the outbreak was found by scientists to have come from a sloth that had died a year earlier.

18 **D6 VALDIVIA**
EARTHQUAKES/TSUNAMIS 1960
LOCATION: Chile
NOTES: See pp.40–41.

19 **D3 HUASCARÁN**
LANDSLIDE/AVALANCHE 1962
LOCATION: Peru
NOTES: The glacier on top of the extinct volcano, Huascarán, broke loose, and 20 million tons of ice and rock thundered down the mountainside, annihilating six villages and killing 4,000 people.

20 **F4 PARANA**
DROUGHT/FIRE 1962
LOCATION: Brazil
NOTES: The seven-month-long drought caused a catastrophic fire that killed 250 people, left 300,000 homeless, and destroyed much of Brazil's coffee crop.

21 **G4 RIO DE JANEIRO**
LANDSLIDE 1966
LOCATION: Brazil
NOTES: The removal of trees on Rio de Janeiro's steep mountain slopes caused the soil to give way during heavy rain. The shanty towns built in their place were swept away and 239 people died.

22 **D3 CHIMBOTE**
EARTHQUAKE/LANDSLIDE 1970
LOCATION: Peru
NOTES: See pp.38–39.

23 **D3 LIMA**
AVALANCHE 1971
LOCATION: Peru
NOTES: More than 600 people perished when the city was engulfed in hundreds of tons of snow that slid off the Andes.

24 **F5 TUBARAO**
FLOOD 1974
LOCATION: Brazil
NOTES: The city was deluged when the Tubarao River burst its banks following heavy autumn rains. The death toll reached 200, and around 100,000 people were evacuated to high ground.

25 **D1 NEVADO DEL RUIZ**
VOLCANO 1985
LOCATION: Armero, Colombia
NOTES: See pp.20–21.

26 **D1 MEDELLÍN**
LANDSLIDE 1987
LOCATION: Colombia
NOTES: Medellin, which nestles in a steep valley between two mountain ranges, was buried under tons of rock during the landslide and 683 of its inhabitants were killed.

27 **F6 BUENOS AIRES**
FLOOD 1993
LOCATION: Argentina
NOTES: Almost ten million acres (four million hectares) of Buenos Aires province was inundated by floodwater, and most of the crops were destroyed.

28 **D3 LIMA**
DISEASE (CHOLERA) 1995
LOCATION: Peru
NOTES: The first cholera outbreak in South America for almost 100 years reached Peru from Indonesia, where it had been raging for 30 years. More than 170,000 people were affected, and 1,200 died.

29 **D3 ICA**
FLOOD 1998
LOCATION: Peru
NOTES: More than 100,000 people were evacuated when a river burst its banks, inundating the city. Across the country, flooding and mudslides caused by freak El Niño rains killed at least 137 people, injured 131, and left 234,000 homeless.

AFRICA AND THE MIDDLE EAST

The map for these listings is on p.133.

1 **I2 CANARY ISLANDS**
LANDSLIDES/TSUNAMIS C. 15,000 YEARS AGO
LOCATION: Atlantic Ocean, off Africa
NOTES: Eruptions on the Canary Islands triggered gargantuan landslides, which created tsunamis. The waves damaged African, American and European coasts.

2 **M2 ALEXANDRIA**
DROUGHT/FAMINE 3500 BC
LOCATION: Egypt, Africa
NOTES: Thousands of people starved to death in the earliest recorded famine.

3 **O2 UR (NOW ELAT)**
FLOOD/TROPICAL CYCLONE C. 3100 BC
LOCATION: Mesopotamia (now Iraq)
NOTES: Noah's flood in the Bible may be an account of flooding of the Tigris and Euphrates River floodplains. According to an earlier account by Gilgamesh, the Mesopotamian king, the flood was due to a six-day-long tropical cyclone.

4 **M2 CAIRO**
DROUGHT/FAMINE C. 2200 BC
LOCATION: Egypt, Africa
NOTES: The Nile flooded insufficiently for several years, which caused widespread famine and contributed to the eventual collapse of Egypt's ruling dynasty.

5 **N2 SODOM AND GOMORRAH**
EARTHQUAKE/SPACE THREAT C. 2200 BC
LOCATION: Dead Sea, Israel
NOTES: The ancient cities of Sodom and Gomorrah sank beneath the Dead Sea during the quake which, some scientists believe, was caused by a meteor shower.

6 **N2 LUXOR**
DROUGHT/FAMINE C. 1708 BC
LOCATION: Egypt, Africa
NOTES: Tens of thousands of people are believed to have died in the "seven-year famine", which is described in the Bible.

7 **N2 JERICHO**
EARTHQUAKE C. 1300 BC
LOCATION: Israel
NOTES: According to scientists, seismic waves, not trumpets, brought the walls of Jericho tumbling down, allowing the Israelites to invade and capture the city.

8 **M2 ALEXANDRIA**
EARTHQUAKE 217 BC
LOCATION: Egypt, Africa
NOTES: The earthquake ruined more than 100 cities and up to 75,000 people died.

9 **N1 ANTIOCH (NOW HATAY)**
EARTHQUAKE AD 115
LOCATION: Syria (now Turkey)
NOTES: Antioch was full of people who had come to pay homage to the Roman Emperor, Trajan, when the city was hit by the earthquake. Thousands of people were crushed by toppled buildings, but Trajan managed to escape by crawling through a window.

10 **N1 ALEPPO (NOW HALAB)**
DISEASE (PLAGUE OF GALEN) AD 164–180
LOCATION: Syria
NOTES: Roman troops returning from Syria brought with them an unspecified contagion that raged through the empire for 14 years. Named after the physician who described it, the epidemic killed up to seven million people across Europe.

11 **M2 ALEXANDRIA**
EARTHQUAKE/TSUNAMI AD 365
LOCATION: Egypt, Africa
NOTES: The earthquake destroyed much of Alexandria, including its lighthouse (the fourth wonder of the world), killing more than 50,000 people. The tsunami that the powerful tremors set in motion devastated Crete's coastline.

12 **M2 CAIRO**
DISEASE (LEPROSY) AD 500
LOCATION: Egypt, Africa
NOTES: The earliest evidence of leprosy's existence in the civilized world comes from 1,500-year-old Egyptian skeletons bearing its marks. By AD 500 the disease had probably spread through Europe and beyond.

13 **N1 ANTIOCH (NOW HATAY)**
EARTHQUAKE AD 526
LOCATION: Syria (now Turkey)
NOTES: The earthquake destroyed virtually every building in the city and killed more than 250,000 people.

14 **L4 LAKE CHAD**
DISEASE (SMALLPOX) C. AD 800
LOCATION: Africa
NOTES: Brief epidemics of smallpox hit the lands south of the Sahara Desert around this time. The disease, which struck people of all ages, affected a large percentage of the populations of these lands and caused many deaths.

15 **P1 DAMGHAN**
EARTHQUAKE AD 856
LOCATION: Persia (now Iran)
NOTES: Damghan, which lies at the foot of the Elburz Mountains, was destroyed by the earthquake and 200,000 of its inhabitants were killed.

16 **O1 ARDABIL**
EARTHQUAKE AD 893
LOCATION: Persia (now Iran)
NOTES: Huge tremors devastated the area of northwest Iran bordering the Caspian Sea. Around 150,000 people perished.

17 **O1 TABRIZ**
EARTHQUAKE 1040
LOCATION: Persia (now Iran)
NOTES: The earthquake left the city in ruins, and 50,000 people lost their lives.

18 **M2 CAIRO**
DROUGHT/FAMINE C. 1064–1072
LOCATION: Egypt, Africa
NOTES: Around 4,000 people died of starvation, and cannibalism became rife throughout Egypt, when crops withered because the Nile kept failing to flood.

19 **N1 ALEPPO (NOW HALAB)**
EARTHQUAKE 1138
LOCATION: Syria
NOTES: Much of the city of Aleppo was destroyed by the earthquake and about 230,000 people were killed.

20 M2 CAIRO

DROUGHT/FAMINE 1199–1202
LOCATION: Egypt, Africa
NOTES: Failure of the Nile to flood during a prolonged drought caused widespread crop failure and 100,000 deaths in Egypt's most severe recorded famine.

21 N2 ACRE

EARTHQUAKE 1202
LOCATION: Lebanon
NOTES: Violent tremors, felt over much of the eastern Mediterranean, destroyed the ancient cities of Acre and Tyre and killed more than 100,000 people.

22 O1 TABRIZ

EARTHQUAKE 1727
LOCATION: Persia (now Iran)
NOTES: Tabriz was wrecked by a strong earthquake, and 77,000 people in and around the city lost their lives.

23 N5 ZANZIBAR

TROPICAL CYCLONE 1872
LOCATION: (now part of Tanzania), Africa
NOTES: Around 150 ships in the harbor were sunk and at least 200 of Zanzibar's inhabitants lost their lives. A party of Europeans, who were searching for the British explorer, Dr. David Livingstone, barely survived this storm.

24 P2 FARAHZAD

STORM 1954
LOCATION: Iran
NOTES: Torrential rain sent a flash flood thundering through a deep gorge. The floodwater swept away a shrine, killing 3,000 worshippers.

25 L5 LEOPOLDVILLE (NOW KINSHASA)

DISEASE (AIDS) 1959
LOCATION: Belgian Congo (now DRC)
NOTES: See pp.120–121.

26 J2 AGADIR

EARTHQUAKE/TSUNAMI 1960
LOCATION: Morocco, Africa
NOTES: The earthquake, with a magnitude of only 5.7, destroyed three-quarters of this coastal city. About 12,000 people were killed, many of whom drowned in the violent tsunami that followed.

27 O1 DAN-ISFAHAN

EARTHQUAKE 1962
LOCATION: Northwest Iran
NOTES: The earthquake lasted only one minute, but it affected 13,000 square miles (33,000 square km), ruining 31 villages, and killing 10,000 people. Dan-Isfahan lost one-quarter of its population.

28 N5 NAIROBI

PEST (LOCUSTS) 1962
LOCATION: Kenya, Africa
NOTES: Following a period of warm, damp weather, a plague of locusts swept across Africa, from Sudan in the east to Cape Verde in the west, and decimated much-needed crops.

29 L4 BIAFRA

DROUGHT/FAMINE 1967–1970
LOCATION: (now part of Nigeria), Africa
NOTES: The famine, caused by drought and exacerbated by conflict with Nigeria, affected 8,000,000 people and prevented Biafra from maintaining independence.

30 P2 BIRJAND

EARTHQUAKE 1968
LOCATION: Northeast Iran
NOTES: The 7.0-magnitude quake rocked Khurasan province in northeast Iran, killing almost 12,000 people.

31 K3 GAO, MALI

DROUGHT/FAMINE 1969–1974.
LOCATION: The Sahel, Africa
NOTES: Severe drought, combined with a deteriorating political situation, caused the deaths of more than a million people through starvation or diseases such as tuberculosis and typhoid.

32 L1 TUNIS

STORM 1969
LOCATION: Tunisia, Africa
NOTES: Severe rains lasting for 38 days flooded 80 percent of the country. At least 500 people died and 50,000 homes were destroyed. On the Kairouan Plain, a Roman villa, a valuable archaeological find, was unearthed by the floodwaters.

33 O2 QIR VALLEY

EARTHQUAKE 1972
LOCATION: Iran
NOTES: The quake affected a 250 mile (400-km) wide area, destroying 58 towns and killing more than than 5,000 people.

34 M4 NZARA

DISEASE (EBOLA) 1976
LOCATION: Southern Sudan, Africa
NOTES: A fever epidemic spread to the Ebola River region of Zaire (DRC) and was identified as a deadly new virus, Ebola, which causes internal bleeding. Of the 318 people affected, 280 died.

35 N2 ASWAN

DISEASE (RIFT VALLEY FEVER) 1977
LOCATION: Egypt, Africa
NOTES: After the Aswan dam was built, a virus carried by the *Aedes* mosquito, which began breeding in the still water, infected thousands of people with Rift Valley fever. Hundreds of them died.

36 M5 NYIRAGONGO (NOW DRC)

VOLCANO 1977
LOCATION: Goma, Zaire (now DRC), Africa
NOTES: Lava erupted from fissures on the volcano's flank, draining the lava-lake in less than an hour. Moving at 40 mph (60 kph), it came within 2,000 ft (600 m) of Goma airport, killing around 70 people.

37 P1 DEYHUK

EARTHQUAKE 1978
LOCATION: Northeast Iran
NOTES: The 7.7-magnitude tremor killed 25,000 people in Khurasan province.

38 O6 ANTANANARIVO

DISEASE (MALARIA) 1980s
LOCATION: Central Madagascar, off Africa
NOTES: An outbreak of malaria, in an area that had previously been clear, affected 100,000 people, killing 20,000.

39 M8 LAINGSBURG

STORM 1981
LOCATION: Karoo, South Africa
NOTES: Around 160 people were killed when rainwater swept down a dried-up riverbed. Much of Laingsburg, which was built on the riverbank, was swept away by a vast wall of water.

40 O3 SAN'A'

EARTHQUAKE 1982
LOCATION: Yemen Arab Republic
NOTES: Around 2,800 people were killed, 1,500 were injured, and 700,000 more were made homeless when 300 villages were wrecked by the earthquake.

41 N4 MEK'ELE

DROUGHT/FAMINE 1984–1985.
LOCATION: Ethiopia, Africa
NOTES: See pp.82–83.

42 L4 LAKE NIOS

VOLCANO 1986
LOCATION: Cameroon, Africa
NOTES: Large volumes of carbon dioxide, bubbled to the surface of the crater-lake and flowed down the volcano's flanks, asphyxiating 1,700 people and most of the other animal life in the area.

43 N3 KHARTOUM

FLOOD 1988
LOCATION: Khartoum, Sudan
NOTES: Heavy rains caused the Nile River to break its banks around the city of Khartoum. Thousands of people died in the flood and more than a million more were left homeless.

44 L4 N'DJAMENA

DISEASE (MENINGITIS) 1988
LOCATION: Chad, Africa
NOTES: Despite a massive vaccination campaign, 4,500 cases of meningitis were diagnosed in Chad. Thousands more cases went unrecorded.

45 O1 RASHT

EARTHQUAKE/LANDSLIDES 1990
LOCATION: Northern Iran
NOTES: The country's worst earthquake struck the area around the Caspian Sea, killing 40,000 people, injuring 60,000, and making a further 400,000 destitute. Landslides wiped out many major roads.

46 M7 BULAWAYO

DROUGHT 1992
LOCATION: Zimbabwe, Africa
NOTES: The ENSO-related drought, which followed a year of poor crop production and rainfall, caused food shortages for 30 million people across southern Africa.

47 J3 KAEDI

PEST (LOCUSTS) 1997
LOCATION: Mauritania, Northwest Africa
NOTES: Swarms of desert locusts severely damaged crops in the area, despite pest control operations to contain them in their breeding areas in the Sahel.

48 N5 KISMAAYO

FLOOD 1997
LOCATION: Somalia, Africa
NOTES: More than 1,700 people died, and cattle herds and crops were wiped out, when heavy rains caused the Shabelle and Juba Rivers to overflow. The flood inundated scores of towns and villages.

49 P1 QAYEN

EARTHQUAKE/LANDSLIDES 1997
LOCATION: Northern Iran
NOTES: The 7.1-magnitude tremor, and the landslides that followed it, killed at least 1,560 people and injured 4,460. A further 60,000 people lost their homes.

50 N3 TESENEY

FLOOD 1997
LOCATION: Eritrea
NOTES: Heavy rains swelled the Blue Nile and Atbara Rivers, inundating farmland in Ethiopia and Sudan. More than 80 people were killed, 3,000 were made homeless, and 6,000 cattle were lost.

51 N5 NAIROBI

FLOOD 1998
LOCATION: Kenya, Africa
NOTES: Floods, caused by heavy rains, killed hundreds of people and led to an outbreak of Rift Valley fever in Kenya. The floodwaters also collapsed several bridges and washed away the East Africa highway, which links land-locked Uganda and Rwanda to the coast.

EUROPE

The map for these listings is on pp.134–135.

1 L8 BOSPHORUS

FLOOD C. 7000 BC
LOCATION: Istanbul, Turkey
NOTES: Thaws at the end of the last ice age raised sea levels by 400 ft (120 m), causing a thin strip of land along the Bosphorus to give way. Saltwater from the Mediterranean submerged a vast area of land and a freshwater lake to create what is now the Black Sea.

2 L8 TROY, HELLESPONT

FIRE C. 2200 BC
LOCATION: (now Dardanelles), Turkey
NOTES: Records suggest that the city was devastated and the whole population perished in a vast conflagration, possibly the same meteor shower implicated in the destruction of Sodom and Gomorrah.

3 L9 THIRA (NOW SANTORINI)

VOLCANO 1500 BC
LOCATION: Greece
NOTES: A massive eruption on the island produced tsunamis that some people believe, engulfed the nearby island of Crete and led to the downfall of the Minoan civilization. This catastrophe has been linked with the Atlantis myth, but recent studies dispute the theory.

4 J9 MOUNT ETNA

VOLCANO 1226 BC
LOCATION: Sicily
NOTES: The first recorded eruption of Europe's largest volcano.

5 K9 SPARTA AND LACONIA

EARTHQUAKE 464 BC
LOCATION: Greece
NOTES: A cataclysmic earthquake affected the whole of Greece, destroying Sparta and Laconia. More than 20,000 people lost their lives in the disaster.

6 K9 ATHENS

DISEASE (PLAGUE) 430 BC
LOCATION: Greece
NOTES: The walled city was under siege by the Spartans when a plague (possibly measles or smallpox) broke out, killing one-third of the 200,000 residents and forcing the Athenians to surrender and the Greek civilization to collapse.

7 K9 BURA

EARTHQUAKE 373 BC
LOCATION: Greece
NOTES: Following the earthquake, Bura, once an inland city, could be seen beneath the waters of the Corinthian Gulf. Thousands of people perished.

8 L9 RHODES

EARTHQUAKE 224 BC
LOCATION: Rhodes Island, Greece
NOTES: Following the earthquake, the mighty Colossus, which is thought to have straddled the entrance to Rhodes Harbor, may have crashed into the sea.

9 I7 COL DE LA TRAVERSETTE

AVALANCHES 218 BC
LOCATION: Italian Alps
NOTES: Hannibal and his army triggered a series of huge avalanches in their rush to descend into the warmth of the Italian lowlands. Snow engulfed 18,000 men, 2,000 horses, and several elephants.

10 J8 ROME

DISEASE (*FALCIPARUM*-BORNE MALARIA) AD 79
LOCATION: Italy
NOTES: Malaria spread rapidly across the Roman Empire from Africa to England. Mosquitoes became endemic in Rome's crop-growing area, the Campagna, where the disease remained rife for centuries.

11 J8 VESUVIUS

VOLCANO AD 79
LOCATION: Italy
NOTES: *See pp.26–27.*

12 J8 ROME

DISEASE (PLAGUE) AD 251–266
LOCATION: Italy
NOTES: At its height, the plague, possibly measles or smallpox, was thought to be killing 5,000 people in Rome every day.

13 M9 KOURION

EARTHQUAKE AD 365
LOCATION: Cyprus
NOTES: The city was abandoned after its population was almost entirely wiped out by a series of tremors and a tsunami that ravaged the eastern Mediterranean.

14 L8 CONSTANTINOPLE

DISEASE (JUSTINIAN PLAGUE) AD 542
LOCATION: (Now Istanbul) Turkey
NOTES: A plague epidemic swept through Constantinople, killing around 10,000 people each day. From there it spread across Europe, preventing the Roman Emperor Justinian from reestablishing the Roman Empire in the West. Accounts of the time suggest that this was the first outbreak of bubonic plague in Europe.

15 G6 SALISBURY

SPACE THREAT AD 550
LOCATION: Wiltshire, southern England
NOTES: Huge fires devastated large areas of land at the start of the Dark Ages. It has been suggested that the fires were due to cometary debris exploding over southern England. The famine that followed forced mass emigration across the English Channel to France.

16 K9 CORINTH

EARTHQUAKE AD 856
LOCATION: Greece
NOTES: The earthquake reduced Corinth to ruins and killed about 45,000 people.

17 G5 DURHAM

DROUGHT 1069
LOCATION: England
NOTES: Poor rainfall destroyed crops in the area three years after the Norman conquest. About 50,000 people died and thousands more sold themselves into slavery to survive.

18 H6 LONDON

TORNADO 1091
LOCATION: England
NOTES: The tornado wrecked more than 600 homes and killed two worshippers in the church of St. Mary le Bow.

19 H5 BOSTON

FLOODS (NORTH SEA) 1099
LOCATION: England
NOTES: The floods, which inundated the areas surrounding the Wash in eastern England, caused the deaths of many thousands of people.

20 J9 MOUNT ETNA

VOLCANO/EARTHQUAKE 1169
LOCATION: Sicily
NOTES: The eruption was followed by a violent earthquake. About 15,000 people died, hundreds of whom were praying in the cathedral in Catania.

21 J8 VESUVIUS

VOLCANO 1198
LOCATION: Italy
NOTES: The violent eruption of Vesuvius activated the nearby Solfatara Lake crater.

22 I4 JUTLAND

FLOOD (NORTH SEA) 1219
LOCATION: Northern Denmark
NOTES: Thousands of people were killed when seawater surged over the exposed, low-lying peninsula of Jutland.

23 M9 SILIFKE (NOW IÇEL)

EARTHQUAKE 1268
LOCATION: Asia Minor (now Turkey)
NOTES: The ancient province of Cieilia was devastated by the earthquake and about 60,000 lives were lost.

24 H5 DUNWICH

FLOOD (NORTH SEA) 1287
LOCATION: East Anglia, England
NOTES: About 500 people died when the North Sea flooded much of East Anglia.

25 G5 BELFAST

FREEZE 1315–1317
LOCATION: Ireland
NOTES: Icy winters ruined crops, causing widespread famine in Ireland and across Europe that claimed thousands of lives.

26 M7 KAFFA (NOW FEODOSIYA)

DISEASE (BLACK DEATH) 1346–1352
LOCATION: Crimea
NOTES: *See pp.112–113.*

27 H6 CHARTRES

STORM (HAIL) 1359
LOCATION: France
NOTES: The ferocious storm pounded the army of Edward III with huge hailstones, killing 1,000 soldiers and 6,000 horses.

28 E2 ÖRAEFA JÖKULL

VOLCANO 1362
LOCATION: Iceland
NOTES: The volcano exploded with such force that the ice on its peak thawed, creating flash floods. About 200 people and large herds of livestock were killed, and around 40 farms were swept away.

29 I5 SCHLESWIG

FLOOD (NORTH SEA) 1362
LOCATION: Germany
NOTES: About 30,000 people drowned when seawater overwhelmed the marshy coastal area around Schleswig.

30 H5 DORT

FLOOD (NORTH SEA) 1421
LOCATION: The Netherlands
NOTES: Despite its vast system of dykes, the country suffered one of its worst-ever floods. Of the 72 villages that were submerged, 20 never resurfaced. More than 100,000 people were drowned.

31 H5 ROTTERDAM

FREEZE (LITTLE ICE AGE) 1431
LOCATION: The Netherlands
NOTES: The bitter winters turned the city's canals into icy roads and froze all the rivers in Germany. Cereal and fruit crops were wiped out across northern Europe, causing widespread famine.

32 J8 NAPLES

EARTHQUAKE 1456
LOCATION: Italy
NOTES: The earthquake killed more than 35,000 people and left Naples in ruins.

33 G9 GRANADA

DISEASE (TYPHUS) 1489
LOCATION: Spain
NOTES: Of the 20,000 Spanish soldiers besieging the Moorish-held city, 17,000 died of typhus.

34 J8 NAPLES

DISEASE (SYPHILIS) 1495
LOCATION: Italy
NOTES: The city was besieged by Charles VIII of France and a mercenary army from all over Europe. A period of debauchery followed its fall, and the troops and camp followers spread the disease across Europe on returning to their native countries. Some of the soldiers are thought to have been part of Columbus's crew who may have brought the disease back from America.

35 H6 LONDON

DISEASE (PLAGUE) 1499
LOCATION: England
NOTES: Henry VII and his court fled to Calais during this outbreak of plague, which killed around 30,000 people.

36 F8 LISBON

EARTHQUAKE 1531
LOCATION: Portugal
NOTES: Violent tremors killed 30,000 people and destroyed 1,500 homes.

37 I6 METZ

DISEASE (TYPHUS) 1552
LOCATION: Germany (now France)
NOTES: The outbreak of typhus claimed the lives of more than 30,000 people, including half of the imperial army under Emperor Charles.

38 O4 GORKIY

FREEZE/FAMINE 1557
LOCATION: Volga Region, Russia
NOTES: Thousands of people perished in the famine, the effects of which were exacerbated by rain and extreme cold.

39 H5 LEYDEN

STORM 1574
LOCATION: The Netherlands
NOTES: During the siege of Leyden by the Spanish army, heavy rainfall caused local dykes to give way. About 20,000 of the Spanish troops were drowned in the ensuing flood.

40 G3 OFF FAIR ISLE

STORM 1588
LOCATION: Shetland Isles, Scotland
NOTES: Ships from the Spanish Armada were wrecked in a gale all around the British coastline during an attempted invasion of Britain. Many of the ships sank off the Shetland Isles, and between 4,000 and 10,000 sailors were drowned.

41 G5 GLOUCESTER

FLOOD 1606
LOCATION: Severn Valley, England
NOTES: The city was inundated, and more than 2,000 people are thought to have drowned, when the Severn Estuary burst its banks in one the United Kingdom's worst-ever flood disasters.

42 I7 CHIAVENNA

LANDSLIDE 1618
LOCATION: Italy
NOTES: Vast chunks of the mountainside fell away, consuming towns in the valley of Chiavenna. None of the 1,500 inhabitants of Plurs survived. In all, 2,427 people were crushed to death. Three survivors dug their way out.

43 J8 VESUVIUS

VOLCANO 1631
LOCATION: Italy
NOTES: The eruption created lahars and streams of lava that engulfed many villages, killing 18,000 people.

44 I5 CUXHAVEN

FLOOD 1634
LOCATION: Germany
NOTES: The North Sea flooded the entire area, drowning more than 6,000 people and destroying about 1,000 homes.

45 G6 WIDECOMBE-IN-THE-MOOR

TORNADO 1638
LOCATION: England
NOTES: The tornado, accompanied by ball-lightning, caused a huge explosion that wrecked the church, killing 50 of the congregation, almost the entire population of the village.

46 J8 ROME

DISEASE (PLAGUE)/FAMINE 1656
LOCATION: Italy
NOTES: Famine followed by plague claimed the lives of 400,000 people. Over a six-month period, the plague had spread from Sardinia to Naples through infected military transport.

47 H5 LONDON

DISEASE (PLAGUE) 1664–1666
LOCATION: England
NOTES: The plague killed about 100,000 people before, according to historians, it was stopped by the "Great Fire" of 1666, which destroyed much of London.

48 P8 SHEMAKHA

EARTHQUAKE 1667
LOCATION: Caucasia (now Azerbaijan)
NOTES: The city, which lies at at the foot of the Caucasus mountains, was rocked by powerful tremors and about 80,000 of its inhabitants perished.

49 J9 MOUNT ETNA

VOLCANO/EARTHQUAKE 1669
LOCATION: Sicily
NOTES: Earthquakes shook the entire island, causing Etna to erupt. Lava flows overwhelmed the city of Catania and killed about 20,000 people.

50 J9 CATANIA

EARTHQUAKE 1693
LOCATION: Sicily
NOTES: The earthquake destroyed Catania, along with many other towns, killing an estimated 60,000 people.

51 F5 ATHLONE

STORM (LIGHTNING) 1697
LOCATION: Ireland
NOTES: Lightning struck Athlone Castle, detonating 260 barrels of gunpowder. The explosion destroyed both the castle and the town.

52 G6 PLYMOUTH

"GREAT STORM" 1703
LOCATION: England
NOTES: The English fleet was damaged at major ports throughout England. Around 300 ships and 30,000 sailors were lost.

53 H5 THE HAGUE
FLOOD 1717
LOCATION: The Netherlands
NOTES: Every coastline was hit in one of the North Sea's worst-ever flood disasters. Around 11,000 people drowned, 2,000 in the Netherlands alone.

54 I7 LEUKERBAD
AVALANCHE 1718
LOCATION: Switzerland
NOTES: The colossal avalanche hurtled down the mountainside, obliterating Leukerbad and killing 50 people.

55 J9 MOUNT ETNA
VOLCANO/EARTHQUAKE 1755
LOCATION: Sicily
NOTES: The eruption was preceded by a massive earthquake, which affected a 5,000-mile (8,000-km) area devastating the city of Lisbon in Portugal.

56 F8 LISBON
EARTHQUAKE/TSUNAMI 1755
LOCATION: Portugal
NOTES: See pp.44–45.

57 J8 CALABRIA
EARTHQUAKE 1783
LOCATION: Italy
NOTES: Five earthquakes in two months rocked the western side of southern Italy, reducing 181 towns to rubble and killing 30,000 people.

58 E2 LAKI
VOLCANO 1783
LOCATION: Iceland
NOTES: Over a period of six months, the volcano emitted vast quantities of lava and clouds of opaque, toxic gas. The lava invaded 123,600 acres (50,000 hectacres) of Iceland, withering crops and the dense gas prevented fishing boats from setting sail. Around 10,000 people died of starvation as a result.

59 J8 CALABRIA
EARTHQUAKE 1797
LOCATION: Italy
NOTES: The earthquake destroyed many towns in the province of Calabria and killed 50,000 of the inhabitants.

60 G5 MANCHESTER
DISEASE (TUBERCULOSIS) 1800
LOCATION: England
NOTES: At the peak of this outbreak of tuberculosis, 20 per cent of Manchester's population died.

61 I7 GOLDAU VALLEY
LANDSLIDE 1806
LOCATION: Switzerland
NOTES: Rossberg Peak broke off and slid down into the valley below with such speed that friction fires started. Four villages were engulfed and 800 people were killed.

62 F5 CORK
PEST/BLIGHT 1817
LOCATION: Ireland
NOTES: Bad weather caused potato crops to fail all across Ireland. Almost 70,000 people died in the ensuing famine.

63 M3 ST. PETERSBURG
FLOOD 1824
LOCATION: Russia
NOTES: The worst recorded flood of the River Neva submerged St. Petersburg and nearby Kronstadt, where a large ship was marooned in the middle of the market place. In all, 10,000 people lost their lives.

64 L2 IISALMI
FREEZE (LITTLE ICE AGE) 1835–1850
LOCATION: Finland
NOTES: The last major glacial advance resulted in the deaths of 137,000 people.

65 F5 GALWAY
BLIGHT/FAMINE 1845–1848
LOCATION: Ireland
NOTES: See pp.108–109.

66 H6 SOHO
DISEASE (CHOLERA) 1853–1863
LOCATION: London, England
NOTES: The third cholera pandemic of the century claimed thousands of lives. In Soho, 700 people died in two weeks.

67 M7 OFF BALACLAVA
STORM 1854
LOCATION: Black Sea
NOTES: The steamship, Prince, foundered in a gale off the coast of Crimea, with the loss of 143 lives.

68 L9 RHODES
STORM (LIGHTNING) 1856
LOCATION: Rhodes Island, Greece
NOTES: Lightning struck the church of St. Jean during a thunderstorm. A large store of gunpowder beneath the church exploded, killing 400 people.

69 J8 CALABRIA
EARTHQUAKE 1857
LOCATION: Italy
NOTES: In Calabria alone, 10,000 lives were lost. Huge fissures appeared in surrounding areas and swallowed up many villages and their inhabitants.

70 G6 OFF BREST
STORM 1870
LOCATION: France
NOTES: The passenger ship, Gorgone, en route to Cherbourg, disappeared in the storm with 122 people on board.

71 G4 TAY BRIDGE
STORM 1879
LOCATION: Scotland
NOTES: Severe winds, a witness claimed, whipped up a waterspout that caused the newly opened Tay rail bridge to collapse. A train plunged into the River Tay and none of the 75 passengers and crew survived.

72 I7 ELM
LANDSLIDE 1881
LOCATION: Switzerland
NOTES: Around 150 people were killed when the village and most of the valley were buried under a mass of rock.

73 L9 SCIO (NOW CHIOS)
EARTHQUAKE 1881
LOCATION: Turkey (now Eastern Greece)
NOTES: One-quarter of the island's 80,000 inhabitants were injured, 7,000 were killed, and 44 villages and towns were reduced to rubble in the earthquake.

74 M9 ANATOLIA
EARTHQUAKE 1883
LOCATION: Asia Minor (now Turkey)
NOTES: In a single tremor lasting only a few seconds, 1,000 people died and 20,000 more were made homeless.

75 G9 MALAGA
EARTHQUAKE 1884
LOCATION: Andalucia, Spain
NOTES: The earthquake, which struck on Christmas Day, killed 745 people and injured 1,253.

76 G9 GRANADA
EARTHQUAKE 1885
LOCATION: Spain
NOTES: The quake devastated Granada, along with the cities of Alhama and Periana, with the loss of 1,000 lives.

77 G6 OFF LAND'S END
STORM 1886
LOCATION: Cornwall, England
NOTES: The British steamship, London, sank in a gale 200 miles (320 km) off the Cornish coast with the loss of 220 lives.

78 I7 LE FAYET/ST GERVAIS
LANDSLIDE 1892
LOCATION: France
NOTES: The two spa towns at the foot of Mont Blanc were washed away by the Tête Rousse glacier, which broke off, thawed, and cascaded down the mountainside. Around 140 people died.

79 F8 OFF PENICHE
STORM 1892
LOCATION: Portugal
NOTES: The British steamer, Roumania, sank, with the loss of 113 lives, off the coast of Portugal en route to India.

80 J8 CALABRIA
EARTHQUAKE 1905
LOCATION: Italy
NOTES: A series of tremors over five days killed 5,000 people across the province, 2,000 in the village of Martirano, which was subsequently destroyed. The effects of the earthquake were felt as far north as Naples and Florence.

81 J9 MESSINA
EARTHQUAKE/TSUNAMI 1908
LOCATION: Sicily
NOTES: A series of earthquakes and a tsunami hit Messina and nearby towns. Around 160,000 people died, including 80,000 of Messina's 147,000 inhabitants.

82 J8 AVEZZANO
EARTHQUAKE 1915
LOCATION: Italy
NOTES: The 7.5-magnitude earthquake devastated the city and killed about 30,000 people.

83 J7 MARMOLADA
AVALANCHE 1916
LOCATION: Tyrolean Alps, Italy
NOTES: The avalanche swept through the town, killing 253 Austrian soldiers in their barracks.

84 H6 FLANDERS
DISEASE (SPANISH INFLUENZA) 1918–1920
LOCATION: France/Belgium
NOTES: See pp.118–119.

85 O4 GORKIY
DROUGHT 1921–1922
LOCATION: Volga region, Russia
NOTES: The drought devastated the entire region and caused widespread famine. More than 20 million people were affected, several million of whom died.

86 K7 SARAJEVO
LANDSLIDE 1926
LOCATION: Bosnia
NOTES: The landslide killed 117 people when the train they were traveling in was crushed on the outskirts of the city.

87 J9 MOUNT ETNA
VOLCANO 1928
LOCATION: Sicily
NOTES: During the eruption, the Messina-Catania railroad was destroyed, along with the town of Mascati and the village of Nunziata. Scores of lives were lost.

88 M8 NORTHERN ANATOLIA
EARTHQUAKE/LANDSLIDES 1929
LOCATION: Turkey
NOTES: The earthquake and the ensuing landslides devastated the province and claimed 1,000 lives.

89 M6 KIEV
DROUGHT/FAMINE 1932–1933
LOCATION: USSR (now The Ukraine)
NOTES: Stalin's brutal transformation of the economy, coupled with drought and famine in Volga and Ukraine, led to the deaths of about five million peasants. Refusing to acknowledge the famine's existence, the USSR spurned foreign aid.

90 N8 ERZINCAN
EARTHQUAKE 1939
LOCATION: Turkey
NOTES: Tens of thousands of homes were destroyed and 50,000 people died.

91 L7 BUCHAREST
EARTHQUAKE 1940
LOCATION: Romania
NOTES: The city was severely damaged and 1,000 people were killed.

92 J8 VESUVIUS
VOLCANO 1944
LOCATION: Italy
NOTES: The eruption caused cessation of hostilities between tens of thousands of allied and German soldiers in the area. Fewer than 100 people lost their lives.

93 D2 HEKLA
VOLCANO 1947
LOCATION: Iceland
NOTES: The eruption caused a massive plume of smoke and steam to rise more than 100,000 ft (30,000 m) into the air.

94 H6 LONDON
STORM (SMOG) 1952
LOCATION: England
NOTES: A deadly smog settled over the city for several weeks, killing thousands of people.

95 H6 OUDE-TONGE
STORM/FLOOD (NORTH SEA) 1953
LOCATION: Belgium
NOTES: See pp.92–93.

96 I7 DALAAS TAL
AVALANCHE 1954
LOCATION: Vorarlberg, Austria
NOTES: For three days, the avalanches hurtled down the Alps, burying towns and villages in Austria, Germany, Italy, and Switzerland, and killing 411 people.

97 H6 PARIS
STORM (BLIZZARD/GALE) 1956
LOCATION: France
NOTES: Almost 1,000 people died in the freezing weather that gripped Europe from England to Siberia.

98 I7 MILAN
STORM (LIGHTNING) 1959
LOCATION: Italy
NOTES: A passenger airliner exploded, killing 68 people, when it was struck by lightning during a storm.

99 H8 BARCELONA
STORM (FLASH FLOOD) 1962
LOCATION: Spain
NOTES: Barcelona was inundated, 445

people were killed, and a further 10,000 were left homeless in Spain's worst flash floods for centuries.

100 I5 HAMBURG
FLOOD (DYKES BROKEN) 1962
LOCATION: Germany
NOTES: Floods along the North Sea coast broke through ancient flood barriers. In Hamburg, on the Elbe, 281 people died and 500,000 were made homeless.

101 J7 BELLUNO
LANDSLIDE 1963
LOCATION: Italy
NOTES: Heavy rains flooded the Piave River Valley and caused the landslide in which 2,000 people were killed.

102 J7 LONGARONE
LANDSLIDE 1963
LOCATION: Italy
NOTES: Vast amounts of rock fell from Mount Toc into the reservoir created by the newly built Vaiont Dam. A huge wave surged over the dam, killing 1,190 people and destroying the town.

103 K8 SKOPJE
EARTHQUAKE 1963
LOCATION: Yugoslavia (now Macedonia)
NOTES: The town was severely damaged by the earthquake. More than 15,000 homes were destroyed, leaving three-quarters of the population homeless. At least 1,000 people died and a further 3,700 were injured.

104 L9 AEGEAN SEA
STORM 1966
LOCATION: Between Piraeus and Crete
NOTES: The Greek passenger ferry, *Heraklion*, went down in a storm with the loss of 230 lives.

105 I7 FLORENCE
FLOOD 1966
LOCATION: Italy
NOTES: The city was inundated and 113 lives were lost. Rome, Naples, and Venice were also damaged. Many priceless works of art were ruined.

106 D2 SURTSEY
VOLCANO 1967
LOCATION: Iceland
NOTES: The island of Surtsey was born when lava spewed out of a rift on the North Atlantic seabed.

107 G4 GLASGOW
STORM ("WIND OF THE CENTURY") 1968
LOCATION: Scotland
NOTES: Savage winds of around 135 mph (215 kph) wrecked 70,000 Glasgow tenement dwellings, killing 20 people. Hurricane-force blizzards swept from Britain to Iran, and snow fell in the Negev Desert in Israel.

108 D2 HEIMAEY
VOLCANO 1973
LOCATION: Iceland
NOTES: See pp.16–17.

109 G6 ENGLISH CHANNEL
STORM 1974
LOCATION: Between England and France
NOTES: The severe gale sank several ships with the loss of 35 lives.

110 J8 ALTAVILLA IRPINIA
EARTHQUAKE 1980
LOCATION: Italy
NOTES: The tremor in this mountainous region east of Naples caused the deaths of 3,114 people.

111 I7 COTE D'AZUR
FIRE 1985
LOCATION: South of France
NOTES: See p.87.

112 H6 SEVENOAKS
"GREAT STORM" 1987
LOCATION: Kent, England
NOTES: The gale wreaked havoc across southern England and northern France. Many hundreds of ancient trees were uprooted, altering landscapes in the southeast of England irrevocably. The final death toll reached 19.

113 O8 SPITAK
EARTHQUAKE 1988
LOCATION: Armenia
NOTES: See pp.34–35.

114 I7 MONT BLANC
EARTHQUAKE/AVALANCHE 1991
LOCATION: The Alps, France
NOTES: Nine people were killed when the earthquake triggered an avalanche.

115 N8 ERZINCAN
EARTHQUAKE 1992
LOCATION: Turkey
NOTES: The 6.7-magnitude tremor was followed by a severe aftershock. Around 500 people were killed and a further 2,200 were injured.

116 H7 VAISON-LA-ROMAINE
STORM 1992
LOCATION: France
NOTES: Torrential rain from continued thunderstorms caused a flash flood of the Ouvèze river. A 49-ft (15-m) wall of water gushed through the town, sweeping 38 people to their deaths.

117 L6 GÖMEÇ
AVALANCHES 1992
LOCATION: Eastern Turkey
NOTES: See p.95.

118 E2 VATNAJÖKULL GLACIER
VOLCANO 1996
LOCATION: Iceland
NOTES: A huge fissure appeared beneath Vatnajökull and began disgorging lava, which thawed the glacier's lower levels and caused the most powerful flood for almost 60 years. No lives were lost, but roads, pipelines, and power cables were severely damaged.

119 J8 ASSISI
EARTHQUAKE 1997
LOCATION: Umbria, Italy
NOTES: The earthquake brought down part of the city's magnificent cathedral, killing 11 people and damaging some of the most important paintings and frescoes in the history of art. Thousands of people were left homeless throughout the state of Umbria.

120 G9 BADAJOS
FLOOD 1997
LOCATION: Extremadura, Spain
NOTES: The city was flooded, and at least 31 people were killed, when sudden severe rain and high winds caused the Guadiana River to burst its banks.

121 K6 KRAKOW
FLOOD 1997
LOCATION: Poland
NOTES: The Oder and several other rivers burst their banks, inundating a 2,000-sq mile (5,200-sq km) area across four countries. About 60 people were killed in Poland, with a further 40 deaths occurring in the Czech Republic.

SOUTH ASIA
The map for these listings is on pp.136–137.

1 D4 DECCAN TRAPS
VOLCANO 65 MILLION YEARS AGO
LOCATION: Jodhpur, India
NOTES: *See pp.98–99.*

2 H8 TOBA
VOLCANO C. 70,000 YEARS AGO
LOCATION: Sumatra, Indonesia
NOTES: The eruption created a huge caldera and dumped millions of tons of ash on the floor of the Indian Ocean over a distance of 1,300 miles (2,080 km).

3 K2 GAOCHENG
FLOOD (YELLOW RIVER) C. 2,400 YEARS AGO
LOCATION: Honan province, China
NOTES: China was prone to vast floods, which were brought under control by a man called Yu. His success was amply rewarded when he became emperor of China's first hereditary dynasty, the Xia.

4 C4 HYDERABAD
FLOOD C. 2,400 YEARS AGO
LOCATION: Indus valley, India
NOTES: The massive floods that occurred at this time are thought to have been triggered by a meteor shower.

5 K5 CANTON (NOW GUANGZHOU)
DISEASE (PLAGUE) AD 610
LOCATION: China
NOTES: The plague affected the southern and coastal provinces predominantly and recurred for 200 years. The number of deaths is unknown, but is likely to have been very high.

6 K2 TAIYUAN
EARTHQUAKE 1038
LOCATION: Shanxi province, China
NOTES: The earthquake affected the entire province. The city was badly damaged and 23,000 people were killed.

7 K2 CHIHLI (NOW BO HAI)
EARTHQUAKE 1290
LOCATION: China
NOTES: The earthquake buried the city with the loss of 100,000 lives.

8 K1 PEKING (NOW BEIJING)
FLOOD/FAMINE 1332–1333
LOCATION: China
NOTES: The flood and subsequent famine caused six million deaths. The disruption they caused may have been responsible for spreading the Black Death.

9 K2 TAIYUAN
EARTHQUAKE 1556
LOCATION: Shanxi Province, China
NOTES: The most destructive earthquake on record also hit Shaanxi and Henan provinces, claiming around 830,000 lives.

10 L6 TAAL
VOLCANO 1591
LOCATION: Luzon, Philippines
NOTES: Taal erupted violently for the first

time, having been relatively active for many centuries. Deadly fumes belched out of the top and side of the mountain, asphyxiating thousands of islanders.

11 M6 MAYON
VOLCANO 1616
LOCATION: Luzon, Philippines
NOTES: In the first recorded eruption of Mayon, dozens of towns and villages were bombarded with huge rocks and engulfed in rivers of lava. Thousands of lives were lost.

12 D5 SURAT
DROUGHT/FAMINE 1669–1670
LOCATION: India
NOTES: An estimated three million people died in the country's first major famine.

13 G5 MOUTH OF HUGLI RIVER
TROPICAL CYCLONE 1737
LOCATION: Bay of Bengal, India
NOTES: The cyclone created a 40-ft (12-m) storm surge along the river that wrecked 20,000 ships and killed 300,000 people in coastal towns and cities.

14 L6 TAAL
VOLCANO 1754
LOCATION: Luzon, Philippines
NOTES: Four villages were wiped out, with the loss of hundreds of lives, when Taal erupted and showered the area with flames, rock, and pumice over a seven-month period.

15 M6 MAYON
VOLCANO 1766
LOCATION: Luzon, Philippines
NOTES: Vast quantities of lava and water flowed down the mountain, forming rivers that destroyed everything in their path. Hundreds of people were either drowned or engulfed in lava.

16 E4 DELHI
DROUGHT/FAMINE 1769–1770
LOCATION: Hindustan, India
NOTES: About three million people, one-third of the province's inhabitants, starved to death during the drought, which lasted for 18 months.

17 F6 CORINGA
TROPICAL CYCLONE 1789
LOCATION: Andhra Pradesh, India
NOTES: More than 20,000 people were killed in the cyclone, which created three huge waves that destroyed the city and blocked the mouth of the Godavari River with mud.

18 D5 BOMBAY (NOW MUMBAI)
DROUGHT/"SKULL" FAMINE 1790–1791
LOCATION: India
NOTES: Thousands of people died when failure of the rains caused the infamous "Poji Bara", or "Skull Famine", so called because cannibalism was rife.

19 M6 MAYON
VOLCANO 1814
LOCATION: Luzon, Philippines
NOTES: Mayon erupted with tremendous force, spewing out rocks, ash, and fire. Four towns vanished beneath a 30-ft (9-m) pile of rocks and 2,200 people died.

20 G5 CALCUTTA
DISEASE (CHOLERA) 1817
LOCATION: India
NOTES: The first cholera pandemic killed 5,000 British soldiers in Calcutta before raging across Asia to the Middle East and Africa. Lasting for six years, it stopped spreading just before reaching Europe.

21 G5 CALCUTTA
DISEASE (CHOLERA) 1826–1838
LOCATION: India
NOTES: See pp.116–117.

22 E6 GUNTUR
DROUGHT/FAMINE 1833
LOCATION: India
NOTES: Poor rainfall caused crops to fail, and at least 200,000 people starved.

23 K5 HONG KONG HARBOR
TROPICAL CYCLONE 1841
LOCATION: Hong Kong, South China Sea
NOTES: British naval ships anchored in the harbor escaped serious damage, but the four-hour storm sank every junk and sampan, drowning thousands of people living or working on the water.

24 L3 SHANGHAI
FLOOD 1851–1866
LOCATION: China
NOTES: Over a 15-year period, 40 to 50 million people drowned in the "rice bowl", the triangle of land between the Huang Ho (Yellow) and Yangtze rivers. These and many other rivers constantly broke their banks and flooded hundreds of towns and villages.

25 L6 MANILA
EARTHQUAKE 1863
LOCATION: Philippines
NOTES: Two huge tremors devastated the city, flattening its tobacco warehouses and decimating the tobacco trade. Up to 1,000 people were killed.

26 G5 CALCUTTA
TROPICAL CYCLONE 1864
LOCATION: India
NOTES: The city was deluged by a 40-ft (13-m) wave. More than 50,000 people were killed and 200 ships were sunk.

27 E5 RAIPUR
DROUGHT/FAMINE 1866
LOCATION: India
NOTES: Drought throughout the Bengal, Orissa, and Behar provinces caused a famine that killed more than 1,500,000 people through starvation and disease.

28 E5 BHOPAL
DROUGHT/FAMINE 1868
LOCATION: India
NOTES: The famine, caused by poor crop yields for several years in succession, killed thousands of people across central and northwest India.

29 G5 BARISAL
TROPICAL CYCLONE 1876
LOCATION: India (now Bangladesh)
NOTES: A storm surge, accompanied by a very high tide, flooded Barisal and submerged every island in the area around the mouth of the Meghna River. At least 100,000 people were drowned within a few minutes.

30 E7 MADRAS
DROUGHT/FAMINE/DISEASE 1876–1877
LOCATION: India
NOTES: In the longest famine on record, three million people died of starvation and a further three million died in the outbreak of cholera that followed. A total of 36 million people were affected.

31 M1 CHANGCHUN
DROUGHT/FAMINE 1877–1878
LOCATION: Manchuria, China
NOTES: Virtually no rain for three years led to the country's worst famine, in the northern and central areas. Up to

13 million people are thought to have perished and cannibalism was rife. Ironically, in neighboring Guangdong province, floods were decimating crops.

32 E2 KASHMIR
EARTHQUAKE 1885
LOCATION: Kashmir Province, India
NOTES: Many cities, towns, and villages were destroyed and more than 3,000 people were killed when Kashmir was shaken for over a month by dozens of powerful tremors.

33 K3 KAIFENG
FLOOD 1887
LOCATION: Henan Province, China
NOTES: The city and hundreds of towns and villages were completely covered in silt, and 1.5 million people perished, when the Huang Ho (Yellow River) burst its dykes and flooded 30,000 sq miles (80,000 sq km) of land.

34 E4 MORADABAD
STORM (HAIL) 1888
LOCATION: India
NOTES: Hailstones the size of oranges smashed through windows and roofs, and 230 farm workers were pounded to death in the fields.

35 M6 MAYON
VOLCANO 1897
LOCATION: Luzon, Philippines
NOTES: Mayon's four-day eruption, the longest in its history, showered the town of Tobaco with white-hot stones and ashes, killing 400 people.

36 D3 LAHORE
DROUGHT/FAMINE 1898
LOCATION: The Punjab, India
NOTES: Around a million people died in the drought and subsequent famine that swept across vast areas of the Punjab and southern and western India. More than 61 million people were affected.

37 D5 BOMBAY (NOW MUMBAI)
DISEASE (PLAGUE) 1904–1908
LOCATION: India
NOTES: In Bombay, Bengal, and the northwestern provinces, 18,000 people were dying of plague each day. The epidemic killed more than three million people across India.

38 E3 KANGRA
EARTHQUAKE 1905
LOCATION: India
NOTES: The 8.7-magnitude earthquake ripped the city of Kangra apart, killing more than 19,000 people.

39 D3 LAHORE
EARTHQUAKES 1905
LOCATION: India
NOTES: A series of earthquakes shook several cities, killing hundreds of people and destroying many historical buildings. The towers of the Golden Mosque in Lahore were toppled.

40 L5 KAGI (NOW CHIAI)
EARTHQUAKE 1906
LOCATION: Formosa, Japan (now Taiwan)
NOTES: The massive tremor devastated the city, killing more than 1,000 people and injuring at least 2,000. More than 5,000 homes were destroyed.

41 K5 KOWLOON
TROPICAL CYCLONE/STORM SURGE 1906
LOCATION: Hong Kong, South China Sea
NOTES: Scores of buildings collapsed and at least 10,000 people were killed,

many of whom were drowned, when the entire district was overwhelmed by gigantic storm surges.

42 L3 SHANGHAI
FLOOD 1911
LOCATION: China
NOTES: The Yangtze River burst its earth embankments, inundating Shanghai and wreaking havoc across four provinces. Of the two million people affected, 100,000 were drowned instantly and a further 100,000 died from starvation within a few weeks.

43 L6 TAAL
VOLCANO 1911
LOCATION: Luzon, Philippines
NOTES: Scolding mud and steam were blown out, obliterating 13 villages and towns. A whirlwind of ash and sulfur dioxide blew across the island. Most of the 1,335 victims were asphyxiated.

44 L5 TAITO (NOW T'AITUNG)
TROPICAL CYCLONE 1912
LOCATION: Formosa (now Taiwan)
NOTES: The cyclone, one of the worst on record, killed 107 people and injured 293. Winds in excess of 190 mph (300 kph) flattened at least 200,000 houses.

45 M6 MAYON
VOLCANO 1914
LOCATION: Luzon, Philippines
NOTES: The eruption ruined the town of Cagsauga, killing hundreds of people.

46 I2 XINING
EARTHQUAKE 1920
LOCATION: Gansu Province, China
NOTES: The violent, 8.6-magnitude tremor decimated the entire province and killed more than 180,000 people.

47 I4 KUNMING
EARTHQUAKE 1925
LOCATION: Yunnan Province, China
NOTES: The earthquake, which was felt across the entire province, killed more than 6,000 people and almost totally destroyed the city of Kunming.

48 H2 TSINGHAI (NOW QINGHAI)
EARTHQUAKE 1927
LOCATION: Gansu Province, China
NOTES: The severe, 8.3-magnitude quake was felt throughout the province and killed around 200,000 people living at the foot of the Nanshan mountains.

49 L3 NANJING
FLOOD/STORM SURGE 1931
LOCATION: Anhui Province, China
NOTES: Heavy, continuous monsoons resulted in flooding of the Yangtze River basin. Six vast waves swept along the river, breaking dykes and inundating a 35,000-sq mile (91,000-sq km) area. More than 40,000,000 people were affected, and several million were killed.

50 I2 LANZHOU
EARTHQUAKE 1932
LOCATION: Gansu Province, China
NOTES: The earthquake left the province in ruins and killed 70,000 people.

51 K2 TIANJIN
FLOOD 1933
LOCATION: China
NOTES: The Huang Ho (Yellow River) burst its dykes, killing 18,000 people. More than three million people were affected by the flood, which inundated more than 3,000 towns and villages.

52 F4 BIRATNAGAR
EARTHQUAKE 1934
LOCATION: Nepal
NOTES: The entire country was rocked by the 8.4-magnitude earthquake, which shook the Himalayan mountains and killed about 10,700 people.

53 K5 CANTON (NOW GUANGZHOU)
LANDSLIDES 1934
LOCATION: Guangdong Province, China
NOTES: Over a two-day period, successive landslides pulverized the entire province and killed more than 500 people.

54 C3 QUETTA
EARTHQUAKE 1935
LOCATION: Pakistan
NOTES: About 60,000 lives were lost when the 7.5-magnitude earthquake destroyed Quetta.

55 K2 JINAN
FLOOD/FAMINE 1939
LOCATION: China
NOTES: Grain and rice crops were wiped out when the Huang Ho (Yellow River) burst its dykes. Within three months, famine had claimed the lives of 200,000 people, and 25 million were destitute.

56 G5 DIAMOND HARBOR
TROPICAL CYCLONE 1942
LOCATION: Bengal, India (now Bangladesh)
NOTES: Winds reaching 140 mph (225 kph) flattened coastal villages and killed more than 40,000 people.

57 L6 SOUTH CHINA SEA
TROPICAL CYCLONE 1944
LOCATION: Off Luzon Island, Philippines
NOTES: The cyclone raged for two days, sinking the US destroyers, Hull, Spence, and Monahan, with the loss of almost 800 lives. The sea had been whipped into such a frenzy that many who had escaped the sinking ships, drowned when the sea ripped off their lifejackets.

58 H4 DIBRUGARH
LANDSLIDE 1949
LOCATION: Northern Assam, India
NOTES: The landslide buried towns across the region, killing about 500 people.

59 M2 SEOUL
DISEASE (HANTAVIRUS) 1950s
LOCATION: South Korea
NOTES: During the Korean War, hundreds of soldiers fell victim to the mouse-borne virus, one of a group of hantaviruses that affect around 200,000 people each year, killing at least 20,000.

60 H4 ASSAM
EARTHQUAKE/LANDSLIDES 1950
LOCATION: India
NOTES: The quake rocked the Himalayan mountains and caused landslides that dammed the Subabsiri River and broke the Bramaputra River dam. The resulting floods killed around 1,500 people and caused extensive property damage.

61 L5 HIBOK-HIBOK
VOLCANO 1951
LOCATION: Camiguin Island, Philippines
NOTES: The eruption shook the tiny island lying off the Luzon coast. Three villages had to be evacuated and 84 people died.

62 J6 HUE
TROPICAL CYCLONE 1953
LOCATION: Vietnam
NOTES: The storm killed around 1,300 people across central Vietnam and badly damaged the old capital. The rice crop

was wiped out, and tens of thousands of straw huts disappeared without a trace, leaving 100,000 people homeless.

63 K3 WUHAN
FLOOD 1954
LOCATION: Hubei Province, China
NOTES: Continued, heavy monsoon rains caused the Yangtze and other rivers to overflow, turning the Yangtze basin into a vast sea. Water levels were 5 ft (1.5 m) higher than in 1931. Despite flood-control measures, 40,000 people died.

64 G4 XIGAZE
FLOOD 1954
LOCATION: Tibet (now part of China)
NOTES: The swollen Nyang Chu River filled Lake Takri Tsoma, finally bursting its banks. Torrents of water gushed on to the city. Around 750 people died, most of whom were Buddhist monks at prayer in the Palace of the Western Paradise.

65 F5 CUTTACK
FLOOD (MONSOONS) 1955
LOCATION: Orissa Province, India
NOTES: Heavy monsoon rains caused vast floods that submerged 10,000 villages and killed 1,700 people.

66 L3 HANGZHOU
TYPHOON WANDA 1956
LOCATION: China
NOTES: The storm struck Zhejiang, Anhui, and Jiangsu provinces, destroying the rice and cotton crops and 38,000 homes. Almost 2,000 people were killed. ,

67 C4 KARACHI
DISEASE (CHOLERA/SMALLPOX) 1958
LOCATION: Pakistan
NOTES: The cholera epidemic lasted for seven months and killed 16,000 people.

68 L6 MANILA
TYPHOON LUCILLE 1960
LOCATION: Philippines
NOTES: Lucille blasted the island, deluging Manila. About 100 people died, many of whom had, hours earlier, survived a tsunami caused by earthquakes in Chile.

69 G5 CHITTAGONG
TROPICAL CYCLONE 1963
LOCATION: E. Pakistan (now Bangladesh)
NOTES: Huge waves swept away millions of mud houses in the Bay of Bengal area, killing 22,000 people. Four cruise ships were carried half a mile (1 km) inland.

70 C4 HYDERABAD
STORM/FLOOD 1964
LOCATION: West Pakistan
NOTES: The freak storm raged across the district to the edge of the Thar desert. Hundreds of people perished when their homes were swept away by floodwater.

71 L6 MANILA
TYPHOON WINNIE 1964
LOCATION: Philippines
NOTES: Winnie wreaked havoc across the Philippines, wrecking Luzon and leaving 300,000 people destitute and 48 dead.

72 G5 CHITTAGONG
TROPICAL CYCLONE 1965
LOCATION: E. Pakistan (now Bangladesh)
NOTES: Huge waves swept across the Ganges Delta for 124 miles (200 km), killing 2,000 people and deluging Dhaka.

73 L6 TAAL
VOLCANO 1965
LOCATION: Luzon, Philippines
NOTES: Water from Taal's crater-lake

began seeping through to the magma below, creating steam. Pressure built up and the volcano exploded. A few hours earlier, experts had decided not to recommend an evacuation, and 200 people living near the crater were killed.

74 D5 GUJARAT
FLOOD 1968
LOCATION: India
NOTES: Heavy rains caused the Tapti River to burst its banks. There was major damage throughout the region and 1,000 people were drowned.

75 L7 ROXAS
TROPICAL CYCLONES 1970
LOCATION: Panay, Philippines
NOTES: Two cyclones struck within ten days of each other, wreaking havoc across 24 provinces in the Philippines. Around 1,500 people were killed and 90,000 homes were destroyed.

76 G5 SANDWIP ISLAND
TROPICAL CYCLONE 1970
LOCATION: E. Pakistan (now Bangladesh)
NOTES: Around half a million people died when a 50-ft (15-m) wave swept along the coast and across the islands on the Ganges Delta. Thousands more had died from disease within weeks.

77 I5 TONGHAI
EARTHQUAKE 1970
LOCATION: Yunnan Province, China
NOTES: The 7.5-magnitude earthquake caused severe damage throughout the province and killed 10,000 people.

78 K5 HONG KONG
TYPHOON ROSE 1971
LOCATION: South China Sea
NOTES: Rose sank scores of boats in the harbor, including a ferryboat in which about 80 people drowned. Another 12 people died when huge sea waves hurtled ashore and created mudslides.

79 D3 DERA GHAZI KHAN
FLOOD 1972
LOCATION: The Punjab, Pakistan
NOTES: The Indus River flooded the entire area. Around 3,000 people drowned and 3,000 villages were swept away.

80 K5 HONG KONG
LANDSLIDES 1972
LOCATION: South China Sea
NOTES: On the third day of a severe rainstorm, two landslides occurred in densely populated areas. One destroyed many huts in a temporary housing area, killing 71 people. The other caused the collapse of a 12-story apartment block in a wealthy area, killing 67 people.

81 G5 MYMENSINGH
TORNADOES 1972
LOCATION: Bangladesh
NOTES: A series of tornadoes covering 800 sq miles (2,070 sq km) killed 200 people and left 25,000 homeless.

82 E5 NAGPUR
DROUGHT 1972
LOCATION: India
NOTES: For almost a month, 50 million people across 14 states were subjected to temperatures of 110°F (43°C) and drought conditions. Crops withered and 800 people died of starvation.

83 M2 SEOUL
FLOOD 1972
LOCATION: South Korea
NOTES: Torrential rains flooded three

provinces in South Korea, killing 450 people and leaving 100,000 others homeless. Landslides in Seoul were responsible for 175 of the deaths.

84 D3 SRINAGAR
EARTHQUAKE 1974
LOCATION: Kashmir province, India
NOTES: The earthquake shook the entire province and claimed the lives of more than 5,000 people.

85 L7 ALICIA
TSUNAMI 1976
LOCATION: Mindanao, Philippines
NOTES: The vast wave, triggered by an undersea earthquake in the Celebes Sea, struck the southwest Philippines. Alicia was devastated and 8,000 people died.

86 L2 TANGSHAN
EARTHQUAKE 1976
LOCATION: China
NOTES: See pp.42–43.

87 I6 BANGKOK
DISEASE (TUBERCULOSIS) 1985
LOCATION: Thailand
NOTES: There has been a resurgence of TB among people in poor health and poor living conditions. It is spreading, in tandem with HIV, across Asia, where it has reached epidemic proportions and is increasing rapidly. The disease affects around 1.7 billion people globally.

88 G5 DHAKA
FLOOD (MONSOON) 1988
LOCATION: Bangladesh
NOTES: Two-thirds of the country was inundated in the worst monsoons in its history. About 2,000 people drowned, 160,000 were affected by disease, and around 28 million were destitute.

89 G4 DHANKUTA
EARTHQUAKE 1988
LOCATION: Nepal
NOTES: Almost 1,000 people died and 6,500 were injured in the Nepal/India border region. Around 65,000 homes were destroyed in eastern Nepal.

90 L6 CABANATUAN
EARTHQUAKE 1990
LOCATION: Luzon Island, Philippines
NOTES: The severe 7.7-magnitude tremor ruined the city and killed 1,653 people.

91 C3 KABUL
EARTHQUAKE 1991
LOCATION: Hindu Kush, Afghanistan
NOTES: The earthquake, felt as far away as Delhi, devastated three provinces and killed more than 300 people.

92 L6 PINATUBO
VOLCANO 1991
LOCATION: Philippines
NOTES: See pp.28–31.

93 G5 SANDWIP ISLAND
TROPICAL CYCLONE 1991
LOCATION: Bangladesh
NOTES: See p.71.

94 E4 UTTAR PRADESH
EARTHQUAKE 1991
LOCATION: India
NOTES: The 6.1-magnitude tremor left around 1,000 people dead throughout Uttar Pradesh.

95 L3 WUXI
FLOOD 1991
LOCATION: China
NOTES: See pp.88–89.

96 E6 OSMANABAD
EARTHQUAKE 1993
LOCATION: India
NOTES: The earthquake devastated the entire area, killing 9,748 people, and injuring about 30,000 more.

97 F4 TARAI PLAIN, KATHMANDU
FLOOD 1993
LOCATION: Nepal
NOTES: The heaviest rains in Nepal's history caused the Bagmati River to overflow. Most of the villages on its eastern banks were deluged and 687 people were drowned.

98 G5 TANGAIL
TORNADO 1996
LOCATION: Dhaka, Bangladesh
NOTES: The tornado, with winds of 125 mph (200 kph) killed more than 500 people, injured at least 50,000, and destroyed 10,000 homes.

99 G5 COX'S BAZAAR
TROPICAL CYCLONE 1997
LOCATION: Bangladesh
NOTES: The tropical cyclone raged over the island and damaged thousands of homes. The low death toll of 67 was due to the timely evacuation of more than 500,000 people, the provision of hundreds of storm shelters, and an unusually low tide.

100 J7 HO CHI MINH CITY
TYPHOON LINDA 1997
LOCATION: South Vietnam
NOTES: Typhoon Linda, one of the worst storms ever to hit Southeast Asia, devastated many coastal villages and destroyed crops. Around 150,000 people were made homeless and 265 were killed, 235 of whom were fishermen who were drowned when their boats were sunk.

101 K5 HONG KONG
DISEASE ("BIRD" INFLUENZA) 1997
LOCATION: South China Sea
NOTES: The influenza outbreak, which killed several people, is thought to have originated from chickens that had been imported from mainland China. The Chinese authorities slaughtered Hong Kong's entire chicken population in an effort to contain the virus.

102 G5 MIDNAPORE DISTRICT
FLOOD 1997
LOCATION: West Bengal, India
NOTES: Prolonged monsoons inundated the district, collapsing 16,000 houses, and leaving 100,000 people homeless. Water supplies were contaminated and crops were destroyed.

103 D2 ROSTAQ
EARTHQUAKE 1998
LOCATION: Afghanistan
NOTES: The town and several nearby villages were devastated when the 6.1-magnitude earthquake shook a remote area in the north, collapsing the hills and leaving a huge crater. More than 4,000 people were killed and a further 15,000 were left homeless in freezing winter conditions.

104 K1 ZHANGBEI
EARTHQUAKE 1998
LOCATION: China
NOTES: The 6.2-magnitude earthquake hit scores of villages in the Yan Mountain area. At least 50 people were killed and tens of thousands were left homeless in freezing winter conditions.

NORTH ASIA & JAPAN

The map for these listings is on p.138.

1 INSET TURA
VOLCANO 250 MILLION YEARS BC
LOCATION: Siberian Uplands, Russia
NOTES: *See pp.100–101.*

2 INSET POPIGAI
SPACE THREAT 39 MILLION YEARS BC
LOCATION: Siberia, Russia
NOTES: A meteor strike left a 62-mile (100-km) crater that covered a vast area in cosmic debris. The impact occurred near the end of the Eocene era and is thought to have killed off some species of giant birds and mammals such as lemur-like primates.

3 INSET NORTHERN YAKUTIA
FREEZE (GLACIATION) 10,000 YEARS AGO
LOCATION: Siberia
NOTES: The greatest mystery surrounding the end of the Last Ice Age is why so many woolly mammoths froze to death in Siberia. One of several theories is that a worldwide displacement of the Earth's crust shunted Russia nearer to the North Pole and shifted America southward. Another is that the Earth shifted on its axis, moving the North Pole from over Hudson Bay to its present position.

4 F6 KAMAKURA
EARTHQUAKE 1293
LOCATION: Honshu, Japan
NOTES: Kamakura was devastated and 30,000 lives were lost when the violent earthquake struck the island.

5 E6 KII
TSUNAMI 1498
LOCATION: Honshu, Japan
NOTES: Around 1,000 people were killed by the tsunami, which followed an earthquake on the Kii coast.

6 C7 IZUMI
EARTHQUAKE 1596
LOCATION: Kyushu, Japan
NOTES: The earthquake decimated Izumi and destroyed the castle at Fushimi. Around 2,000 people were killed.

7 D7 URYA-JIMA
TSUNAMI 1596
LOCATION: Japan
NOTES: A 50-ft (15-m) wall of water overwhelmed the tiny island, drowning 700 of its 5,000 inhabitants. The island sank beneath 180 ft (55 m) of water and never resurfaced. The survivors reached the mainland in fishing boats.

8 F5 INAWASHIRO
EARTHQUAKE/TSUNAMI 1611
LOCATION: Honshu, Japan
NOTES: The earthquake obliterated the city, killing 3,700 people. The ensuing tsunami submerged the entire area, turning it into a permanent lake.

9 F6 EDO (NOW TOKYO)
EARTHQUAKE 1703
LOCATION: Honshu, Japan
NOTES: The old capital was destroyed and about 200,000 lives were lost in the earthquake and ensuing tsunami.

10 C8 OKINAWA
TSUNAMI 1703
LOCATION: Japan
NOTES: More than 100,000 people were killed in what is possibly the most destructive tsunami on record.

11 F3 KAMIKAWA
EARTHQUAKE 1730
LOCATION: Hokkaido, Japan
NOTES: Many towns and villages across Hokkaido were badly damaged by the earthquake, and 137,000 lives were lost.

12 F5 KAMAISHI
EARTHQUAKE 1737
LOCATION: Northeast Honshu, Japan
NOTES: Thousands of people were killed and Kamaishi was destroyed in the earthquake and ensuing tsunami.

13 F4 HIROSAKI
EARTHQUAKE/TSUNAMIS 1766
LOCATION: Northern Honshu, Japan
NOTES: More than 1,000 people died and about 7,500 buildings were destroyed when the earthquake precipitated a series of tsunamis.

14 C7 ONTAKE
VOLCANO 1779–1780
LOCATION: Sakurajima, off Kyushu, Japan
NOTES: Day became night when the volcano showered both Sakurajima and Kyushu with ejecta, burying at least 20 villages and killing around 300 people.

15 E6 ASAMAYAMA
VOLCANO 1783
LOCATION: Honshu, Japan
NOTES: The eruption of one of Japan's most active volcanoes sent lava bombs raining down like meteors on 48 villages, crushing them to dust and killing 5,000 inhabitants. A huge rock landed in the river, creating a new, permanent island.

16 C7 OMUTA
TSUNAMI 1792
LOCATION: Kyushu, Japan
NOTES: The 30-ft (9-m) wave crashed in from the Ariake Sea, obliterating the town and killing almost 10,000 people.

17 C7 UNZEN
VOLCANO 1792
LOCATION: Kyushu, Japan
NOTES: The cities of Higo and Shimabara were annihilated and 15,000 inhabitants were killed following this eruption, one of the worst in Japan's history.

18 F6 TOKYO
EARTHQUAKE 1857
LOCATION: Honshu, Japan
NOTES: Violent tremors devastated Tokyo and surrounding provinces. Multiple fires broke out and, fanned by 60-mph (96-kph) winds, quickly spread through the city, causing most of the 107,000 deaths.

19 E6 MINO
EARTHQUAKE 1891
LOCATION: Honshu, Japan
NOTES: The huge earthquake reverberated over three-fifths of Japan. Lasting no more than six seconds, it flattened 20,000 buildings and killed 6,000 people outright. Around 1,000 more people died of their injuries within a few weeks.

20 F5 KAMAISHI
TSUNAMIS 1896
LOCATION: Northeast Honshu, Japan
NOTES: A series of tsunamis smashed Honshu's Sanriku coast. The first wave hurtled inland, submerging Kamaishi and killing 4,700 of its 6,557 inhabitants. The death toll reached 28,000 as scores of other towns and villages were deluged.

21 INSET NAMANGAN
EARTHQUAKE 1902
LOCATION: Eastern Ubekistan
NOTES: The 6.4-magnitude earthquake caused major damage throughout the region and killed 4,500 people.

22 INSET TUNGUSKA
SPACE THREAT 1908
LOCATION: Siberia
NOTES: A fragment of cometary material disintegrated in the air over a sparsely populated area, creating a fireball that incinerated 770 sq miles (2,000 sq km) of forest. Shock waves were felt 2,500 miles (4,000 km) away, and the sky was light enough to read by at midnight as far away as Europe and North America.

23 C7 KAGOSHIMA
TSUNAMI 1914
LOCATION: Kyushu, Japan
NOTES: Dozens of the city's residents, who were fleeing an earthquake, were trapped in the narrow streets near the seafront when a 16-ft (5-m) tsunami smashed inland. The death toll reached 35, with a further 21 people missing.

24 F6 TOKYO
EARTHQUAKE/FIRES 1923
LOCATION: Honshu, Japan
NOTES: The 8.3-magnitude tremor rocked the entire Great Eastern Plain, flattening 600,000 homes. Most of the 143,000 victims were consumed by the fires that raged out of control across several cities.

25 F5 KAMAISHI
TSUNAMI 1933
LOCATION: Northeast Honshu, Japan
NOTES: Following a severe underwater earthquake, the Sanriku coastline was assaulted by a huge wave that swept up thousands of tiny, phosphorescent sea creatures, causing the wave to glow. In local folklore, a huge, glowing sea dragon was responsible for the 3,000 deaths and 10,000 wrecked homes.

26 E6 OSAKA
TROPICAL CYCLONE 1934
LOCATION: Honshu, Japan
NOTES: Most of Osaka's buildings were made of wood, and 87 schools, unable to withstand the severe winds that battered them, disintegrated, killing 420 pupils. The city's textile industry was wiped out when 3,082 factories were ruined with the loss of 4,000 lives.

27 E6 KII
TSUNAMI 1944
LOCATION: Honshu, Japan
NOTES: The huge 25-ft (8-m) wave swept through Kii, causing immense damage and killing almost 1,000 people.

28 D6 HIROSHIMA
EARTHQUAKE/TSUNAMIS 1946
LOCATION: Honshu, Japan
NOTES: An undersea earthquake shook and demolished 25 new buildings in Hiroshima. The tsunamis created by the tremor left 50 towns and cities in ruins and 2,000 people dead. More than 40,000 homes were ruined.

29 INSET KAMCHATKA
TSUNAMI 1952
LOCATION: USSR (now eastern Russia)
NOTES: Pacific-wide tsunamis, caused by an earthquake off Kamchatka, wrecked the Russian coast. They also seriously damaged Midway Island, 1,875 miles (3,020 km) to the south, and Hawaii.

30 F4 HAKODATE
TYPHOON MARIE 1954
LOCATION: Hokkaido, Japan
NOTES: Marie devastated the entire island, crippling the road and railroad systems, and killing hundreds of people. Another 1,000 lives were lost when the *Toya Maru* sank outside Hakodate harbor.

31 F6 TOKYO
TYPHOON IDA 1958
LOCATION: Honshu, Japan
NOTES: Heavy rains and high winds devastated the Izu Peninsula, causing widespread flooding and about 2,000 landslides. More than 1,000 homes in dozens of villages were washed away with the loss of more than 600 lives. The area's rice crop was decimated when 120,000 acres (48,600 hectacres) of rice fields became small lakes

32 E6 NAGOYA
TYPHOON VERA 1959
LOCATION: Honshu, Japan
NOTES: The worst typhoon in Japan's history wreaked havoc across several provinces. More than 5,000 people were killed, mostly in Nagoya, which was lashed by 15-ft (5-m) waves that ruined almost 6,000 homes within minutes.

33 E6 ISHIKAWA
FLOOD 1964
LOCATION: Honshu, Japan
NOTES: Torrential rains caused major flooding across five provinces. Swollen rivers broke through dykes in more than 200 places, and 150 bridges collapsed. Landslides wiped out many villages. A total of 108 people died, and a further 44,000 were left homeless.

34 F5 OGA PENINSULA
TSUNAMI 1983
LOCATION: Honshu, Japan
NOTES: The colossal wave, the result of an earthquake, rose 49 ft (15 m) out of the Sea of Japan overwhelming Oga and killing 107 people.

35 C7 UNZEN
VOLCANO 1991
LOCATION: Kyushu, Japan
NOTES: Pyroclastic flows tore down the mountainside, killing a team of scientists and journalists monitoring the eruption.

36 E4 OKUSHIRI
TSUNAMI 1993
LOCATION: Okushiri Island, Japan
NOTES: The town, which was built on a promontory on the island, was hit from both sides by the 35-ft (11-m) wave. Virtually every building was smashed to matchwood and 240 lives were lost.

37 D6 KOBE
EARTHQUAKE 1995
LOCATION: Honshu, Japan
NOTES: *See pp.46–49.*

38 INSET PAROMAY
EARTHQUAKE 1995
LOCATION: Sakhalin Island, Russia
NOTES: The 7.5-magnitude tremor caused severe damage across the entire island and killed 2,000 people.

SOUTH PACIFIC

The map for these listings is on p.139.

1 P8 TAUPO

VOLCANO C. AD 150

LOCATION: North Island, New Zealand
NOTES: This eruption, probably more powerful than any other of the last 2,000 years, including Krakatau, is thought to have turned the North Island into a gray desert. All that can be seen there now is the volcano's caldera, Lake Taupo.

2 O9 TAPANUI

SPACE THREAT AD 1200

LOCATION: South Island, New Zealand
NOTES: Maori myths and legends tell of the skies' falling, the earth's upheaval, and strange, destructive fires from space. Evidence suggests that a meteor strike created the immense "Landslip Crater" and extensive fires around this time.

3 I4 PAPANDAYAN

VOLCANO 1772

LOCATION: Java
NOTES: The 8,750-ft (2,652-m) mountain was reduced by 4,000 ft (1,212 m) when it sank like a stone into a heaving sea of lava, taking with it 3,000 people and 40 towns and villages.

4 J4 MIYI-YAMA

VOLCANO 1793

LOCATION: Kiousiou, Java
NOTES: The eruption caused the volcano to explode. Tons of mud and water rained down on the surrounding plains, killing around 53,000 people.

5 K5 MAUMÈRE

TSUNAMI 1800

LOCATION: Flores Island, Indonesia
NOTES: The gigantic wave crashed over the island, wiping out the town and killing around 500 islanders.

6 J5 TAMBORA

VOLCANO 1815

LOCATION: Sumbawa, Indonesia
NOTES: All but 26 of the 12,000 islanders were killed. Most were swept up in violent clouds of gas and ash. A British administrator, Sir Thomas Raffles, described the volcano as "a body of liquid fire [that] raged until the darkness caused by...falling matter obscured it". Debris in the atmosphere affected the climate around the world. Vast amounts of ash fell on farmland and fishing areas. The resulting famine brought the death toll to more than 90,000.

7 J4 GALUNGGUNG

VOLCANO 1822

LOCATION: Java
NOTES: During the eruption, mud, ash, and rocks were blown over a 40-mile (65-km) area. Streams of burning mud slid down the mountain, engulfing dozens of villages and killing 1,000 people. A second eruption four days later killed a further 4,000.

8 P8 AUCKLAND

DISEASE 1840-1860

LOCATION: North Island, New Zealand
NOTES: In the 20 years following the arrival of Europeans on the island, whooping cough, smallpox, measles, and influenza swept through the Maori population, reducing their numbers from 100,000 to 40,000.

9 L7 ADELAIDE

PEST/BLIGHT (RABBITS) 1859

LOCATION: South Australia
NOTES: Rabbits, introduced into Australia by settlers in 1859, flourished in the absence of natural predators. Spreading across the continent over many years, eating the grass grown for sheep, rabbits became a major pest. In 1950, humans intervened by transferring the virus, myxomatosis, which is related to the human smallpox virus, to the rabbit population. This measure has controlled their numbers effectively throughout Australia to this day.

10 P5 FIJI

DISEASE (MEASLES) 1874

LOCATION: Polynesia
NOTES: The disease, which was carried into Polynesia by Europeans, went on the rampage on Fiji, killing 20 percent of the native population.

11 I4 KRAKATAU

VOLCANO 1883

LOCATION: Sunda Straits, Indonesia
NOTES: See pp.24–25.

12 P8 TARAWERA

VOLCANO 1886

LOCATION: North Island, New Zealand
NOTES: The eruption sent a huge cloud of ash 6 miles (10 km) into the air that affected the weather halfway across the world. Ash and rocks rained down on three villages to the north of the island, killing 150 people, and burying the hydrothermal deposits at the Pink and White Terraces.

13 J4 KELUD

VOLCANO 1919

LOCATION: Java
NOTES: Following Kelud's eruption, its crater-lake gushed down the mountain and formed vast lahars, which swept down into the surrounding valleys and killed 5,500 people.

14 J5 MERAPI

VOLCANO 1931

LOCATION: Java
NOTES: For three weeks following the eruption, a river of lava 80 ft (24 m) deep and 600 ft (182 m) wide streamed down the mountain, and claimed more than 1,300 lives.

15 P8 NAPIER

EARTHQUAKE 1931

LOCATION: North Island, New Zealand
NOTES: The country's largest ever earthquake claimed the lives of 256 people. Most of the town center was demolished, and fires broke out, gutting the commercial area. The land around the town lifted 6 ft (2 m), causing the rivers to change course.

16 M8 MELBOURNE

FIRE 1937

LOCATION: Victoria, Australia
NOTES: The entire state of Victoria was ravaged by bushfires, which claimed the lives of 71 people.

17 M4 RABAUL

VOLCANO 1937

LOCATION: Papua New Guinea
NOTES: During the eruption, at least 441 people were killed by a violent steam explosion, ejecta, and pyroclastic flows.

18 M5 LAMINGTON

VOLCANO 1951

LOCATION: Papua New Guinea
NOTES: The eruption produced ash flows that claimed the lives of 6,000 people; the entire population of the island's northern coast.

19 P8 RAUPEHU

VOLCANO 1953

LOCATION: North Island, New Zealand
NOTES: The eruption created a lahar that swept along the Tongariro river and washed away the railroad bridge. The Wellington to Auckland train plunged into the river, killing 155 people.

20 M7 MAITLAND

FLOOD 1955

LOCATION: New South Wales, Australia
NOTES: A cyclone caused seven rivers to overflow, flooding 20 towns. About 10,000 homes were badly damaged and 22 lives were lost.

21 J5 AGUNG

VOLCANO 1963

LOCATION: Bali, Indonesia
NOTES: Agung emitted a poisonous black cloud that killed hundreds of people worshipping beside the Besakih temple, erected to ward off evil spirits. For five days, scalding lava poured over three villages, bringing the death toll to 1,200.

22 P8 HAMILTON

FIRE 1967

LOCATION: Tasmania, Australia
NOTES: Unusually high temperatures, low humidity, and severe north-westerly winds turned a few small fires into a blazing inferno that engulfed south Tasmania, including the northern and western suburbs of Hobart. The largest ever loss of property and life on the Australian continent in any one day razed more than 1,300 homes to the ground in 14 municipalities and claimed the lives of 62 people.

23 M6 TOWNSVILLE

CYCLONE ALTHEA 1971

LOCATION: Queensland, Australia
NOTES: Cyclone Althea, with winds of up to 122 mph (196 kph), ripped through Townsville, causing major damage and killing several people. A storm-warning system was set up in the wake of this severe cyclone.

24 K5 DARWIN

CYCLONE TRACY 1974

LOCATION: Northern Territory, Australia
NOTES: See pp.68–69.

25 M7 MACEDON

FIRE (ASH WEDNESDAY) 1983

FIRE Victoria, Australia
NOTES: See pp.84–85.

26 P8 RUAPEHU

VOLCANO 1986

LOCATION: North Island, New Zealand
NOTES: The eruption caused a massive steam explosion. Hot, highly acidic water from the volcano's crater-lake poured down the mountain, melting the ice and snow on the slopes. A vast lahar was formed, posing a threat for skiers on nearby slopes.

27 M7 NEWCASTLE

EARTHQUAKE 1989

LOCATION: New South Wales, Australia
NOTES: The 5.6-magnitude tremor shook Newcastle, Australia's sixth largest city, causing severe damage and the deaths of 13 people. It was the first earthquake in the country to hit an urban area.

28 M6 QUEENSLAND

FLOOD 1990

LOCATION: Queensland, Australia
NOTES: Torrential rain following a drought caused major floods across one-third of the state. Many outback towns were inundated in some of the worst flooding for a century.

29 M4 MARKHAM VALLEY

EARTHQUAKE 1993

LOCATION: Papua New Guinea
NOTES: The earthquake resulted in major landslides that dammed the Ume River. A total of 60 people were killed, many of whom were drowned in the resulting floods, and several more were injured.

30 M7 GRAFTON

DROUGHT 1994

LOCATION: New South Wales, Australia
NOTES: The start of the El Niño weather system in the Pacific Ocean led to a drought across eastern Australia that affected both New South Wales and Queensland. When this phase of the drought ended, six months later, 93 percent of New South Wales was severely affected, and the wheat crop throughout the state was reduced by 90 percent.

31 M7 SYDNEY

FIRE 1994

LOCATION: New South Wales, Australia
NOTES: More than 100 homes were razed to the ground and four people were killed when bushfires raged across the state. The city's beaches were covered in a layer of ash.

32 M7 LITHGOW

FIRE 1997

LOCATION: New South Wales, Australia
NOTES: Two firefighters were killed as the worst bushfires in 30 years ravaged New South Wales. The fires threatened the suburbs of Sydney, forcing hundreds of residents to evacuate the area.

33 M5 PORT MORESBY

DROUGHT/FREEZE 1997

LOCATION: Papua New Guinea
NOTES: At least 60 people perished when repeated frosts in high-altitude areas decimated the sweet potato crops and the Fly River dried up, which effectively severed the country's main food and fuel supply line. In all, around 700,000 people were affected.

34 M8 THREDBO

LANDSLIDE/AVALANCHE 1997

LOCATION: New South Wales, Australia
NOTES: The country's premier ski resort, built on steep slopes, suffered a landslide that buried 20 people in two ski lodges. The sole survivor was dug out after 65 hours.

35 M6 TOWNSVILLE

FLOOD 1998

LOCATION: Queensland, Australia
NOTES: The flood inundated the town and swept cars and the wreckage of homes into the ocean. One person was swept off a bridge and drowned, and another disappeared into the churning, muddy waters of a nearby river.

GLOSSARY

AFTERSHOCKS
Smaller seismic events that occur after an earthquake, and which can persist for days or weeks after the main shock.

AGE
A passage of time in the Earth's history distinguished by special characteristics.

AMPLITUDE
A measurement of the size of a wave form that can be used to determine the magnitude of an earthquake.

ANTIBIOTIC RESISTANCE
The ability of a microorganism to resist the effects of antibiotics.

ANTIBIOTICS
Literally meaning "destructive of life," antibiotics are chemical substances that are highly toxic to bacteria but relatively harmless to animals and are used in the treatment of bacterial infections.

ANTIBODIES
Special molecules that are produced in the blood of animals in response to the presence of an antigen. By attaching themselves to the antigens on infectious organisms, antibodies can render them harmless or cause them to be destroyed.

ANTIGEN
A substance that stimulates the release of antibodies.

ASTEROID
A rocky or metallic body orbiting the Sun in the same plane as the planets. Most asteroids orbit between Mars and Jupiter, and are thought to be fragments of a planet that exploded early in the history of the Solar System, or material that failed to condense into a planet. However, there are also about 100,000 asteroids orbiting between the Earth and Mars, some of which are close enough to be captured by Earth's gravity.

ATMOSPHERE
The gaseous envelope that surrounds the Earth. It consists chiefly of oxygen and nitrogen and is made up of several distinct layers that are progressively less dense the higher up they are.

ATMOSPHERIC PRESSURE
The force that is exerted by the air in the atmosphere. Atmospheric pressure depends primarily on the weight of overlying air and it therefore varies according to altitude. Air movements also affect the pressure. In regions where air is rising the pressure is lowered, and in regions where air is falling the pressure is increased.

BACTERIA
A big and diverse group of single-celled microorganisms that commonly multiply by cell division. Bacteria are thought to have been the earliest life forms on Earth. Some live on or inside the human body, particularly within the intestine, without causing any harm. However, other types of bacteria cause infectious diseases.

Some of these infectious bacteria have evolved an immunity to every antibiotic developed to date.

BAROMETER
An instrument for measuring atmospheric pressure. The most accurate type is the mercury barometer, which records the pressure of air by measuring how far mercury is forced up a glass tube.

CAMBRIAN
The first period (570 to 510 million years ago) of the Paleozoic Era witnessed the emergence of complex life forms, which included a wide range of brachiopods, arthropods, and mollusks.

COMET
Sometimes known as "dirty snowballs," comets are masses of ice, frozen gases, and dust that orbit the Sun elliptically. On nearing the Sun, comets are heated, and the gases evaporate and form into a long, bright tail.

CORE
The center of the Earth is composed of dense metals, particularly iron. At the very center, the pressure is so great that the metal is solid despite the enormous heat. This moon-sized inner core is surrounded by a layer of molten iron.

CORIOLIS EFFECT
The effect of the Earth's rotation on the direction of the movement of air and water. In the Northern Hemisphere winds and ocean currents moving toward the equator are deflected to the right, and in the Southern Hemisphere to the left. The Coriolis effect also causes rising and falling air to spiral.

CRETACEOUS
The final period (146 to 65 million years ago) of the Mesozoic Era and the last period in which dinosaurs were the dominant land animals. In the Cretaceous, North and South America separated from Europe and Africa, and the continents moved northward, causing temperatures to drop. The mass extinction at the end of the period wiped out up to 75 percent of species, including all the dinosaurs.

DEPRESSION
A region of low atmospheric pressure also known as a low.

DEVONIAN
The fourth period (408 to 362 million years ago) of the Paleozoic Era. The climate throughout the Devonian period was warm, and much of the land was covered by shallow swamps. New fish species evolved, including those with bony fins that, later in the period, became the first vertebrates to venture onto land. There was also a series of mass extinctions, the worst of which wiped out more than 70 percent of the species living at that time.

DIKE
A bank of earth built on coasts or along river banks to protect land from flooding

when the water rises. Dikes are often known as levees in the United States.

DOPPLER RADAR
An instrument that uses radio waves to detect the movement of air. Doppler radar is used to identify thunderclouds that are likely to generate tornadoes before their spiraling funnels appear from the base of the cloud.

EARTH
The Earth is the third planet from the Sun, orbiting it at an average distance of about 93 million miles (150 million kilometers). The Earth is estimated to have formed about 4.6 billion years ago.

EL NIÑO
The name that is commonly given to a shift of currents in the Pacific Ocean that affects weather patterns around the world. El Niño is Spanish for "The Child," or "Christ child," the name that Peruvian fishermen give a warm current that flows near to the Peruvian coast for a few weeks around Christmas. In El Niño years, these waters remain warm for several months and countries to the east of the Pacific experience unusually heavy rain, while countries to the west of the Pacific have less rain than usual.

ENSO
An acronym for the change in Pacific weather patterns, commonly known as El Niño, combined with the Southern Oscillation, a change in air pressure over the Pacific. Scientists combined the two names when the oscillating weather patterns, which had been observed in the South Pacific and southern Asia, were found to be linked to El Niño.

EPICENTER
The point on the surface that is directly above the focus or hypocenter of an earthquake. The seismic waves are at their highest amplitude and the damage is greatest at the epicenter.

EPOCH
A division of geological time that is most commonly used to describe the subdivision of the two periods in the Cenozoic Era (65 million years ago up to the present day).

FAULT
A fracture in a rock formation caused by the shifting or dislodging of the Earth's crust due to tectonic movement.

FIREBREAK
An open space, with very little or no vegetation or other combustible material, that is designed to stop the spread of a fire. When a fire is driven by strong winds, firebreaks have to be very wide in order to be effective.

FLOOD
The inundation of land by either sea or freshwater. Freshwater floods can occur in the form of a flash flood, which is the result of a single, torrential rainfall. A freshwater flood can also be caused by a long period of unusually high rainfall. Sea floods may also be of long or short duration. When a storm strikes at a time of high tide, the sea briefly invades the land. Long-term sea flooding is caused by sea-level rises due to tectonic upheavals or the melting of ice caps.

FOCUS
The place within the Earth where rock breaks and from which seismic waves emanate during an earthquake.

FUNGI
A diverse group of living organisms, the majority of which live by decomposing organic matter. The fungi group includes single-celled organisms such as yeast and multicellular organisms such as mushrooms. Many fungi have evolved to form close relationships with a plant species. This relationship can be mutually beneficial but in some cases the presence of the fungi damages or kills the plant. Most plant diseases are caused by fungi, but a few fungi cause disease in humans and other animal species.

GALAXY
A vast collection of stars that is held together by gravity. Our own galaxy is a spiral galaxy known as the Milky Way and contains in the region of 500 billion stars.

GLACIER
A long-lived mass of ice that flows over land under the force of gravity. Glaciers are formed by compacted snow falling on mountains or on land near the poles where the rate of new snow deposited is greater than the rate of thawing.

GREENHOUSE EFFECT
The accumulation of heat in the lower atmosphere caused by the buildup of gases such as methane and carbon dioxide. Heat energy radiating from the Earth's surface is reflected back by these gases, so the higher their concentration in the atmosphere, the greater the level of heat energy that gets trapped.

HANTAVIRUSES
A group of viruses causing epidemics of hemorrhagic fever or pneumonia. They are thought to be transmitted to humans through contact with infected rat feces.

HOT-SPOT VOLCANO
Volcanoes that form in the middle of a tectonic plate rather than at a plate boundary. They occur where a plume of extremely hot rock is welling up from deep within the mantle and manages to melt its way through the crust. This is most likely to take place on the seabed and creates midocean islands such as the Hawaiian and Canary Islands.

HURRICANE
The name usually given to the tropical cyclones that hit the Caribbean and American coasts. The word is derived from the Caribbean word "urican," meaning strong wind.

ICE AGE
A phase during an ice epoch when the global temperatures are particularly low and the ice caps spread out from the poles. At the peak of the Last Ice Age, about 18,000 years ago, glaciers covered almost half of North America, and large areas of Eurasia and South America.

ICE CAP
A thick sheet of glacial ice that covers a large area of land or frozen water. The current position of the continents has caused an ice cap to form at both the North Pole and the South Pole.

ICE EPOCH
A period in the Earth's history when an ice cap covers one or both of the poles and the mean global temperature is cooler than normal.

LAHAR
The Javanese word for mudslide, a lahar often occurs as a result of the eruption of a subduction volcano when volcanic ash mixes with water to form a sticky slurry of mud that flows rapidly down the sides of a volcano.

LAVA
Molten rock that flows onto the surface from an erupting volcano.

LEVEE
See Dike.

LIQUEFACTION
A change in the composition of soil and other sediments into a soft slurry that is caused by the upward movement of water during an earthquake. Liquefaction increases the damaging effects of an earthquake because the ground can no longer support the weight of buildings.

MAGMA
The molten rock and dissolved volcanic gases that are trapped beneath the Earth's crust. The chemical composition of magma influences the force of an eruption. Usually, the more dissolved gas in the magma, the more explosive the eruption.

MAGNITUDE (EARTHQUAKE)
The severity of an earthquake is based on the amount of energy released by fracturing rock. This is calculated in several different ways depending on the scale used. The oldest and best-known is the Richter scale.

MANTLE
A 1,800-mile (2,900-kilometer) thick layer of hot rock that lies between the Earth's metallic core and the thin layer of cool rocky crust on the surface. Although the rock of the mantle is hot enough to be molten, the enormous pressure created by the weight of the rock above causes it to be very viscous, and it therefore circulates extremely slowly.

METEOR
A bright trail or streak visible in the sky when a piece of extraterrestrial rock or metal captured by the Earth's gravity passes through the atmosphere. The object glows with the heat caused by the friction of its passage through the air and the outer layers vaporize. All but the largest of these objects disintegrate before reaching the ground.

METEORITE
The name given to a meteor or comet that hits the Earth's surface.

MISTRAL
A cold, dry wind that blows from the Alps across the south of France. The wind is strongest on the coast, reaching speeds of up to 85 mph (135 kph), and is most frequent in winter and spring.

MODIFIED MERCALLI INTENSITY SCALE
A scale used to describe the extent of earthquake damage that uses Roman numerals to describe the level of damage.

In areas where all the buildings have collapsed, the value is XII. When there is only minor damage, but the earthquake can be felt, the value is VI. When the tremors are so weak that they can only be detected by instruments, the value is I.

MONSOON
Seasonal rains that are caused by a change in wind direction, and occur in much of Southeast Asia, north Australia, Africa, and Central America.

PANDEMIC
Rapid spread of a disease over a wide geographical area, usually the world.

PERMIAN
The final period (290 to 250 million years ago) of the Paleozoic Era. During this period landmasses moved toward the equator, forming a single continent known as Pangaea. The movement of the continents caused most of the shallow seas to disappear and brought a sharp rise in temperature. At the end of the period, huge volcanic eruptions may have triggered a climatic upheaval that led to the greatest mass extinction in the Earth's history, in which more than 90 percent of species died out.

PRION
An abnormal protein found in the brains of animals suffering from certain fatal brain diseases such as Creutzfeldt-Jakob disease, which affects humans, the sheep disease scrapie, and bovine spongiform encephalopathy (BSE) in cattle.

PUMICE
A low-density rock that forms when lava solidifies with bubbles of volcanic gases still trapped inside. The density is often so low that the rock floats.

PYROCLASTIC FLOW OR SURGE
A glowing cloud of hot toxic gas that contains droplets of molten rock erupted from a subduction volcano. The mixture is heavier than air, so the cloud flows down gullies like a river. When the cloud contains a high proportion of gas, it is known as a pyroclastic surge.

RESONANCE
A rise in the amplitude of a vibration that occurs when the frequency of the vibrations is equal to or very close to the natural undamped frequency of the matter through which the vibrations are passing. The composition of certain natural features and buildings resonate seismic waves, increasing their effects.

RICHTER SCALE
A scale for expressing the severity of an earthquake developed in 1935 by the American seismologist, Charles Richter. It is a measurement of the total energy released during an earthquake and is calculated from the amplitude of the shock waves detected by seismographs. The scale, which ranges from 1 to 10, is logarithmic so that each increase of 1 represents a 32-fold increase in the level of energy released by the earthquake.

RIFTING BOUNDARY
A tectonic plate boundary at which the plates are being slowly forced apart and new crust is formed by solidifying lava. The rise of plumes of hotter rock in the mantle splits the solid rock of the crust,

allowing lava to rise to the surface. Most rifting boundaries are beneath the sea, but the Great Rift Valley in Africa is the most notable exception.

SEISMIC WAVES
Shock waves that radiate in all directions from the focus of an earthquake. They consist of primary or "P" waves, which travel like sound waves and produce a rushing wind noise at the surface that people often hear before the shaking of an earthquake begins. Most earthquake damage is caused by the secondary or "S" waves, which travel more slowly and cause the ground to shake.

SOLAR SYSTEM
The Solar System consists of the Sun, nine planets, more than 60 moons, and countless asteroids and comets. The Solar System occupies a disk-shaped volume of space that is more than 7.4 billion miles (12 billion kilometers) across.

STORM SURGE
A rise in the sea level caused by the low air pressure and strong winds of a large storm. Surges frequently cause serious flooding, especially when their arrival coincides with a high tide.

STRATOSPHERE
An upper layer of the atmosphere in which the air is very dry and there is virtually no weather activity.

SUBDUCTION BOUNDARY
This type of boundary occurs where two tectonic plates are pushing together and the rock at the edge of the plates is of a different density. In these conditions the heavier plate is forced under the lighter plate and melts to become part of the rock in the mantle. Since the rock of the seabed is of higher density than the rock of land masses, subduction often occurs at the boundary between a plate carrying a continent and a plate carrying the ocean floor.

SUBDUCTION VOLCANO
The most explosive and deadliest sort of volcano. Such volcanoes are created as a result of crustal subduction, which takes rock, sediment, and water down into the heat and high-pressure environment of the mantle. Here it becomes a mixture of molten rock and dissolved gas that slowly rises and collects beneath the crust. When the pressure is too great, the molten rock bursts to the surface.

SULFUR DIOXIDE
A gas often released during violent volcanic eruptions that is responsible for global cooling. The gas is shot high up into the atmosphere, where it remains for many months acting like a planetary sunscreen that reflects part of the Sun's radiation back into space.

SUN
A star, located 30,000 light years from the center of the Galaxy, that contains over 99.9 percent of the Solar System's mass and acts as the gravitational pivot around which all planets in this system orbit. The Sun is also the Solar System's energy source, reaching temperatures of 27 million degrees Fahrenheit (15 million degrees Celcius) at its core and about 9,900°F (5,500°C) at the surface.

SUPERCELL
A thunderstorm that is large enough to produce tornadoes. The columns of rising and falling air in average-sized thunderstorms are not wide enough to be influenced by the Coriolis effect, but in supercells the updrafts and downdrafts are large enough to spiral.

TECTONIC PLATE
The crust of solid rock covering the surface of the Earth is broken up into seven large and more than eight smaller pieces, known as tectonic plates. These plates are moved at the rate of about an inch a year by the circulation of magma in the mantle. Most of the Earth's volcanoes and earthquakes are located near to the boundaries of these plates.

TORNADO
A rapidly spinning column of air, usually funnel-shaped, that extends down from the largest thunderclouds to the ground. Here it creates a vortex over 2,640 feet (800 meters) in diameter in which winds rotate inward and upward at speeds of more than 300 mph (500 kph).

TROPICAL CYCLONE
A storm also known as a hurricane and typhoon, several hundred miles in diameter and thousands of feet high, that rotates around a central eye and generates winds in excess of 73 mph (118 kph). These storms form only over oceans near the equator when the water temperature is more than 76°F (24°C) and when winds are calm. The storms travel at 10 to 60 miles (16 to 100 kilometers) per hour away from the equator. Tropical cyclones that form to the north of the equator rotate in an counterclockwise direction and those that form in the Southern Hemisphere rotate in a clockwise direction.

TSUNAMI
A wave or series of waves generated when an earthquake, landslide, or volcanic eruption disturbs the ocean floor. They are sometimes called tidal waves or, if caused by an earthquake, seismic sea waves. "Tsunami" is a Japanese word meaning "port" (tsu) "wave" (nami).

TYPHOON
The name given to the tropical cyclones in many parts of Asia – derived from Chinese words "tai," meaning "great" and "feng" meaning "wind."

VECTOR
An animal that spreads disease-causing microorganisms.

VIRUS
A disease-causing microbe consisting of a small number of genes surrounded by a protective coat. A virus is not a cell, but exists as a cellular parasite. Viruses do not grow or reproduce independently but, upon entering a host cell, they use the host's biochemical machinery to either integrate their genes among the host's genes or to replicate themselves.

VOLCANIC ASH
Tiny fragments of rock created by the solidifying droplets of lava that explode from volcanoes and are shot high up into the atmosphere, where they darken the sky, before falling back to earth.

INDEX

ACKNOWLEDGMENTS

I WOULD LIKE TO THANK for their help and advice David Booth, Paul Henni, and Roger Musson at the British Geological Service; the International Tsunami Information Center, NOAA; Dr R Scott Steedman, Director of Engineering, GIBB Ltd, Reading; the Institute of Hydrology; The Fire Service College; The Meteorological Office; Dr Bill McGuire at the Centre for Volcanic Research and UCL; Simon Day; Juan Carracedo; Colin Tudge; Dr P.B. Wignall at the University of Leeds; and EQE International. I would also like to thank my agent, Lavinia Trevor, and the editors and designers at Dorling Kindersley, particularly Peter Adams, Teresa Pritlove, and Philip Ormerod.

Dorling Kindersley would like to thank:
Professor Michael Benton, University of Bristol; Peter Burkill, Plymouth Marine Laboratory; Paul Henni, Professor Antony Hallam, University of Birmingham Dr Benny Peiser, Liverpool John Moores University; and Dr Michael Blackford at the International Tsunami Information Center.

Illustrated locator maps
Sallie Alane Reason

Computer generated artworks
Jason Little; Philip Ormerod

Additional editorial assistance
Vicky Wilks; Heather Jones

Additional design assistance
Jo Earl; Pete Byrne

Index
Hilary Bird

French translations
Jonathan Hurrell

Cartographic research
David Perry

Dorling Kindersley would also like to thank the following for their kind permission to reproduce the photographs:

a=above, c=centre, b=below, l=left, r=right, t=top

AKG: 96bl;
Arquivo Nacional de Fotografia/Instituto Portugues de Museus: 45cl;
Tony Arruza: 45cl;
Associated Press Service: 41, 62cb;
Associated Press: Topham Picture Source: 62bl, 71l & r, 74bl;
Australian Picture Library: 53br;
Australian Picture Library: Evan Collis 84b;
Benelux Press: 92clb & bl;

Bishop Museum: 40br;
Bonnier-Alba: Lennart Nilsson 115;
Bridgeman Art Library: 26cl, Giraudon 45bl;
Camera Press: 88 cla & clb, Hoflinger 61;
J Allan Cash: 92cb, 97, 99tl;
China Features: 88cr; Liu Dong 42–3b, Di Yun 77tr, 88cr;
Bruce Coleman: 44b, 108ca, Alain Compost 13cb, Christopher Fredriksson 80cl;
Colorific!: 38, Alon Reininger 35bl, 38,121br, Rick Rickman 50tra, Michael Yamashita 49c;
Colorific!/Black Star: Cindy Karp 33cl, Boccon Gibod 83br, Herman Kokojan 7 & 33br, Malcolm Linton 104bl & 116, Marshall Lockman 32b;
Corbis: 36cl, 36clb, 36–7b, 37tr, 40bl;
Corbis/Bettman/UPI: 40l, 44cl, 59r, 76tr, 81br;
Keith Cox, Department of Earth Sciences, Oxford: 100tl;
Culver Pictures Inc: 118c, 105tl;
Dallas Morning News: David Leeson 89tc;
Environmental Images: 9cr, John Arnould 97tr, Jimmy Holmes 48tl, Doug Perrine 52cr;
E T Archive: 14bl, 96cr, 112bl, 114bl;
Mary Evans Picture Library: 24tr, 25b, 23br, 104tc, 114tl, 117cb & b;
Xue Fengchun: The Tangshan City Reborn: 42bl, 43tr, c & cb;
Werner Forman: 105cl , Musee Royal de L'Afrique Centrale Tervuren 52clb;
Getty Images: 59l, 76bl, 81bl, 118t& br, 92bl, 109cb, Paul Chesley 16tc, Mike Vines 99b, Ted Wood 85;
Robert Harding Picture Library: 16ca, Robert Francis 18bc;
Michael Holford: 12cl;
Mats Wibe Lund/Icelandic Photo & Press Service: 6t, 16tl, 17br, Kristinn Ben p17bl, 50tr, Kristjon Haralds 12tr;
Illustrated London News Picture Library: 109br;
Image Bank: Eric Meold 60–1, A T Willett 54tc, 74t;
Images: 18clb;
Images of Africa: Friedrich von Horsten 80b;
Imperial War Museum: 95tc;
International Stock Photo: Bill Stanton 73bc, Warren Faidley 6clb, 64cr, 64cl;
JMA: 63cl & c, cb, cbl;
Frank Lane Picture Agency: Australian Information Service 68cl & 68b, Bob Stone 58t;
Lunar and Planetary Institute: V L Sharpton 98tr;
Magnum: P Jones Griffiths 90, & 91tr, Steve McCurry 89b, F Scianna 82cl & 83tc;
Tim Marshall: 59t;
Alan Moller: 58;
Montreal Gazette: 72b;
Names Project Foundation: Paul Margolies 121cl;
NASA: Jet Propulstion Laboratory 78c;
NASA: 4–5, 54c, 63b, 103br;
National Geographic: 120, Chris Johns 102–3b, O L Mazzatenta 26bl;

National Medical Slide Bank: 107tr;
National Meteorological Library: JMA 63cla & ca;
Natural History Museum: 98bl;
Natural History Photographic Agency: 107, 109t;
Network: Barry Lewis 27tr;
Peter Newark's Western Americana: 114bc;
Lennart Nilsson: 115;
Novosti: 35br;
Orion Press: Nishiinoue p10–11;
Oxford Scientific Films: Mike Hill 69b;
Palm Beach Post: Jeff Gere 93, Loren Hosack 65b, David Lane 75tr, John L Lopinot 65t, C J Walker 65c;
Panos Pictures: J Hartley 80tr;
Pictor International: 24b, 79, 119tr;
Planet Earth: 25cl, 108b, P Bourseiller 15, 27br, 30–1, 31b, Krafft 19tr;
Rex Features 8tc, 20bc, 29tr,47, 77tl & br, 84cl, 86b, 86–7, 87bc (inset), 87 crb (inset), 95bl, 102ca, Carlos/Angel 20cl, Nina Bermann 73br, Laurent Chamussy 53cr, Dearrmas 103, Richard Jones 123b, Akihiro Nishiaura 48, Nunez 67bl;
Rosenberg Library, Galvaston 70cl & b;
Saba: Alberto Garcia 28–9b, 29br (inset), 50clb, Shawn Henry 13br, 28cl, Tom Wagner 49tr;
Science Photo Library: 12tr, 24cr, 52–3, 57tc, CVL/Eurolios 123cr, Gregory Dimijian 16b, Barry Dowsett 111br, Earth Satellite Corporation 91crb, Eye of Science 106ca, Keith Kent 57tc, Krafft/Explorer 100, Dr Kari Louriatmaa 123tl, Professor Stewart Lowther 18–19, Peter Menzel 12bl, 32tc, 56tl, 70cr, 119b, NIBSC 104br, NOAA 64b, NOAASS 124–5 & 140–153, David Parker 15tr & 43tr, Roger Ressmeyer/Corbis 50cl, David Scharf 112cr, Fred K Smith 55, Sinclair Stammers 115tr, Soames Summerhays 2, US Geological Survey 16cl, Tom van Sant/Geosphere Project, Santa Monica 12–13;
Asahi Shimbun Photo Service: 22;
Frank Spooner: 5tl, 31tr, 32cra, 44t, 73tl, 76cr, 79tr, 82–3, 102bl, 105bl, Gamma 12crb, 20cl, 34bl, Giboux/Liaison 44tr, Lysaght 51;
State Journal Register: 52bl, 62bc;
Stockmarket: 66b & cla, W Bacon 32tr, A & J Verkair 4cr;
Sygma: 3c, 5b, 29tl, 34br, 54–5 b, 57b, 62cr, 67tr, 69cr, Michael Owen Baker 8b, Balder 122bl, Alan & Sandy Carey 85tr, Friday 46t, Julien Frydman 21cr, L Gilbert 110–1, Jon Jones 84tc, B Kraft 9tc, 91bl, V Miladinovic 86tr, P P Poulin 72cr, J Reed 62cr, P Robert 46bl & 46bc, 122c, A Tannenbaum 21l , Randy Taylor 21br, Lannis Waters/Palm Beach Post 74–5b, Haruyoshi Yamaguchi 13tr;
Topham Picture Source: 62bl, 72;
US Geological Survey: 39r, 52tr, 56cla & br;
C J N Wilson: 23bc;
Woodfin Camp & Associates Inc: 29tl, 35br, 77bl, Alexandra Avakian 13cl, Jonathan Blair 99cr, David Burnett 77bl, Chuck Nacke 35br, 91cl
Woodfall Wild Images: Tom Murphy 94.